BY KEVIN BALES

BLOOD
AND
EARTH

RANDOM HOUSE
NEW YORK

BLOOD AND EARTH

—

MODERN SLAVERY, ECOCIDE, AND
THE SECRET TO SAVING THE WORLD

—

KEVIN BALES

Published in the United States by Random House, an imprint
and division of Penguin Random House LLC, New York.

RANDOM HOUSE and the HOUSE colophon are registered
trademarks of Penguin Random House LLC.

LIBRARY OF CONGRESS CATALOGING-IN-PUBLICATION DATA
Bales, Kevin.
Blood and earth : modern slavery, ecocide, and the secret to
saving the world / Kevin Bales.—First edition.
pages   cm
Includes bibliographical references and index.
ISBN 978-0-8129-9576-3 (hardback)
ISBN 978-0-8129-9577-0 (ebook)
1. Slavery—Environmental aspects—Developing countries—
History—21st century.   2. Slave labor—Environmental
aspects—Developing countries.   3. Environmental
degradation—Developing countries.   4. Consumption
(Economics)—Environmental aspects.   I. Title.
HT867.B347 2016
306.3'62091724—dc23   2015008438

Printed in the United States of America on acid-free paper

randomhousebooks.com

468975

Book design by Simon M. Sullivan

FOR MY MOTHER AND FATHER

FELIX QUI POTUIT RERUM COGNOSCERE CAUSAS.

VIRGIL, *GEORGICS,* BOOK 2

CONTENTS

BLOOD
AND
EARTH

1

SECRETS

It's never a happy moment when you're shopping for a tombstone. When death comes, it's the loss that transcends everything else and most tombstones are purchased in a fog of grief. Death is a threshold for the relatives and friends who live on as well, changing lives in both intense and subtle ways. It's the most dramatic and yet the most mundane event of a life, something we all do, no exceptions, no passes.

Given the predictability of death it seems strange that Germany has a tombstone shortage. It's not because they don't know that people are going to die; it's more a product of the complete control the government exerts over death and funerals. Everyone who dies must be embalmed before burial, for example, and the cremated can be buried only in approved cemeteries, never scattered in gardens or the sea. Rules abound about funerals and tombstones—even the size, quality, and form of coffins and crypts are officially regulated. All this leads to a darkly humorous yet common saying: "If you feel unwell, take a vacation—you can't afford to die in Germany."

Granite for German tombstones used to come from the beautiful Harz Mountains, but now no one is allowed to mine there and risk spoiling this protected national park and favorite tourist destination.

So, like France and many other rich countries, including the United States, Germany imports its tombstones from the developing world.

Some of the best and cheapest tombstones come from India. In 2013 India produced 35,342 million tons of granite, making it the world's largest producer. Add to this a growing demand for granite kitchen countertops in America and Europe, and business is booming. There are more precious minerals of course, but fortunes can be made in granite. In the United States, the average cost of installing those countertops runs from $2,000 to $8,000, but the price charged by Indian exporters for polished red granite is just $5 to $15 per square meter—that comes to about $100 for all the granite your kitchen needs. The markup on tombstones is equally high. The red granite tombstones that sell for $500 to $1,000 in the United States, and more in Europe, are purchased in bulk from India for as little as $50, plus a US import duty of just 3.7 percent.

Leaving aside what this says about the high cost of dying, how can granite be so cheap? The whole point of granite, that it is hard and durable, is also the reason it is difficult to mine and process. It has to be carefully removed from quarries in large thin slabs, so you can't just go in with dynamite and bulldozers. Careful handling means handwork, which requires people with drills and chisels, hammers and crowbars gently working the granite out of the ground. And in India, the most cost effective way to achieve that is slavery.

"See the little girl playing with the hammer?" asked a local investigator. "Along with the child, the size of the hammer grows, and that's the only progress in her life." Slavery in granite quarries is a family affair enforced by a tricky scheme based on debt. When a poor family comes looking for work, the quarry bosses are ready to help with an "advance" on wages to help the family settle in. The rice and beans they eat, the scrap stones they use to build a hut on the side of the quarry, the hammers and crowbars they need to do their work, all of it is provided by the boss and added to the family's debt. Just when the family feels they may have finally found some security, they are being locked into hereditary slavery. This debt bondage is illegal, but illiterate workers don't know this, and the bosses are keen to play on their sense of obligation, not alert them to the scam that's sucking them under.

Slavery is a great way to keep your costs down, but there's another reason why that granite is so cheap—the quarries themselves are illegal, paying no mining permits or taxes. The protected state and national forest parks rest on top of granite deposits, and a bribe here and there means local police and forest rangers turn a blind eye. Outside the city of Bangalore, down a dirt track, and into a protected jungle area, great blocks of granite wait for export. "People have found it easy to just walk into the forest and start mining," explained Leo Saldanha of the local Environmental Support Group. "Obviously it means the government has failed in regulating . . . and senior bureaucrats have colluded to just look the other way."

Supriya Awasthi has been an anti-slavery worker in India for nearly twenty years. Her work takes her through the halls of government and down into the depths of human suffering. A fearless woman, she is especially good at talking her way into places slave masters try to hide. Not long ago she took this remarkable photograph, tricking a slave master into showing off his quarry and his slaves:

The slave master showing off his families of hereditary slaves

We've all got a picture in our minds of what a slave master looks like. Here's the twenty-first-century version: clean, well-fed, and proud of his business. This quarry, carved out of a protected national forest, is producing not granite but the big sandstone slabs used in European cities for paving squares and plazas. You can see the slabs stacked in the lower right. Near the slabs are clusters of small children chipping and shaping the stone. Their fathers are toiling along the rock face on the left, and their mothers are carrying the quarried stone to where they and their children will work it into shape. The forest is long gone, along with the soil, and when this quarry is worked out and abandoned the area will simply be wasteland, useless as forest or farmland.

German filmmakers researching the tombstone shortage were the first to follow the supply chain from European graveyards to quarries in India—and they were shocked by what they discovered. Expecting industrial operations, they found medieval working conditions and families in slavery. Suddenly, the care taken to remember and mark the lives of loved ones took an ugly turn. Back in Germany the filmmakers quizzed the businessmen that sold the tombstones; these men were appalled when they saw footage from the quarries. The peace and order of the graves surrounding ancient churches was suddenly marred by images of slave children shaping and polishing the stone that marked those graves.

Our view of cemetery monuments is normally restricted to what we see when we bury our loved ones or visit their graves. If we think about where the markers come from at all, we might imagine an elderly craftsman carefully chiseling a name into a polished stone. The "monuments industry" in America promotes this view. One company explains there are two key factors that affect the price of tombstones. First, they point out the "stone can come from as close as California and South Dakota or as far away as China and India," adding that "more exotic stones will have to be shipped and taxed, which will add to the overall cost." And, second, this company notes that granite takes thousands of years to form and it is "heavy, dense, brittle, and many times sharp, requiring great care and more than one person in its handling." Because of this there must be "techniques and processes that require skill as well as time to make your memorial beautiful and lasting." All of this helps us to feel good about what we've spent for the stone at our loved one's grave, but the facts are different. We know that, even though it comes all the way from India, slave-produced granite is cheap. We also know that, while some polishing and skillful carving of names and dates is needed, those heavy, dense, and sharp tombstones will first be handled by children, though they will be taking "great care," of course, since the slave master is watching.

Some of the most ancient objects we know are tombstones, dating back to the earliest moments of recorded human history. Our civilization, even today, is built of what we pull from the earth, stone and clay for bricks, salt and sand and a host of other minerals that meet so many of our needs. There's an intimacy in the stone we use to mark the final resting place of someone we love; there's another sort of intimacy in the less obvious but still essential minerals that let us speak with our loved ones on phones or write to them on computers.

Cellphones have become electronic umbilical cords connecting us with our children, our partners, and our parents with an immediacy and reliability hardly known before. Our lives are full of ways that we connect with other people—the food we serve and share, the rings and gifts we exchange—and we understand these objects primarily from the point at which they arrive in our lives. We think of Steve Jobs in his black turtleneck as the origin of our iPhones, or imagine a local funeral director carving a loved one's name into a tombstone. Whether we are grilling shrimp for our friends or buying T-shirts for our children we generally think of these things as beginning where we first encountered them, at the shop, at the mall, in the grocery store. But just as each of us is deeper than our surface, just as each of us has a story to tell, so do the tools and toys and food and rings and phones that tie us together. This book is a collection of those stories united across continents and products along a common theme: slaves are producing many of the things we buy, and in the process they are forced to destroy our shared environment, increase global warming, and wipe out protected species.

· · ·

It makes sense that slavery and environmental destruction would go hand in hand. In some ways they spring from the same root. Our consumer economy is driven at its most basic level by resource extraction, pulling things from the earth, an extraction that we never actually see. We pull food from the earth, of course, but we also pull our cellphones from the earth, our clothing, our computers, our flat-screen televisions, our cars—it all comes from the earth, ultimately. And pulling things from the earth can be a dirty business. To make our consumer economy hum and grow and instantly gratify, costs are driven down as low as they can go, especially at the bottom of the supply chain; this can lead to abusive conditions for workers and harm to the natural world. Taken to the extreme it means slavery and catastrophic environmental destruction. But all this normally happens far from any prying eyes. It's a hidden world that keeps its secrets.

But there's no secret about the engine driving this vicious cycle. It is us—the consumer culture of the rich north. Shrimp, fish, gold, diamonds, steel, beef, sugar, and the other fruits of slavery and environmental devastation flow into the stores of North America, Europe, Japan, and, increasingly, China. The profits generated when we go shopping flow back down the chain and fuel more assaults on the natural world, drive more people toward enslavement, and feed more goods into the global supply chain. Round and round it goes—our spending drives a criminal perpetual motion machine that eats people and nature like a cancer.

How closely linked are these two crimes? Well, we know environmental change is part of the engine of slavery. The sharp end of environmental change, whether slow as rising sea levels and desertification, or disastrously sudden like a hurricane or a tsunami, comes first to the poor. I've seen men, women, children, families, and whole communities impoverished and broken by environmental change and natural disasters. Homes and livelihoods lost, these people and communities are easily abused. Especially in countries where corruption is rife, slavers act with impunity after environmental devastation, luring and capturing the refugees, the destitute, and the dispossessed. This has happened in countries like Mali, where sand dunes drift right over villages, forcing the inhabitants to flee in desperation, seeking new livelihoods, only to find themselves enslaved. It happens in Asia every time a tidal wave slams into a coastline, pushing survivors inland, and in Brazil when forests are destroyed and the land washes away in the next tropical storm, leaving small farmers bereft and vulnerable.

Slaves lured or captured from the pool of vulnerable migrants are then forced to rip up the earth or level the forests, completing the cycle. Out of our sight, slaves numbering in the hundreds of thousands do the work that slaves have done for millennia: digging, cutting, and carrying. That cutting and digging moves like a scythe through the most protected parts of our natural world—nature reserves, protected forests, UNESCO World Heritage Sites— destroying the last refuges of protected species and, in the process, often the slave workers. And as gold or tantalum or iron or even shrimp and fish are carried away from the devastation, these commodities begin their journey across the world and into our homes and our lives.

Surprisingly, slavery is at the root of much of the natural world's destruction. But how can the estimated 35.8 million slaves in the world really be that destructive? After all, while 35.8 million is a lot of people, it is only a tiny fraction of the world's population, and slaves tend to work with primitive tools, saws, shovels, and picks, or their own bare hands. Here's how: slaveholders are criminals, operating firmly outside of any law or regulation. When they mine gold they saturate thousands of acres with toxic mercury. When they cut timber, they clear-cut and burn, taking a few high-value trees and leaving behind a dead ecosystem. Laws and treaties may control law-abiding individuals, corporations, and governments, but not the criminal slaveholders who flout the gravest of laws.

When it comes to global warming, these slaveholders outpace all but the very biggest polluters. Adding together their slave-based deforestation and other CO_2-producing crimes leads to a sobering conclusion. If slavery were an American state it would have the population of California and the economic output of the District of Columbia, but it would be the world's third-largest producer of CO_2, after China and the United States. It's no wonder that we struggle and often fail to stop climate change and reduce the atmospheric carbon count. Slavery, one of the world's largest greenhouse gas producers, is hidden from us. Environmentalists are right to call for laws and treaties that will apply to the community of nations, but that is not enough. We also have to understand that slavers—who don't adhere to those laws and treaties—are a leading cause of the natural world's destruction. And to stop them, we don't need more laws. We need to end slavery.

The good news is that slavery *can* be stopped. We know how to bust slaveholders and free slaves, we know how much it costs and where to start, and we know that freed slaves tend to be willing workers in the rebuilding of our natural world. Ending slavery is a step forward in fixing our earth. There's always been a moral case for stopping slavery; now there's an environmental reason too.

■ ■ ■

There is a deadly triangular trade going on today that reaches from these threatened villages and forests in the most remote parts of the earth all the way to our homes in America and Europe. It is a trade cycle that grinds up the natural world and crushes human beings to more efficiently and cheaply churn out commodities like the cassiterite and other minerals we need for our laptops and cellphones. To stop it, we have to understand it. My initial comprehension of this deadly combination was purely circumstantial. I knew what I *thought* I had seen all over the world, but suspicions weren't good enough. I needed to collect real and careful proof, because if the link between environmental destruction and slavery proved real, and our consumption could be demonstrated to perpetuate this crime, then breaking these links could contribute toward solving two of the most grievous problems in our world. I thought if we could pin down how this vicious cycle of human misery and environmental destruction works, we could also discover how to stop it.

To get a clear picture has taken seven years and a far-reaching journey that took me down suffocating mines and into sweltering jungles. I started in the Eastern Congo, where all the pieces of the puzzle are exposed—slavery, greed, a war against both nature and people, all for resources that flowed right back into our consumer economy, into our work and homes and pockets. I knew if I could get there—and stay clear of the warlords and their armed gangs—I could begin to uncover the truth.

2

UNDER THE VOLCANO

The helicopter dropped like an elevator in free fall to dodge any rebel-fired rocket from the surrounding forest. We landed inside a tight circle of UN soldiers on a small soccer field. The soldiers stood with their backs to us, aiming their automatic weapons at the tree line, as the blast from the rotors whipped the tall grass around their legs. As we touched down, jeeps and four-by-fours roared up, bringing injured soldiers for evacuation, goods and gear to ship out, then reloading with arriving people and equipment. Yet children stood a few feet from the soldiers, complaining about the disruption to their soccer game.

■　■　■

Moments later, after our papers were checked, the UN pilot, a Russian with a rich baritone, called the children together and got them singing French folk songs. From the way the kids mobbed him, this had to be a feature of every landing. Their voices rippled with giggles, like water flutes. As I listened, I took in the mountains ranged so beautifully around us. It seemed, for a moment, like paradise. But there was trouble here. No electricity, no running water, and the enemy at the gates.

• • •

For months I'd been searching for a way to reach a rebel-controlled mine in the chaos of Eastern Congo. The only way in, I discovered, was on a UN forces helicopter, since rebels control all the roads. Now I had arrived at the jungle settlement of Walikale (pronounced "Wally-cally"), about thirty miles from the mine. Walikale is like Fort Apache, an isolated outpost surrounded by hostile forces, dense forests, and sheltering a handful of locals who scurried here through the bush to avoid capture after their villages were overrun by rebels.

As we climbed the hill from the landing field, I took my cellphone from my pocket, out of habit more than anything. I assumed it would be useless here, but then watched as the little bars built up on its screen. No electricity or running water, no paving on the roads, and good luck if you needed a doctor, but incredibly I had a signal. "This is why I am here," I thought, "I can't live without my phone, and people here are dying because of it."

• • •

Let's talk about our phones for a moment. Yours is probably within arm's reach right now. Our phones are so ubiquitous, we tend to forget that they only arrived on the scene about twenty years ago. Sure, there had been "radio telephones" for decades, but those were big brick walkie-talkies that only worked in a few areas. It was when scientists figured out how to assemble the hexagonal "cells" linked to towers, and then switch and share all the calls through the phone system, that the explosion came. In 1995 about fifty million cellphones were purchased worldwide, by the end of 2013 sales were up to two billion and there were more phones in the world than people. By 2014, 91 percent of all human beings owned a cellphone. It's a phenomenal success story, greatly improved communication supporting and supported by new businesses and super-clever design teams, together fueling an economy that spouts money out of Silicon Valley like a fountain.

The scientists who made the packets of our conversations jump from tower to tower, the engineers that made our phones smaller and smarter, the designers that made our phones fit snugly into our lives, together they changed everything. The idea that people once had to call a telephone wired to a building in the hope of reaching a person who *might* be there seems quaint, clunky, and a little absurd to our children. All the power of modern technology transformed a world of copper wires into a world where billions of conversations fill the air. It was brilliant, but it had a cost. The ideas might have come from Silicon Valley, but to make our phones we needed other minerals, like tin and coltan. And while silicon is found everywhere, tin and coltan are concentrated in only a few parts of the world. The frictionless genius of our creative class, which we see every day in our lives and in advertising, leads us to support environmental destruction and human enslavement that we never see. We want our clever phones, the market needs resources to make them, and getting those resources creates and feeds conflict. It turns out that the foundations of our ingenious new economy rest on the forceful extraction of minerals in places where laws do not work and criminals control everything. Places like Walikale.

· · ·

The threat looming over Walikale, the cause of all the lawlessness, is the echo of a much larger conflict. The two provinces in the eastern part of the Democratic Republic of Congo are like the elbow pipe under your sink, the place where ugly stuff sticks and festers. After the 1994 genocide in next-door Rwanda, first many of the Tutsi refugees, and then many of the perpetrators, Hutu militias and soldiers, as well as an even larger number of Hutu civilians, fled across the weakly policed border and settled in the Eastern Congo. The militia men took over villages and stole land, goods, food, and even people at gunpoint. Nineteen years later they are still there, living like parasitic plants, their roots driven deeply into the region. Chaos reigns, government control has collapsed, and ten different armed groups fight over minerals, gold, and diamonds—and the slaves to mine them. The big dog is a Hutu group called the Democratic Forces for the Liberation of Rwanda (FDLR), a force that is not democratic and has never tried to liberate anyone or anything. The one thing that all these warring groups have in common is that they make slaves of the local people.

These eastern provinces are called North Kivu and South Kivu, and they hold some of the wildest, most deeply beautiful and seriously dangerous terrain on the planet. The mixture of mountains, river valleys, great lakes, and volcanoes is spectacular, though the endemic parasites and diseases, including typhoid and plague, are a constant threat. The nature reserves and national parks in the Kivus are some of the last places to find a number of threatened animal species, like the great gorillas. Two kinds of elephants roam the forests, and hippos work the riverbanks. High in their treetop nests, this is the only place in the world to find our closest relative, the bonobo chimpanzee. Sometimes called the "hippie chimp," bonobos are known for resolving conflicts peacefully, through sexy cuddling rather than violence—a trick humans haven't quite mastered. But when the rebel groups pushed into these protected forests and habitats, deforestation and illegal poaching followed, and the bonobo population fell by 95 percent. But this isn't the first time the Congo has been trampled.

At the very beginning of the twentieth century there was an unquenchable demand in America and Europe for an amazing new technology—air-filled rubber tires. The Age of the Railroad was ending. Henry Ford was making cars by the million, bicycles were pouring out of factories, freight was moving in gasoline-powered trucks, and they all ran on rubber. The Congo had more natural rubber than anywhere else. To meet this demand King Leopold II of Belgium, in one of the greatest scams in history, tricked local tribes into signing away their lands and lives in bogus treaties that none of them could read. He sold these "concessions" to speculators who used torture and murder to drive whole communities into the jungle to harvest rubber. The profits from the slave-driving concessions were stupendous. Wild rubber, as well as elephant ivory for piano keys and decoration, was ripped out of the forests at an incredible human cost. Experts believe that ten million people died. It is the great forgotten genocide of the twentieth century. One witness was an African-American journalist named George Washington Williams. He coined the phrase "crimes against humanity" to describe what he saw.

The genocide, the killers, and the corrupt king were exposed by a whistle-blower, an English shipping clerk named Edmund Morel. Assigned to keep track of the goods flowing in and out of the Congo, he realized that rubber and ivory worth millions were arriving in Europe, but the ships going back carried little besides weapons, manacles, and luxury goods for the bosses. Nothing was going *in* to pay for what was coming *out*. Morel kept digging, getting the facts. He was threatened and then thrown out of his job, but he didn't stop. By 1901, he was working with others in a full-time campaign against slavery in the Congo that brought in celebrity supporters like Mark Twain.

It's just over one hundred years later and anti-slavery workers are back in the Congo; the sense of déjà vu is strong. Armed thugs still run the place. More fortunes are being made, more people are being brutalized, and slave-produced commodities are still feeding the demand for new technologies. It's not rubber this time though— instead slaves wielding shovels clear-cut forests and tear away hilltops to expose the grubby gray-brown pebbles of coltan. Once smuggled out of the Congo, the mineral will be transformed into "legal" Rwandan coltan and lawfully exported. It's magical geology; Rwanda has few coltan deposits but has become one of the world's biggest exporters of the mineral. It's going to take more than an alert shipping clerk to expose the human slavery at the heart of this trade—the thugs are better at hiding these days. But the truth is out there in the rain forests and protected habitats suffering the on-slaught of slave workers driven by rogue militias. That's why I'm in Walikale with my co-worker Zorba Leslie, lugging my backpack along a dirt track with ruts that would swallow a motorcycle.

Walikale used to be a sleepy little village, but now it is crowded with refugees from the countryside. War has swept through many times in the last fifteen years, and everywhere is ruin. Rusty half-tracks and jeeps are shot up and crushed along the road. Along the dirt track, three boys, homemade drumsticks flying, are doing their own version of *STOMP* on a battered and derelict Russian army truck. The tin-roofed school where we'll sleep was used as a rebel base for months. The walls are pocked with bullet holes, windows are smashed, and our food is cooked over an open fire. As soon as we've dropped our packs, an order comes to report to the local Congolese army commander, so we walk back through town and climb the bluff to the fortified camp. In the old colonial office, the atmosphere is genial but chilly.

"You can't go to the mine."

"Hold on, we've got clearance and permission," I say. It's taken us days to get here, and there's no way I want to stop now.

"I have a spy in the rebel camp, their leaders were alerted that foreigners were coming in on the helicopter."

"So? They can't know why we're here. We'll just slip in, shoot some film, and get out."

"No," the commander says. "They know two Americans came on the helicopter, and Americans make a great target, worth lots of ransom. There's a squad waiting to ambush you as soon as you leave town."

I swallow hard and give in. He knows this war-torn jungle like we never will. We'll just need to be patient and cunning.

．　．　．

To visit any town or village in Eastern Congo is to walk on rubble. Children play, people do their best to get by, but destruction is everywhere. And yet, there is a paradoxical air of paradise. The land is a high plateau, so even though the region sits almost on the equator, the air is cool and fresh, the sunlight crisp. Daytime temperatures are surprisingly comfortable all year round. The rich volcanic soil is dark, crumbly, and fertile. Most nights there is short, intense rainfall that refreshes the lush greenery and riot of flowers. The low mountains are covered to their peaks with forests. Lake Kivu, one of the African Great Lakes, holds fish, and about a thousand feet below the surface is a cache of 72 billion cubic yards of natural gas ready to fuel a new economy. Mountains, flowers, sun, water, fresh fish, fresh vegetables, fruit, and dark rich soil—this place has it all.

Nature is willing, but the people are broken. War has shattered minds and bodies and any semblance or expectation of order; life has become a scramble for survival in a population divided between those with guns and those without. This chaos is the perfect breeding ground for slavery. When valuable minerals are stirred into the mix, the odds of a slavery outbreak are even higher.

The same cycle that fueled the slavery and genocide of 1901 continues to revolve today, not just in Congo but around the world. It's a four-step process; simple in form yet complex in the way it plays out. In the rich half of the world step one arrives with great advertising fanfare. A new product is developed that will transform our lives and, suddenly, we can't live without it. Consumer demand drives production that, in turn, requires raw materials. These materials might be foodstuffs or timber, steel or granite, or one of a hundred minerals from glittering gold and diamonds to muddy pebbles of coltan and tin. Step two is the inevitable casting of a curse—the "resource curse" that falls on the poorest parts of the world when their muddy pebbles, little-used forest, or some other natural resource suddenly becomes extremely valuable. In a context of poverty and corruption the scramble for resource control is immediate and deadly. Kleptocratic governments swell with new riches that are used to buy the weapons that will keep them in power. But for every bloated dictator there are ten lean and hungry outsiders who also know how to use guns, and they lust for the money flowing down the product chain. Soon, civil war is a chronic condition, the infrastructure of small businesses, schools, and hospitals collapses, the unarmed population is terrorized and enslaved, and the criminal vultures settle down to a long and bloody feed.

Step three arrives as the pecking order stabilizes and gangs begin to focus less on fighting each other and more on increasing their profits. A little chaos is good for criminal business, but too much is disruptive, even for warlords. Black markets also need some stability, and with territories carved up and guns pointing at workers instead of other armed gangs, the lean and hungry men begin to grow fat themselves. Step four builds on this new stability that serves only the criminals. Secure in their power, the thugs ramp up production, finding new sources of raw materials and new pools of labor to exploit. Thus the curse has reached its full power. In that lawless, impoverished, unstable, remote region, slavery and environmental destruction flourish.

■   ■   ■

A few days before flying to Walikale we arrived at the border city of Goma, a good place to start if you want to understand what is happening in Eastern Congo. It's the gateway, the depot, the UN's eastern headquarters, basically the transportation hub for the provinces of North and South Kivu. It is also the home of hundreds of international non-governmental organizations that stepped in when the government collapsed. These groups work to protect human rights and women's rights, end sexual violence, meet the needs of children and orphans, and promote disarmament, environmental justice, rule of law, medical care, food security, education, religious tolerance, democracy, and more. Today these organizations fill the buildings with their offices and the streets with their distinctive four-wheel-drive SUVs. The result is a town like no other. Billboards and posters line the streets, advertising not consumer goods, but how to prevent infectious diseases and domestic violence. A good-sized city whose main industry is foreign aid has a strange feel. It's as if the Salvation Army mounted a revolution and took over a city the size of Tallahassee, Florida, and the only jobs available for local people were servicing a bunch of do-gooders.

And looming over the city is the volcano. Called Nyiragongo, it has erupted some twenty-four times in the past one hundred and thirty years. Large eruptions occurred in 1977, 1982, and 1994, culminating in a devastating explosion in 2002. That year a fissure eight miles wide opened on the side of the mountain and lava boiled out toward Goma. Nyiragongo's unusually fluid lava sped down streets at up to sixty miles per hour, swept away buildings, covered part of the airport, destroyed 12 percent of the city, and made 120,000 people homeless. Fortunately, early evacuation kept the death toll to 150. Today the hardened lava is everywhere and streets end abruptly at a low wall of rippled black rock, a frozen torrent. Life persists on top of the hardened lava while Nyiragongo continues to churn and smoke. It's ominous, but in Goma the volcano is not the main worry, for the city also sits on political and ethnic fault lines whose eruptions are more deadly and widespread than Nyiragongo's.

What is happening in the Eastern Congo today is the reverberation of the political and ethnic explosion that occurred in Rwanda in 1994 and left all of East Africa reeling. In April of that year, the world watched in horror as genocide swept through Rwanda. Nearly a million people were murdered and another two million fled the country. Large numbers of refugees, mostly ethnic Tutsis who were the target of the genocide, escaped across the border into Congo. An unstoppable river of twelve thousand people *per hour* smashed through the no-man's-land on the edge of Goma. Most of these refugees ended up in vast and ragged camps built on the lava fields around the city. When cholera hit two months later, killing fifty thousand people in just a few weeks, the rock was too hard to dig graves, and bodies piled up along the roadsides.

Just a hundred days later, in July 1994, the genocidal regime in

Rwanda was overthrown. Vicious Hutu militias (also called *Intera-hamwe*) were now fleeing into Congo, along with detachments of Rwanda's Hutu-dominated army. Once they crossed the border the Hutu militias began attacking the Tutsi refugees who lived around Goma and in turn Tutsi militias committed brutal attacks on Hutu refugees. Because the Tutsis had long opposed the rule of Congo's dictator, Joseph Mobutu, he refused to protect them, and a free-for-all erupted. As violence escalated, neighboring countries and ethnic groups piled into the fight, some supporting the Tutsis, some the Hutus, some wanting to support Mobutu, some wanting to attack him, and some just making a grab for the region's diamonds, gold, and coltan. The conflict expanded into what's now called the First Congo War. When the smoke cleared about a year later, some half a million people were dead, and Mobutu was gone, replaced by a new president backed by Rwanda and Uganda. But the peace was short-lived. In 1998 conflict broke out again, the flash point for the Second Congo War being those same Hutu militias that now controlled the refugee camps in Goma.

The Second Congo War is the modern world's greatest forgotten war. Raging from 1998 to 2003, and overshadowed on the global stage by the events of September 11, 2001, and the subsequent "War on Terror," it involved eight countries and about twenty-five armed groups. By its end 5.4 million people were dead, a body count second only to the two world wars. It was a war of unimaginable savagery. Rape was a key weapon, suffered by many hundreds of thousands of women and a large number of men and children. The Batwa pygmies, the original inhabitants of Congo's forests, were hunted like animals, killed, and eaten. In 2003 a journalist for the British newspaper *The Independent* interviewed refugees in a protected camp and reported their firsthand accounts of massacre and terror:

> "Katungu Mwenge, 25, saw her daughters aged seven and nine gang-raped and her husband hacked to death by a rebel faction. She fled with

her four other children to Eringeti, where they were using banana tree
leaves for blankets under a leaking plastic roof.

"Tetyabo-Tebabo Floribert, 18, was badly traumatised. Rebels de-
capitated his mother, three brothers and two sisters. Anyasi Senga, 60,
fled her village with 40 others and lived in the bush for two months,
surviving on wild fruits and roots. Ambaya Estella's three children and
her husband were killed by the rebels, who killed most of the inhabitants of her village using axes and machetes."

No one "won" the Second Congo War; it simply collapsed from
exhaustion as resources and energy ran out. Despite agreements to
set up a central government, the provinces of North and South Kivu
were left as a patchwork of armed camps, each area under the complete control of one of the hostile militias. Roads, schools, hospitals,
water supplies, electricity, homes, and farms were destroyed; most
of the region was in ruins. All services, including the rule of law, had
ceased to exist. This was the crucial next step in the creation of an
environmentally destructive slavery enclave.

At the end of the war the militias turned to new ways to control
and exploit local people. With "peace" they began a transition from
being mobile fighting units to established garrisons controlling
fixed areas of land. Settled into their new territories, more and more
of their attention became devoted to the lucrative trade in minerals.
Their mining profits increased and bought more luxury items, sta-
ples, weapons, and, without the fighting, more ways to enjoy their
power.

Each militia staked a claim to as much land as they could control
and defend. The boundaries set in this landgrab, however, remain
fluid and armed groups who think they have a chance will invade the
land of a neighboring militia. It's hard to understand this much
chaos, but imagine a city where the police and government have
simply run away and five or six mafia gangs are running everything,
each based in a different neighborhood. The thugs have total control and can do whatever they please, so just crossing from one part
of town to another means paying a tax or risking attack or even en-

slavement. It's a kind of feudalism, but these feudal lords have no sense of responsibility toward the people on their turf and there is no overlord king to keep order. For the thugs the townspeople are more like stolen cattle; there's no investment beyond the effort of capture and little reason to keep them alive. Now imagine that when the government sends in the National Guard to confront the mafia, the Guard just carves out its own territory, settles in, and becomes another mafia. That's the Eastern Congo.

When they're looking for territory to grab, the militias first seek out minerals. Throughout this part of the world, there's gold, diamonds, coltan, cassiterite (the ore that gives us tin), and niobium for electronics, as well as molybdenum and wulfenite for making high-grade steel; all of these are near the surface and easily mined. For years local people have been supplementing their crops with money earned gathering minerals from streams and along cliffs and fissures. The armed gangs want much more; they want all the minerals, no matter how deeply they must dig, and they want them now.

Once they've pinpointed a desirable area to attack, the militia will surround the village at night and take it by force. They want to catch the villagers at home and prevent them from running away into the forest. If the land around the village has plentiful minerals, the soldiers just move into the houses. One, two, or three soldiers will force their way into a family's home, announcing, "We're living with you and you will do as we say." Anyone who resists will be killed. Then the men and boys are put to work digging and hauling minerals. Women and girls also dig and sort stone, do the housework, cook, and suffer regular sexual assaults. The violence and rape increase when the soldiers get drunk or stoned.

■ ■ ■

While the violence and atrocities continue, some armed groups came to realize that slave-driven mining paid better and brought less attention than rape and massacre. And to supply more and bigger mining, these thugs developed "legal" ways to enslave people.

There are many paths into slavery. The most obvious is the blatant physical attack that captures a person and overpowers him with
violence. But throughout history people have been lured and tricked
into slavery as well, sometimes even walking into slavery in the belief that it is opportunity not bondage. In the Congo today, just as in
America not long ago, there is yet another way—a slave-catching
machine constructed from a corrupt, often completely bogus, legal
system that feeds workers into mines.

This fake legal system is an almost foolproof way to get slaves and
is most efficient when there are ethnic, tribal, or racial differences to
exploit. It works like this: a traditional chief, a policeman, a local
official, or a member of a militia will arrest someone. The charge
might be anything from loitering to carrying a knife or being a "ter-
rorist." Whatever the charge, the arrest has either no basis in law or
rests on some petty and rarely enforced minor ordinance. It is simply a way of gaining control over a person. Playing out this charade,
the arrest will then be followed by one of three outcomes. The victim may simply be put straight to work in the mines as a prisoner
under armed guard. Alternately there may be a sham trial in which
the individual will be "sentenced" to work and again taken to the
mines as a prisoner. Finally, the fake trial may result in the arrested
person being "convicted" and then fined a significant sum of money.
Unable to pay the fine, either the individual will be sent to the mine
to "work off" the fine, or the debt will be sold to someone who
wishes to buy a mineworker. All outcomes lead to the same place: an
innocent person is enslaved in the mines. And the charade shows
how the vacuum of lawlessness can be filled by a corrupt system that
maintains a veneer of legitimacy.

This system has an eerie parallel with a virtually identical slave-
catching machine called "peonage" that existed in the American
Deep South from about 1870 until the Second World War. The
parallels between the enslavement of mine workers in Alabama at
the beginning of the twentieth century and Congo today are so close
as to be uncanny. This isn't the result of some sort of criminal cross-

fertilization—I couldn't find a single person in the Congo who had ever heard of the American "peonage" slavery, or knew it had been practiced in the Deep South for more than fifty years with duplicate results to what is happening in the Congo. But both were driven by the same dynamic and can perhaps be undone in the same way.

Peonage slavery had an evil elegance, a simplicity that meant slaves were easy to come by and easy to control. Alabama, with rapidly expanding iron and coal mines from the 1880s, operated the system on a huge scale. Under Jim Crow laws virtually any African-American man could be arrested at any time. Sometimes no charge was made, but to keep up appearances such minor crimes as vagrancy, gambling, hitching a ride on a freight train, or cussing in public might be listed as the cause for arrest. If you were a young, strong-looking African-American male, you were fair game. Brought before a local justice of the peace or sheriff, the prisoner would invariably be found guilty and ordered to pay a fine well beyond his means. At that point the sheriff, another official, or a local businessman would step forward and say that they would pay the fine, and in exchange the convict would have to work off the debt under their control. The magistrate would agree and the prisoner would be led away by their new "owner." The number arrested and convicted was pretty much determined by the number of new workers needed by the mining companies or other white-owned businesses. Once enslaved, the prisoners could be worked any number of hours, chained, punished in any way—including confinement, whipping, and a technique resembling water-boarding—and kept for as long as their "owner" chose. Some men who were arrested and never charged still labored in the mines for decades. A long stint in the mines was the exception, however, not because the slaves achieved their freedom, but because mortality was as high as 45 percent per year due to disease (pneumonia and tuberculosis were common), injury, malnutrition, and murder.

By the twentieth century local governments in at least twenty counties in Alabama were dealing directly in slaves, taking contracts from the United States Steel Corporation and other companies to deliver a fixed number of "convicts" per year. The demand for iron ore miners was so great that U.S. Steel let it be known they would buy as many prisoners as the local sheriffs could arrest on top of the number already contracted. Local officials made fortunes from these lease contracts. No one knows how many African-Americans were enslaved in this way, but since the practice was common in all the Southern states, and especially in Georgia and Alabama, few would dispute that hundreds of thousands of black American men were illegally enslaved under peonage.

Understanding American peonage slavery is important because it helps us to see Congo slavery as part of the long history of bondage. The close link between conflict, prejudice, and slavery unites the two stories. In 1865 the American South was shattered and destitute. The Civil War had killed at least 620,000 soldiers and an unknown number of civilians. The postwar chaos worked nicely for those who still retained some power, setting the stage for them to act with impunity and supporting the emergence of armed groups like the white supremacist Ku Klux Klan. If anything, the turmoil following the Second Congo War was even greater than that after the American Civil War, but some of the outcomes have been almost identical. For the poor South, it was cotton and iron ore that carried the "resource curse," and kleptocratic and racist local governments moved quickly to stabilize and legitimize their control. Whether it was sharecropping or peonage slavery, the result was great riches for a white elite, and an ongoing degradation of the land and destruction of the vast Southern forests.

■ ■ ■

The rebel troops who were waiting to ambush us outside Walikale went back to their camp after a few days, which allowed us to slip around to another site nearer the militia-controlled coltan and cassiterite mines. Led to a ruined school by local human rights activists, I spoke with young men who had managed to escape the mines.

They told me that the threat of enslavement came from both the armed groups and the local chiefs. As one man explained, "They *always* need workers." Because tribal chiefs control much of the land, he continued, "they make up charges against people when they need more labor. You might be walking through a village or across their land, you might have brought something to sell, but suddenly you are grabbed and charged with stealing, owing someone money, or being from a rebel group. No one knows what the laws are, so how can we defend ourselves? This happens all the time!"

These escaped slaves said that people weren't arrested just to feed the mines. Another young man explained: "A tribal chief will decide he wants to dig a big fishpond, so he will make a deal with a local militia captain. The captain will arrest people and find them guilty of some crime and then sell them to the chief to 'work off' their fines." Businessmen buy workers this way as well. As one man put it, "A businessman will pay the police to arrest people, and then sentence them to three or six months of work, but once they are in the mine they just belong to the businessman, they're not allowed to leave." He went on, "Any incident can be used as an excuse to arrest people. Just north of here a dead body was found in the forest. When the body was found, everyone around there was arrested, one whole family was arrested. The local administrator ordered that every member of the family be fined $50 and each one had to dig a fishpond for the local boss. Then the police took up the case, and they arrested the whole family again, there were seventeen of them, fining them even more money. The police worked them hard for ten days and then gave them back to the local administrator. All of these arrests were done with the complicity of local chiefs who either get a cut of the money or the labor."

Another escaped slave jumped in, shouting in his agitation, "The chief gets a cut! The leader gets a cut! The militia gets a cut! We get nothing! You can pay your fine and *still* be sent off to the mines and forced to work!"

I asked the men if any proof was needed for an arrest. "No," one man said, "it can be done without proof, without a piece of paper, without even any testimony. There are lots of people in the [nearby] Bisie mine who are trapped this way, I think more than half the workers. Some are even sent from towns far away."

Having been in the mines, the men had a deep understanding of how the peonage slavery played out—"The fines or debts are usually for $100 or more, but at the mine the debt is recalculated into the number of tons of ore you have to dig and supply. When you're on the site, any food you eat, any tool you use, anything at all, is added to the debt and the number of tons of ore you have to dig. The number of tons depends on the boss and how hard or easy it is to get the ore out of the ground."

These young men understood that the fine and the debt were just a trick to enslave more workers, a ruse aimed at convincing workers that someday they might pay off their debt and leave. One of them explained it this way: "Once you're at the mine, in that situation, you are the boss's slave. Many people are taken that way and then die there from disease or cave-ins, and your family never even knows you've died; you just disappear. Miners can start with this false debt and then spend ten to fifteen years as a slave to the boss." Enslaved miners often disappeared in early-twentieth-century Alabama as well; as Blackmon, a writer on American peonage, explains, "when convicts were killed in the [mine] shafts, company officials sometimes didn't take the time to bury them, but instead tossed their bodies into the red-hot coke ovens glowing nearby."

The peonage system of enslavement is also a good way to settle scores and intimidate people. One of the young men in the Congo explained, "Let's say someone owes me money, but doesn't want to pay. I go to the chief, the chief has him arrested and he's sent to the mine to dig ore. I get a cut of the ore he digs, the chief gets a cut, and the person running the mine gets a cut. The man who owed me money gets nothing, and he can end up being there for years."

Peonage slavery was used in the same way to keep the black population intimidated in the Deep South. Blackmon gives the "crimes" listed by one Alabama county when "felons" were sold to the mines: "There were twenty-four black men digging coal for using 'obscene language,' . . . thirteen for selling whisky, five for 'violating contract' with a white employer, seven for vagrancy, two for 'selling cotton after sunset'—a statute passed to prevent black farmers from selling their crops to anyone other than the white property owner with whom they share-cropped—forty-six for carrying a concealed weapon, three for bastardy, nineteen for gambling, twenty-four for false pretense [leaving the employ of a white farmer before the end of a crop season]." Just swearing at or even near a white person could send a black man to the mines. Men and some women were arrested for any behavior that was thought to threaten authority. In a chilling demonstration of racist power in that Alabama county, the crimes of eight more men were listed as "not given."

On one hand it is discouraging to see how history repeats itself, but on the other hand the parallel between peonage slavery in the Deep South and in the Congo today helps our understanding. There is no wide-scale legally concealed slavery in the American South today. With luck we can learn from how Americans brought that cruel system to an end what lessons might help the Congolese end their peonage slavery today.

A shortcut to success would be to attack the problem with more resolve than was demonstrated by the US government in the late nineteenth and early twentieth centuries. Resistance by Southern congressmen to violate "states' rights," a careful concealment of the peonage slavery by major American corporations, and the readiness to believe that African-Americans were always guilty of *something*, meant those who exposed this slavery were sidelined and their stories suppressed. For decades it was Department of Justice policy to ignore this slavery, leaving it to local judges to try any cases that somehow surfaced. Often these were the same judges who were accomplices in the crime. The ultimate deciding factor that ended this travesty was not concern for those enslaved, but fear on the part of President Franklin Roosevelt. In the lead-up to World War II, Roo-

sevelt worried that "the second-class citizenship and violence im-
posed on African Americans would be exploited by the enemies of
the United States." But it was not until five days *after* the Japanese
attack on Pearl Harbor that Attorney General Francis Biddle issued
a directive ordering the Department of Justice investigators and
prosecutors to build "cases around the issue of involuntary servitude
and slavery." Like the United States in the 1870s, the Congo waits
for justice, and that requires the rule of law.

Fortunately, unlike the United States in the nineteenth century,
the Democratic Republic of the Congo, however shambolic, is a
member of an international community of countries with shared
legal conventions and treaties. While corrupt politicians often rule,
today they know they are in the wrong. Congo, and all other countries, have agreed that the international law against slavery is para-
mount, taking precedence over any national law and enforceable by
any government anywhere. So far, no country has decided to use
this international law to help Congo end slavery, but the tools are
there.

■   ■   ■

The parallels between peonage slavery in the United States and the
Congo are important, but that isn't the only way slaves are brought
to the mines. As I spoke to more people who had been caught up in
slavery I was amazed to learn that there are at least six distinct types
of slavery in Eastern Congo: forced labor by armed groups; debt
bondage slavery; peonage slavery; sexual slavery; forced marriages;
and the enslavement of child soldiers. All of these types of slavery, in
one way or the other, also support the destruction of this rich and
unique environment. The most well-known slavery, related to me
time and again, is forced labor at gunpoint.

Forced labor at the hands of military groups exists along a con-
tinuum. At the extreme end the villagers are rounded up by an
armed group, beaten and assaulted, and put to work under threat of
violence. No payment is offered, there is no freedom of movement

or choice, and resistance is met with violence such as rape, torture, and murder. The work may entail digging minerals, hauling ore, or sorting or washing mineral ore.

While some workers are captured and forced into the mines, others actually travel to the mines on their own in hope of securing a livelihood. That sounds like a very risky thing to do, and it is, but the war left many people without land, tools, or work of any kind, and they're desperate. With no press or media, they live on rumors, so when they hear that people are getting rich at the mines, some decide to take a chance.

At the mine, overseers happily greet them with the promise of a job, knowing they'll soon have them locked into debt bondage slavery. Money, food, and tools are advanced to the worker, at an unknown interest rate, to get them started. In a system reminiscent of sharecropping, other costs (real or fraudulent), extortionate interest, and false accounting are then piled on top of the original debt. In the mining area around Walikale, the medium of exchange isn't money but bags of cassiterite ore that are bartered for food and other goods. Free workers who come to the mine soon find they can't dig fast enough to buy the food they need to stay alive. If they take out a "loan" of food, they fall further into debt. They quickly find themselves in a situation where they must do anything required by the lender—and all freedom is lost. One man who had been in the mines told me it was common for workers to be held for ten to fifteen years in debt bondage slavery (if they didn't die first), and that lenders would often sell or trade these slaves to other people.

Different types of slavery support different segments in the supply chain. For instance, a local human rights worker explained to me how businessmen who buy minerals collude with the armed groups at the mines to enslave workers. The mineral buyer will approach a military leader to say that he has ten tons of minerals stored at a mine and needs to have the ore transported over dangerous territory to the border so it can be smuggled out of the country. Once the businessman pays the militia commander to transport the minerals, the commander sends out troops to arrest people. These "convicts" are then forced, without pay or choice, to carry the bags of minerals through the bush to the border—ore mined by forced labor and debt-bond slaves is now loaded on the backs of peonage slaves. A local man told me that near his village, "several people I knew were arrested but refused to carry the minerals. When they refused, one man was shot dead in front of the others and another man had his biceps sliced open with a machete, leaving him handicapped." Terrified, the other "convicts" shouldered the bags and moved out.

Another type of slavery is less about profit and more about supporting the rule of terror and exploitation by the militias. This is the enslavement of children to turn them into fighters. During raids on villages young boys, and sometimes girls, are kidnapped by the armed groups and trained to kill. As part of their brainwashing they are often forced to rape other children or young people or to murder members of their own family or village. Brutalized, traumatized, and often drugged, the children will soon obey any order. UN forces and relief workers regularly report that children taken this way are put to work carrying assault weapons and patrolling mining zones. These children are cannon fodder for the militias, disposable fighters that can be thrown at the enemy and easily replaced. Whether they are boys or girls, they will also be raped. Recruitment of child soldiers is forbidden in both Congolese and international law, and the UN forces in Eastern Congo make it a priority to rescue these children when they can. In spite of this effort, the practice remains widespread.

■   ■   ■

Females occupy a special place within this system. Girls and women carry the greatest burden of enslavement in Congo: their bodies are used as both tool and battlefield. While some male slaves are sexually abused, sexual assault is the norm for enslaved women. Whatever the nature of their recruitment or passage into slavery, whatever type of work they are forced to do to benefit their slaveholder, women in slavery will inevitably be sexually assaulted. This is the rule, not the exception. It applies to the very young and the old, it applies in the field, factory, and house. The sexual abusers extend beyond the slaveholder to his sons, friends, relatives, free workers, and customers. It is rare to be able to make a definitive statement about any human activity, but I do not hesitate to state: *for women, slavery means rape.*

Male slaves are primarily seen as beings of labor potential; female slaves are seen as sources of labor *and* as bodies that can be used as sexual outlets, for their reproductive potential, and, like diamond jewelry or expensive cars, as items of conspicuous consumption. This leads to a paradox: while enslavement is the total control of one person by another, the enslavement of women achieves a totality, a horror, exceeding that of men.

Both men and women in Eastern Congo described to me how militias and the Congolese army target women and girls in their attacks on villages, taking them into the bush to serve as sexual slaves. Some women and girls wind up in the mines this way, while others, especially orphans, are lured to the mines by older women who promise to provide for them but in fact sell them for sex in exchange for small quantities of mineral ore. These older women profit by meeting a great demand for young girls and teenagers. One human rights worker explained to me, "Men assume that young girls are less likely to have sexually transmitted diseases such as HIV/AIDS. And since younger girls can't negotiate their own prices, they are less expensive, if not free."

The problem is compounded by culture. A local man explained to me that girls and women are traditionally seen as objects, as tools for reproduction. In the mining zones, away from their traditional roles, their worth is even less—"they are simple commodities," he said, "merchandise for barter for a few dirty rocks [mineral ore] collected from the ground." Another local activist echoed this, underscoring the lack of opportunities: "For the girls, their sex is their merchandise." Some women, often widowed in the wars, come to the mines looking for work. They end up in the less-skilled jobs like mineral processing or cooking for the workers. Soon saddled with debts, they feel the pressure to turn to prostitution to feed their children or just survive; from there it is a quick descent into slavery. In any event, no woman or girl is free to refuse sex to the armed thugs who control the mines. All of this is part of a larger and common pattern—the use of rape as a weapon of war, resulting in the destruction of the social fabric of communities by pervasive sexual violence.

There is one further distinction made by witnesses concerning the treatment of some enslaved women. In addition to rebel and government forces taking women by force for sexual slavery, Congolese National Army soldiers also take women by force to keep as "wives." This usually involves the holding of a woman by a single individual, and over time this relationship is transformed into one of traditional (though clearly forced) "marriage." One woman described her experience:

> It was a night in 2007 and my family and I were sleeping in our home. There was a knock from outside; assailants ordered my husband to open the door. A group of six men in military uniform, four armed with guns and two unarmed, came into the house. They started to loot all our valuables. They took us outside and forced us to follow them to the forest. Once we arrived in the forest, they freed my husband but forced me to continue going deeper into the bush with them. A commander had chosen me to be his wife and he kept me in the forest for seven months, raping me anytime he wanted. Because he did not think I was capable of escaping, he allowed me to wander alone and this is when I escaped.

While this woman escaped, this type of forced marriage can become permanent. When a woman has lost all other family members and found a place of slight safety within an army unit as the "wife" of a commander, there can be a giving up and giving in. In some ways it is similar to what's known as Stockholm syndrome, the paradoxical condition in which hostages begin to identify and sympathize with their captors. Psychologists describe the hostage as viewing the perpetrator as "giving life by simply not taking it." In the violent universe of the Eastern Congo, where a woman's survival can be precarious, this reaction is not unusual.

Forced marriage, forced labor, peonage, sex slavery, debt bondage, child soldiers—it is a measure of the lawlessness and chaos of the Kivu provinces that it is possible to find so many distinct types of slavery. Conflict and disorder create very fertile ground for slavery, and here its different forms all seem to be emerging at once. In the chaos of war, in the free-for-all scramble for minerals, the resource curse of the Congo kicks in and the rule of law collapses. In the thriving black markets that fill the vacuum, slavery and destruction flourish.

■ ■ ■

One of the most remarkable investigations of the impact of this disorder on people was carried out in 2010 by a team based at Harvard. This team did something that is very rare—instead of simply collecting personal stories or case studies, they collected data covering the whole population of the Kivu provinces. Because of the danger to teams of researchers needed to carry out random sampling, this type of representative survey in the Congo is pretty much unheard of, but it is desperately needed when it comes to areas afflicted with slavery, war, and sexual violence.

The researchers found that out of the 6.1 million people in the region, nearly one in five adults reported being forced into the conflict—abducted to carry weapons, serve as a sex slave, or affected in some other way. Some of these victims of violence and rape were themselves, at times, perpetrators. Children forced to be soldiers were raped and abused by their captors, and also forced to rape and abuse others. Even more people, about 2.5 million women and 1.4 million men, altogether more than half the population, suffered sexual violence, usually rape.

To give this some scale, note that the Eastern Congo has a population roughly the same as Greater Chicago. Imagine all the houses and apartments in Chicago, the leafy suburbs and downtown blocks. Now imagine that two out of every three homes have been assaulted by armed thugs, the families living in them killed or raped or both, their property taken, their children carried off, and their home set on fire and left to burn. It's a vision beyond the worst horror film, yet that is the reality in the Kivus.

Not surprisingly the Harvard team found that chaos and violence on this scale drove people out of their minds. Half of the surviving population were showing symptoms of post-traumatic stress, just under half were deeply depressed, a quarter of the population had been actively thinking about suicide, and one person in six had actually tried to kill themselves. That last fact needs repeating: out of six million people, one million had attempted suicide. No one knows how many others succeeded.

Walking around Walikale it was hard to see the true depth of the Kivus' tragedy and instead it was possible to see a way out of it. Children still played, mothers carried their babies on their backs, a choir was having an afternoon practice in a church, their clear voices wafting over the road.

As we walked along one dirt road a growing throng of children began to walk with us. Laughing and larking about, we noticed the ominous fact that almost every child was carrying a newly sharpened machete. Their laughter and flashing weapons made a strange contrast, and my co-worker joked aloud, "What is this? Take your machete to school day?" then turned to a local man and asked him in French what was going on. "Oh!" replied the man, also in French. "Today is called 'Take your machete to school day!'—all the children spend part of today cutting grass and weeds around the school." The children were pitching in and having fun at the same time and the adults were also finding ways to forget.

There was no electricity in the town, but at night the local priest would fire up a gas-powered generator for two hours. A select few were granted access to this power for two essentials deemed more important than lighting or cooking—charging cellphones and watching soap operas on a battered television. Near the equator the transition from day to night is abrupt, and the deep darkness would bring our work to an end. Sometimes we'd stop in a rough open café for a drink as dusk fell. Sitting under a palm frond shelter around a wobbly table made of scraps, we'd sip lukewarm sodas while insects swarmed. Sometimes Congolese army officers would be drinking beer while their squad of six or eight young soldiers lounged around the entrance gate. Looking over these young men, I was struck by the weaponry they so casually looped around their shoulders. One teen cradled a rocket-propelled grenade launcher. His buddy wore a vest loaded with rockets. Nearby a young man held a heavy machine gun. All the rest carried Kalashnikov assault rifles, and some wore pistols as well. Grenades hung from their belts. The squad was armed to the teeth—it was a lot of firepower for a visit to a café. I tried not to stare at the sharp contrast between the sophistication of the weapons and the complete lack of basic amenities like running water or electricity.

Underneath the bubble of UN protection Walikale is slowly finding some order. Even in the tortured ground of an abandoned strip mine, tough weeds and wildflowers push up through the slag. Though its buildings are shot up and supplies are few, the school keeps going and the classes are crowded. Men and women who have lost everything make a little business, and try to rebuild. Some of the toughest weeds are the homegrown activists, the human rights and environmental workers who face up to government and rebels alike. Their pay, when it comes, is minimal, and some have a price on their heads, but they keep going, sinking roots and growing justice. It was an honor to be with them, like getting to hang out with Frederick Douglass and Harriet Tubman.

Not long before we got to Walikale a government minister had come from the capital "to look into the situation." In the minister's presence one of the local human rights activists spoke up in public about the killings and slavery. Before the day was out he was arrested, taken off to Goma, and charged with "communicating with the enemy." After being pushed around for a few days, he was taken before an official who gave him this warning: "Don't talk about how the big people eat at the big table." I said I'd like to meet this brave man and asked his name, but I was told: "Maybe where you come from you can name such an activist, but to name a person here is to expose them to death." My informant went on to explain that to get reliable information on the human rights violations and environmental destruction, witnesses have to be hidden away, and that, "If the military finds a report or a witness, everyone will be arrested and then disappear."

These activists were taking a risk just meeting with us. Word of mouth had spread the news of our arrival around the region. One local activist told us the local Congolese army commander had flown out to Walikale to warn his troops that we were coming and that it was important to "be careful of these white people, whatever they hear about, they tell." The military called the activists we were working with *"bouche trou"* (open mouths) because they were willing to talk about the crimes and destruction. And whenever the Congolese military or the rebel groups feel the threat of exposure, they close those open mouths.

I wish I could tell you more about these heroes, but they work under threat every day, and their identities need to be kept quiet. The militias want them dead, and many government officials want them silenced; yet they keep working. Some are focused on safeguarding the people of Eastern Congo and fighting slavery, others are trying to protect the environment; nearly all of them understand the link and work for both. These men and women are ready to give everything, and sometimes they do. Like most abolitionists, these frontline workers see the risks they take as simply part of their jobs. They also live on a shoestring since the wider world, except for a few anti-slavery groups, doesn't even know they exist.

The activists slip stealthily around the mines helping slaves to escape and documenting the vast destruction that open-pit mining brings to the forest and the streams that run through it. But not all of the armed gangs have settled in areas where mining is an option. Some groups, ranging up toward the border with Uganda, swarm across the weak boundaries of international nature reserves, pushing their slaves before them. The destruction is hard to comprehend; rare gorillas are butchered as their "protected" forest homes are burned to make charcoal for sale. Hippos are slaughtered for their meat and ivory, and as species after species is crushed, the interlocking ecosystem around them collapses.

· · ·

As I was writing this chapter sad news arrived from one of these nature reserves. A rocket-propelled grenade had killed three park rangers and five soldiers as they were helping refugees to safety in the Virunga National Park. Since 1996 more than 130 park rangers have been killed protecting this nature reserve or caught up in combat between the different armed groups. The 3,000-square-mile Virunga Park is the oldest in Africa, established in 1926, and home to around one third of the world's population of rare mountain gorillas, as well as elephants, hippopotami, buffalo, and antelope. It is such a precious ecosystem that UNESCO declared it a World Heritage Site. But after nearly ninety years Virunga Park is at risk; the armed thugs who are smashing and grabbing the resources of North and South Kivu look at this protected forest reserve and see rich pickings ripe for the taking, and they're willing to use and expend any number of slaves to do so.

Nature doesn't stand a chance against their firepower. In 2006 a German conservation group carried out a census of the hippos in Virunga Park. What they found shocked them and the global conservation community. Where the previous census had found more than 30,000 hippos, one of the largest and healthiest hippo populations on earth, this time they could find only 629 animals. The researchers flew in small planes to count the hippos along the shore of Lake Edward and the rivers that feed it, but instead of the expected hippo herds they saw Mai Mai rebels killing and butchering animals, and heaps of dismembered carcasses spread along the shore. It was slaughter on an industrial scale using machine guns and grenade launchers. Soldiers hacked out the teeth to sell as ivory, and long lines of enslaved porters carried away haunches of hippo meat to sell in town and village markets outside the park. Elephants and buffalo coming to the shore to drink were also killed and butchered. The lake turned red with blood and stained the shoreline.

The slaughter had a disastrous impact not just on the hippo population, but also on the ecosystem of the lake, and on the refugees who fled there to avoid the conflict. Lake Edward has supported fishing communities for centuries, their main catch being tilapia fish, a crucial protein source. But the size of the fish population depends on the number of hippos and so collapsed after their massacre. Richard Ruggiero, an African specialist in the U.S. Fish and Wildlife Service, explained it this way, "Any animal that eats enormous quantities of bio-mass, as do hippos eating grass, has an important effect on the . . . ecosystem. Hippos not only consume lots of grass, but they digest it and deposit it into the aquatic ecosystem, thus fertilizing it." That's a very nice way of explaining that every day every hippo poops around sixty pounds of dung into the lake. Plankton feast on that dung and are then eaten by the worms and larvae that feed the tilapia and other fish. So, no hippos means no fish—and communities around the lake, swollen with refugees from the conflict, go hungry as the fish stocks collapse. But the armed groups don't care about the fish or the lakeside villages—butchering hippos brings in quick cash when the meat is sold in nearby towns.

Unlike the hippos, the mountain gorillas of Virunga have never had a population numbering in the thousands, and conservationists are especially worried about a new trend in gorilla killing. In the past gorilla poaching was driven by one of two possible reasons. At the local level, the armed gangs or starving villagers and refugees killed the gorillas for meat. At the international level, professional hunters sold a baby gorilla for thousands of dollars in the illegal wildlife market. But in recent killings, Emmanuel de Merode, former director of WildlifeDirect, a group that supports the park rangers in Virunga, explained, "None of the gorillas was cut up, and there was a baby still on one of the mothers. In the history of gorilla conservation, there've never been incidents like these where a group is attacked not for meat or baby gorillas. We believe this was an act of sabotage by the people in the charcoal business who want to see the gorillas dead."

These great and normally gentle apes live in small family groups. They eat mainly plants, and spend most of each day grazing in the misty cloud forest in the mountains above the lake, often stopping to groom each other and play, especially with the juveniles. Females carry their infants as they forage, and breast-feed till their young are about three years old. The bond between mother and offspring is powerful, and females also tend to mate for life with a single silverback male. This slow and bucolic life and the tight fit between gorillas and their narrow ecological niche means that reproduction rates are low. Females give birth to a single infant every six to eight years, and just two offspring over a mother's forty-year life is not unusual.

In spite of their great physical power, mountain gorillas are rather timid: they fear lizards and crocodiles, avoid chameleons and caterpillars, and do their best to cross any stream without getting their feet wet—sometimes using a stick to test the depth of the water. Researchers have found they use simple tools, such as rocks to break open palm nuts or clubs improvised from tree branches. Gorillas are our nearest relatives after chimpanzees and bonobos, sharing around 97 percent of our DNA.

The gorillas are a clear gauge of the link between slavery and environmental destruction. They are the canaries in the coal mine, powerful but sensitive hominids whose annihilation would mark the beginning of the end for the great cloud forest. They are a rare and important species, but also precious in a country starving for outside investment. In the Eastern Congo there are about 6 million people, but only around 700 gorillas, mostly living in the Virunga Park.

While the gorillas are small in numbers, they have the potential to generate much more for the Congolese economy than almost any human being. Per capita income in the Congo is $280 per year, meanwhile—even as the conflict rages—gorilla tourism brings in $3 million in payments for gorilla watching and another $20 million in indirect profits for hotels, restaurants, transportation, and so forth. Put simply, every gorilla brings in about $25,000 a year to the Eastern Congo, and this is a resource that, if it is not destroyed, keeps producing (and slowly reproducing). The part of the Virunga Park on the Rwanda side of the border clearly shows this is possible. There, new trails have been built so that tourists can visit a mountaintop, Lake Ngazi, and the grave of Dian Fossey, author of *Gorillas in the Mist*. Three groups of golden monkeys, a gorgeous species found only in the park, have been habituated to the human presence and can be visited daily, all in addition to the chance to watch gorillas. It's good business that pumps money into the local economy and keeps the forest safe.

At the same time, the gorillas sustain their habitat. Think of them as the hippos of the cloud forest. Like the hippos, these big herbivores are "processing" a lot of vegetable matter every day. Unlike the hippos, they don't just produce fertilizer. Gorillas love fruit and fruit has seeds. Gorillas pass these seeds through their digestive tracts and then leave them to grow in a fresh pile of manure. Or, as the primatologists put it a little more delicately: "gorillas removed significant quantities of seeds . . . [that were] deposited in dung on trails or scatter-dispersed under or away from parent canopies." This sounds like gorillas are carefully removing seeds by hand and then surgically inserting them in dung, until you get to the term "scatter-dispersed"—a waste disposal method I'd rather not think about—but it means gorillas don't just eat the forest, they help it to spread and grow as well.

Unlike many species that draw tourists, gorillas are gentle souls. While they can be susceptible to human diseases like pneumonia, it's possible to create space for tourists in their habitat in a way that keeps everyone safe. But to the armed gangs invading Virunga the rarity and grace of the gorillas doesn't matter—the gorillas, like the hippos, are simply food. Easy to track and shoot, they are eaten by the gangs, and excess meat is sent down to the towns for sale. Killed in the jungle, most murdered gorillas simply disappear, but when two well-known silverback males were killed three years ago park wardens found their severed heads and feet in a latrine at a rebel camp. "The stench was terrible, a mixture of rotting flesh and human excrement," reported a conservationist on the scene. One of the gorillas had become habituated to humans, thus making him an especially easy target. The wardens who discovered the remains could do nothing against the heavily armed rebels.

The fighters who killed those gorillas weren't the Mai Mai who butchered the hippos but yet another of the armed gangs called the Rally for Congolese Democracy (RCD)—an army of about two thousand men led by a man named Laurent Nkunda. Nkunda established his own "mountain state" near Virunga, and used his soldiers to rape, terrorize, and enslave local people in order to steal gold, timber, coltan, and other natural resources, as well as butcher protected species for sale. He was especially well known for forcing thousands of children to become soldiers. In 2009, a joint Rwandan-Congolese force captured Nkunda, but his "mountain state" just passed into new hands. It seems that he was driven out because more powerful groups wanted to exploit not just the animals of Virunga but the great forest itself.

Around the world, tropical forests are being destroyed at incredible speed and every tree that falls releases CO_2 increasing global warming. The Congo holds the world's second-largest rain forest, but satellite images show ever-growing parts of North and South Kivu stripped of trees. While the trees of Virunga Park might be useful as timber, for the rebels they are even more valuable when burned to make charcoal, a process that simply increases the speed of the greenhouse gas emission. Without roads it's very difficult to get large logs out of the forest, but a fifty-pound bag of charcoal can be lifted to the shoulders or balanced on a bicycle and carried out of the forest by a teenage slave herded along at gunpoint. As the forest recedes, these slaves, mostly boys, trickle down the slopes and join the road into Goma. In that city most people use charcoal for cooking and heating, and supplying them is worth an estimated $30 million a year to the armed gangs. The cooking fires of Goma, however, use only a small part of the charcoal made in the protected forest; even more flows across the border into Rwanda. In 2004, Rwanda, in order to protect its own forests, passed a law banning the production of charcoal anywhere in the country. This meant some nine million Rwandans had to look elsewhere for their supply, and the only available source near Rwanda is the Virunga National Park.

A witness to this destruction is Paulin Ngobobo, one of the Virunga Park rangers. He explained that the culprits are both the rebel groups and the Congolese army troops sent to protect the park and local people. The soldiers maintain roadblocks and do regular patrols, but they are also looking for ways to make money. Some soldiers have not been paid in years and turn to charcoal-making as a source of revenue. Ngobobo explained, "The military is put in the park because of the armed bandits that operate there, but they're not paid, so they start making charcoal instead."

The Congo has a long history of putting army units in the field but not paying their salaries. Ex-president Mobutu, the dictator who held power in the Congo for thirty-two years, "once asked his soldiers why they needed salaries when they had guns." According to Ngobobo, the army uses military activities as a cover for the charcoal trade. "We'll get a report," Ngobobo noted, "from a military commander saying we cannot patrol the park for a certain time because of military maneuvers, but what they are actually doing is cutting down trees and poaching."

"The gorillas have become a hindrance to the charcoal trade," explained Emmanuel de Merode. "The last fifteen years of Congo's history have been defined by the illegal exploitation of natural resources," de Merode stated. "The charcoal trade definitely fits into that reality. Rwanda is unsustainable in terms of natural resources within its own borders, so it has to look to the outside. What's happened is that there's only one real source of charcoal for Rwanda, and that's Virunga National Park." At the same time, the people near the park, many of them refugees from the fighting, are desperate to earn money any way that they can. Ngobobo tries to convince local people of the value of the forest, but it is a hard sell. "The population is very poor. It's impossible for them to see the value of the park. They see it as another obstacle," he says. The armed groups resent Ngobobo's interference in the charcoal trade. In 2007, while meeting with villagers about preserving the forest, he was arrested by militia, stripped, and flogged in front of the villagers he had come to visit. A year later he was arrested by the Congolese army and charged with furnishing false information about the charcoal trade and obstructing the investigation into the gorilla killings.

This is a tragedy at so many levels, it is hard to know where to begin. The environmental destruction, death, and slavery feed into each other in cycles that, once begun, stop only when they hit the limit of annihilation. Armed gangs drive people from their homes with brutality and sexual assault; thousands are enslaved. Their weapons, their bullets, are paid for by the riches they tear from the forest, sometimes meat and charcoal for the local markets, sometimes for the minerals that go into the products we buy. The rule of law disappears and anything goes. Since the militias have no reason to preserve or maintain communities or nature, they destroy and consume everything they can. Local agriculture is disrupted or abandoned and hunger creeps in. Corruption feeds on the chaos, and the human vultures descend, each trying to make off with a piece of the region's rich resources.

It is hard to see a way out of this mess, but there is one place where reason might prevail and lead to real and positive change—and that is the role that you and I play in this calamity. Let's return to the phones in our pockets. We don't buy charcoal made from the Virunga forest or feast on gorilla flesh, but the real money propping up the criminals of the Eastern Congo comes not from gorillas or charcoal, but from minerals used in vast amounts in electronics. Because it's filtered through a global supply chain that whitewashes and green-washes the ore, concealing its devastating origins, we both drive the demand and benefit from these minerals every time we speak on a cellphone or open our laptop. If these minerals can be traced from the hands of slaves and into our phones and laptops, we can find out where and how to stop this catastrophe. Standing in the burnt-out forest, now devoid of its rich and precious life, I knew that was my next step—I had to dig hard and follow the minerals.

Back in Walikale I walk up a ridge and look down into the river that rages through the settlement. Taking a battered old Nokia from my pocket, I press the long string of numbers that connect me to my sweetheart in London. . . .

3

THE CITY OF RAGS

This was once a mountain, now it's rubble. A great hollowed-out pile of debris drenched in human waste, toxic chemicals, and blood. This is the Bisie (pronounced *bee-cee-a*) mine about thirty miles from Walikale. It's a mountain of tin and coltan rapidly disappearing as antlike slaves swarm over it and tunnel through it. Twenty thousand people live on this mountain in a city of rags.

From a distance it doesn't look like a city, just thousands of discarded plastic bags left to whip themselves to shreds in the wind, catching on random wires and crooked sticks, caked with mud, piled and jumbled in every direction. Open pits dot the landscape filled with rainwater and sewage, wriggling with mosquito larvae and parasites. Exhausted, hollow-eyed children, wasted sinewy men, and women with blank stares float through the mist like ghosts and cower when swaggering soldiers pass. Their fear is real; as one woman told me, "This is where the girls are butchered like goats. And if anyone is suspected of swallowing precious minerals, they just cut open their bellies."

There was a time when the belly of this forest, the heart of this mountain, hadn't been cut open and looted. But before we go back in time, look around you right now. Somewhere close to you there is probably a circuit board, one of the key components of the information age. But circuit boards won't work without the ore slaves are digging in the Bisie mine: cassiterite. Cassiterite is simply tin ore. Tin is used to make solder, and solder is what, literally, holds electronics together. The solder (the word comes from the Latin "make solid") used in electronics is a mixture of 63 percent tin and 37 percent lead. That precise mixture of tin and lead can be very accurately applied to link one electrical circuit to another, to fix a chip to a computer motherboard, or to do thousands of other jobs necessary in the production of our cellphones, laptops, and any other object (cars, toys, baby monitors, all the way up to jumbo jets and supertankers) that needs electronics.

Which brings us back to the Congo and the Bisie mine. In the 1980s the villagers living in this part of the forest found that the bed of the shallow little Bisie River was full of cassiterite pebbles and gathered them to sell to visiting traders. With the explosion in cellphone and laptop use, the price of tin shot up and the traders wanted more. Spreading out along the river the villagers picked up more of the pebbles and worked their way upstream to find the source. Deep in the forest, where the river had cut into the side of the mountain, the tin ore pebbles were everywhere. When villagers dug into the mountainside they found it was packed full of black cassiterite pebbles. The small mountain on the other side of the river turned out to be compacted red cassiterite ore. These two, the Black Mountain and the Red Mountain, along with the river and its floodplain, now make up the mining site. The original villagers who found the ore are gone. No one knows what happened to them. During the Congo Wars, armed gangs were drawn to the mineral riches of the site and killed, enslaved, or drove away anyone already there.

Pockmarked with pits and ditches, the mountain looks as if it has been carpet bombed. Perched along its top and along its edges is the city of rags. The trees have all been cut down, boulders and rubble, mud and gravel are everywhere, and no plants grow. Mine shafts drive into the sides of the mountain. The mountain's heart is almost pure tin ore where the tunnels converge into a central room. With dim flashlights strapped to their heads, men and boys pound with hammers and chisels on the walls and in the tunnels. Over time they've hauled millions of pounds of waste rock out of the mines on their backs and dumped it on the mountainside. Once mined, the tin ore is taken to the riverside. Put in old oil cans with the tops cut open and holes punched in the sides and bottom, the ore is washed free of dirt and sand.

The miners are a motley mix and in poor shape. Some are orphaned ex–child soldiers, freed after UN intervention. Promised government help but receiving none, they've come to the mine hoping to earn enough to eat. Many miners are enslaved, through the tricks of peonage or false debt, and others were just rounded up at gunpoint. Women and girls tend to be used for cleaning the ore, for cooking, or for sex. Some were captured, raped, and then brought here. Others, their families and villages destroyed, have come looking for a chance to survive. Of the 20,000 inhabitants most are sick and injured; only the bosses, soldiers, and some merchants are well fed.

Without safety equipment the work quickly takes its toll. Worst, and most prevalent, is silicosis, which occurs when the lungs fill with microscopic sharp-edged rock dust. The dust makes the lungs bleed and form scar tissue. As the scar tissue expands, the lungs can't bring oxygen to the body. In time even an otherwise healthy person withers away, slowly but irreversibly suffocating to death. Flying shards of rock from the chisels regularly damage eyes, and rock falls and other accidents break bones. So many people sleep piled together in the "safety" of the tunnels that most miners suffer from scabies and are covered with angry red rashes. Poor health and overcrowding mean infectious disease spreads rapidly, and deaths from normally preventable illnesses are common. Sexually transmitted diseases also seethe through the site. The few women present, with little control over their bodies and no protection, are raped or used by many men and infection spreads. Trapped in this hell many miners trade their ore for drugs, usually marijuana and a locally pressed hashish, and work stoned, increasing their chance of accidents.

One night I sat under an open shelter and talked with two young men who worked in Bisie as a lightning storm raged around us. It was as if the tricks of a cheap B movie had taken control of my life: ragged, blinding bolts underlining every word of trickery and violence, nearby trees rendered stark and abstract by the weird bleaching light. Ominous lowering clouds, the rumble and crack, foreshadowed each turn in their stories. The thunder often drowned out their voices, and though we huddled together I had to shout for them to hear me. These men spoke softly and slowly about the diseases and the dangers. "Last month," one said, "cholera broke out, two of our friends died." "And then there was the earthquake," added the other, "down in the holes the walls collapsed, rocks fell, many were injured, some were buried alive."

Both had come to the mine looking for work, both now carried debts they couldn't begin to pay. One of the young men had been told to lock up some bags of ore, but while he waited for the keys to arrive one of the bags was stolen. Told he was responsible for the lost 50 kilos of ore, he now hauls bags of ore out of the mines to pay his debt. The dust is taking its toll, and he's coughing and has chest pains, a hernia gives him constant pain. When he gets sick he has to borrow again for treatment. He's trapped in a downward spiral of backbreaking work, exhaustion, illness, and more debt. He has no idea how long he'll have to work like this, or when his debt will be paid off.

The mining at Bisie could have happened without the rape, slavery, and murder. The ownership of the mountains, under Congolese customary law, should fall to the two clans that lived around the site. As the Second Congo War came to an end, a mining company called Mining and Processing Congo (MPC) worked to develop the Bisie site. Granted exploration rights by the national government, they also negotiated with the local clans and agreed to build schools, a health center, a hydroelectric plant, a manioc mill, and to train and employ the local workers. The company built a compound of clapboard houses on the mountain, a workers' canteen, and a helicopter pad. But just as the company was preparing to ramp up production, the local military strongman made his move.

During the war Colonel Samy Matumo led a renegade Mai Mai force in the same area. After the war, he took up the government's offer to bring his troops into the Congolese National Army, and his force was renamed the Eighty-fifth Brigade. The government's plan was to absorb these rebel soldiers and then disperse them across the army, but Matumo refused to let his men go, instead setting up a camp at the mining site and quickly moving into the protection racket. Soon MPC workers were being roughed up. One was shot in the leg and had to be helicoptered out. More violence followed, along with random arrests, harassment, and death threats. Then Matumo made his pitch to the mining company—for $10,000 per month all these problems would go away. Faced with extortion, MPC pulled out staff and ceased work, so Matumo turned to less scrupulous businessmen he knew from the illegal arms trade to take over the mines. Soon a tight web of corruption and payoffs to district officials linked Matumo to a shadowy mining company in Goma that was ready to buy minerals no questions asked. Matumo began mining the site his own way, no building infrastructure for the local people, simply enslaving workers and setting his fighters over them. MPC still owns the legal right to Bisie, but all they can do from their office in Goma is watch a constant relay of old Russian airplanes pass overhead smuggling their ore out of the country.

■　■　■

It might have been different. The government of Congo might have enforced the rule of law and MPC might today be legally and responsibly mining the tin ore of Bisie. Samy Matumo's soldiers might have been dispersed and would now be learning to be citizens again. Slaves might not have been taken, women and girls not raped, and the profits from the smuggled tin ore might not be flowing into the pockets of criminals and supporting horrific crimes. It might have been different, but it wasn't. The government, already corrupt, can't control the armed groups and local officials who simply cave in to the offers of bribes by the gangs. The rule of law doesn't protect people, much less mining contracts, so there's no remedy there. And behind all that is the fact that you and I *need* this stuff. We demand so much of it that the criminals (both inside and outside government) can't resist taking a cut, enslaving people, and destroying the environment in the process.

■   ■   ■

The supply chain that reaches from the Bisie mine to the phone in your pocket has around eleven steps, the last two being the retailer where we buy our goods and ourselves, the ultimate consumers of the cellphones, laptops, and everything else. Since most businesses don't want slavery in their products, the lies told to hide slavery cluster most thickly at the beginning of the supply chain. The sense of guilt or responsibility for the origin of the base materials fades at every step on the chain—until it is completely extinguished in the minds of many consumers.

Let's examine that supply chain closely, but instead of following the minerals let's examine the people along the chain and explore their motivations for passing the ore along. That way we can properly determine who is criminally guilty, who is culpable, and who may not be guilty, but still has to take on part of the responsibility for what is happening in Congo. The first link in the chain is the miners, those who dig and chisel the ore and who suffer most. They don't know what happens to the ore except that it is hauled away and that their masters are making a lot of money from these bags of dirty pebbles. These miners, enslaved through peonage, trickery, or capture, and the girls and women used and abused at the site are neither guilty nor responsible. They are victims. They are involved in this chain because they were forced to be. They mine because they have no choice.

The second link, the thugs and criminals who have enslaved these men and women, boys and girls, are immediately and precisely guilty. Whether they are part of a rebel group or the Congolese army, if they are driving slaves they are guilty. Equally guilty are the parasites feeding on this crime—the officials, tribal chiefs, corrupt police, moneylenders, brothel keepers, and mineral dealers—who levy taxes, harvest slaves through false arrest, enslave through debt, trade in the flesh of children, and buy and sell the ore in full knowledge of its ugly human cost. They participate in this with the motive of making money in a part of the world where money is scarce. At the higher levels of this link, the money is used to fund their militias, pay off officials, and gain relative wealth and power. At the lower levels—at the level of the common soldier—the motive is scarcely distinguishable from the motives of the slaves themselves: they are trapped in a cruel system and trying to survive it, which in no way excuses the violence they mete out on those a single step below them in this chain.

It's at this stage in the supply chain that we are likely to find "ecocide"—the large-scale destruction of the natural environment. This is where the cycle connecting slavery and environmental crimes starts to spin: ecocide pushes local people into greater vulnerability as their normal livelihoods disappear, making them more vulnerable to slavery—the slavery in turn drives further destruction of the local and planetary environments. The same thugs and criminals, whether they are officials, rebels, or "businessmen," who drive slavery at this level of the supply chain are guilty of ecocide. What's their motivation? Militia leaders in desperate, war-traumatized, lawless parts of the world don't spend a lot of time thinking about the environmental impact of the slave-driven operations that keep them in power. In their violent quest for money and power, the destruction of local habitats and species, the damaging of ecosystems, and the unleashing of greenhouse gases are hardly priority concerns. Surrounded by other armed gangs, they know they might be displaced at any moment. Smash and grab is the order of the day, as well as keeping an open escape route and a pile of ready gold and cash.

The third link in the human supply chain is the mineral-dealing middlemen and their pilots and truck drivers, their bookkeepers and other employees. Most of the armed groups or local officials don't export the minerals themselves; they simply sell ore to these middlemen (known in the Congo by the French term *négoçiants*). It is the *négoçiants* that buy ore at the mine and arrange for its transportation, sometimes trucking it to Goma, sometimes smuggling it out by air to a neighboring country. These are criminals that don't carry weapons or dress in combat fatigues. With enough education to manage accounts and international transfers, they cluster in the settlements, towns, and cities around Eastern Congo taking a top slice of profits as the minerals pass through their hands. These white-collar middlemen are *willing accomplices* in the crimes of slavery and ecocide, they know exactly what they are buying, transporting, and selling. They are firsthand witnesses who stand by while horrific crimes are committed and then step in to take their fees and profits.

The *négoçiants* deliver their bloody minerals to fourth-link trading houses and exporters, known as *comptoirs*. They may be in Goma, or in Rwanda, Burundi, Uganda, Kenya, or another country. The *comptoirs* are businessmen who are *aiding and abetting* the crimes of slavery and ecocide. They and their companies knowingly profit from the crimes and act in a way that shows that they want the crimes to succeed—which in most countries meets the legal requirement for criminal guilt. Even if they don't dirty their own hands with the violence of slavery or the destruction of the environment, these men are dealing in stolen goods, acting as a fence for the thugs and their accomplices, and covering up for them. This is in some ways the hardest step: the placement of the stolen goods, money, or minerals into a seemingly legitimate business so that tainted minerals can be illegally converted into "lawful" goods and introduced into the market. In spite of the fact that there is a rash of denials from trading houses and exporters, there can be no plausible deniability; too many investigators have followed the trail of conflict minerals to the doorsteps of the *comptoirs*. The crimes of slavery and ecocide rely upon the support of these trading houses and exporters.

The guilt of these *comptoirs* is simply compounded by their lies. Their motivation is easily understood, "hot" goods always cost less than legitimate goods, and the *comptoirs* get to buy low and sell high, making fat profits.

These *comptoirs* who run the trading houses and export depots either blend tainted minerals with other minerals that may be clean of both slavery and ecocide or relabel the minerals as "Rwandan cassiterite," and then they sell them on to the fifth link, businesses in Europe, North America, China, Russia, and Australasia. It is at this step, when the ore leaves Africa, that a mask is drawn over the minerals, disguising their origin. The companies buying the now disguised ore run smelters and process the minerals further, making pure tin or solder, or converting raw coltan into the fine powder that can be manufactured into electronic capacitors. Three companies dominate this processing consuming about 80 percent of minerals: the US-based Cabot Corporation, German-based H.C. Starck, and the Chinese state-owned Ningxia Nonferrous Metals Import and Export Corporation. The people who run Cabot Corporation and H.C. Starck have strict policies against buying coltan or other conflict minerals from Congo, and mount their own inspections. But I have been unable to find any such policy issued by Ningxia Nonferrous Metals. Telephone calls to their agents in Great Britain and the United States were fruitless. The number in the UK was "no longer in use," and the US number reached a message that stated, "The person you are trying to reach does not accept calls from unknown numbers. Goodbye [click]."

Underneath the big players are a series of smaller processors. Some of these are doing the right thing and taking part in a tracing project called the ITRI Tin Supply Chain Initiative, or "iTSCi." The iTSCi project is a solid way forward—these smaller processing companies know Africa and they know minerals. The iTSCi project provides the inspections, uses bar-coded tagging, as well as including a role for local officials to do the right thing. Through the project ITRI feels certain that they can tag clean minerals at source, including from mines in Eastern Congo. The Bisie mine is at the top of their list for mines they want to inspect.

You'd think that everyone would be lining up to support this project, but in January 2011 it was "in very real danger of failing" because of a shortage of funds, according to the head of the Tantalum-Niobium Research Center. This was especially disheartening because, once established, the project was designed to be self-supporting based on a small levy paid by mineral processors. This is exactly the sort of work that should be supported by those further along the supply chain, starting with electronic component makers all the way up to major retailers, and it has a powerful recommendation. When I talked with small-scale family miners and human rights workers in Eastern Congo, they told me about ITRI and how they wanted to participate. Their stumbling block wasn't the iTSCi project, it was getting the legal permit they needed for the sites they were already mining from corrupt officials—without it they couldn't prove they were the actual mine operators. By 2014 the project hadn't shut down, but it was still in a stage of slow expansion. There's a virtuous cycle here waiting to spin—and it needs the participation of more companies at more levels to start it rolling. Sadly, some companies stay away because they are uncertain which way to best address and inspect their supply chain, and others hold back hoping that the problem will go away, solved by someone else, and so save them trouble and expense.

When minerals leave these smelter and processor companies, both big and small, the sixth link in the chain splits into two distinct streams. Both streams are made up of companies that make basic components such as capacitors from coltan or solder from tin. The split occurs because some companies choose to buy slave-free and ecocide-free raw minerals and some don't. But it is also at this point on the supply chain that another layer of fog descends, since some of these manufacturers are small factories in Asia that move into and out of production in response to market demand, while others are big-name corporations. Of the larger manufacturers it is surprising how few of them have taken active measures to avoid slave-produced minerals. Most have some sort of "corporate social responsibility" policy, but it often seems nothing more than cobbled-together vague generalizations. In March 2011, a review by the Triodos Bank found that Sharp and Panasonic were clearly refusing to use conflict minerals, but that Sony, Garmin, Casio, and Sanyo were failing to make clear and measurable attempts to stay clean of slavery.

Here at the sixth link it is important to distinguish between guilt, culpability, and responsibility. None of the people running these companies are guilty of slavery or ecocide in any direct way, and while they may not be requiring (or sometimes even requesting) their suppliers to make sure raw materials are clean, it is also true that they are not legally bound to do so. At the same time, when slavery and ecocide are clearly documented and there is evidence that the chain of dirty minerals leads to your front door, then if you are not taking *responsibility* and dealing with that problem, you are morally *culpable*, if not legally guilty. Sharp and Panasonic are responsible for the minerals they use and, happily, are acting responsibly and so avoid culpability. The surprising thing is that the men and women leading these companies haven't leapt into the iTSCi project by simply joining the process and paying a small levy on the minerals they use. These are adjoining links in the supply chain, and they probably already know each other. So why does the plan that would deliver clean minerals languish for lack of funds? One reason is that company lawyers are quick to point out that publishing corporate responsibility statements has no liability, but admitting you might have had slavery in your products by actively joining a project that keeps your supply chain clean carries reputational risk. It is the old conundrum in the question "when did you stop beating your wife?" or in this case "using slave materials?" Some businesses think that doing too much to solve the problem is an admission of guilt and fear that creates liability.

The same fears and obfuscation occur in the split at the seventh link in the chain, between those who work to exclude tainted minerals and those who don't seem to care. That's when these electronic bits and pieces are sold to the companies that assemble them into circuit boards used in the phones and computers we buy. The men and women in this business are likely to have factories in China, other parts of Asia, or Mexico. You've probably never heard of most of them, companies like Jabil, Asustek, or Sanmina. One of the largest is Flextronics, and they have a policy requiring documentation from suppliers and use their website to explain the problem of conflict minerals. The other circuit board assemblers also tend to have a policy, but the problem is that these policies rely on "due diligence declarations." In other words, they ask suppliers if they're selling dirty goods and accept what they answer. That just doesn't cut it. They'd get closer to the truth with monitoring and inspection, but no law requires that in any of the big consumer countries. So at the seventh link, some companies, like Flextronics, are trying to be responsible and others are failing to be good corporate citizens.

Armed with the diligence declarations from their suppliers, the men and women running these companies pass these assurances up to the eighth link: the big companies that use their circuit boards to assemble consumer products. At this level we are far removed from Congo and the companies are keenly focused on getting their components cheaply so they can outperform their competitors. The company accountants are pointing out that it's a liability to do more diligence or inspections or restrict the company to suppliers who don't engage in slavery at any point. Price competition for these companies is fierce, driven by the pressure on prices at the consumer level. Yet, while accountants are pressing hard on their suppliers, it is that same pressure that echoes all the way back to the mines in the Congo. Back in the mines, money is driving slavery, high up the supply chain, money is driving a blind eye to slavery. And the money that ultimately drives both is the spending and bargain hunting by consumers.

One of the best known of these assembler companies is the Chinese firm Foxconn, Apple's largest supplier, which has a clear policy that they do not buy minerals from Congo. As these bits and pieces get closer and closer to being our phones and laptops the culpability and responsibility gets more and more diluted. The people making circuit boards into products are not guilty of direct enslavement or environmental destruction, but they're still culpable if they are not doing the work necessary to be certain their circuit boards and products are clean. Like everyone else on this chain, it is their responsibility to do so, and in many ways Foxconn's response is determined and shaped by their biggest customer—Apple.

We're almost home—the ninth link in the chain is the people who finish the assembly and sell you your phone or laptop—the people at Apple, Dell, IBM, Nokia, or some other brand-name company. I'm going to use the folks at Apple as an example because I use Apple computers, have an iPhone and an iPod, and, full disclosure here, own five shares of Apple stock (Steve Jobs used to own 5.5 million shares). The bottom line on Apple, and this goes for most of the brand-name computer companies, is that they *are* taking responsibility, just a little late, and trying to find ways to ensure a clean supply chain. As of summer 2014, they are headed in the right direction, but simply aren't there yet. The people at Apple are absolutely right when they say:

> The supply chain for tantalum consists of many types of businesses—including mines, brokers, ore processors and refiners, component manufacturers, and board assembly manufacturers—before reaching final assembly manufacturers. The combination of a lengthy supply chain and a refining process makes it difficult to track and trace tantalum from the mine to finished products—a challenge that Apple and others are tackling in a variety of ways.

For Apple this involves working with other big firms in the Extractives Workgroup, a joint effort of the Electronics Industry Code of Conduct and the Global e-Sustainability Initiative (GeSI). The Extractives Workgroup focuses on minerals used by the electronics industry and the supply chain. Their key actions so far have been a detailed study of the supply chain and a requirement that suppliers ensure their goods are clean. That's all well and good, and they've certainly done the right thing by bringing a lot of companies together to address the problem.

In 2012 the Enough Project on conflict minerals reviewed and published their second set of scores for the major electronics companies—grading them on their own inspection regimes and how well they worked with others, both politically and over the supply chains. Apple scored fairly well with a score of thirty-eight, and ranked ninth out of twenty-four major companies. Intel topped the list with a score of sixty and Nintendo, to its shame, lay at the bottom with a score of zero. At the same time the Enough Project pointed out that "four leading companies—Intel, Motorola Solutions, HP, and Apple—have been pioneers of progress." These firms had moved forward while other companies held back waiting for rules to be made by the U.S. Securities and Exchange Commission (SEC). Apple and the other companies had developed conflict minerals programs, including "a smelter auditing program and an aid project for lagging smelters, direct sourcing and aid projects to help Congo develop a clean minerals trade, and tracing projects to dig deeply into their supply chains to identify precise numbers of smelters." Apple still needs to enforce its own rules on smelters, work to adhere to the new guidelines set by international bodies, and implement the new regulations set by the U.S. Securities and Exchange Commission. It also wouldn't hurt if they'd publicly oppose the U.S. Chamber of Commerce's lawsuit against the SEC that is trying to quash the new rules on conflict minerals.

The popular media never stops reminding us that the CEOs of the big brand-name computer companies are visionaries and thought-leaders. So, how about a vision of a laptop that is absolutely free of slavery and ecocide? And how about some thought leadership to make that happen? Maybe instead of horizontal organizations at each step of the chain, they could assemble a vertical, multi-link, industry-wide group, like the Extractives Workgroup, to crack the problem. Tainted minerals are easier to identify the closer you are to the mines, so why not get behind the iTSCi project and the mineralogy nerds and crystallography boffins supported by the big German processor H.C. Starck who already know how to tag clean ore? Why not work with the anti-slavery groups that could introduce them to sources of minerals that give a good job and decent life to miners and their families? These heroes of the new economy are not half-starved militia soldiers, or local officials brutalized and corrupted as they grew up in a world of war, they're billionaires and stewards of some of the wealthiest companies in the world. They get to make choices about the world they are creating.

One of the tech visionaries we hear a lot about is Peter Thiel, best known as the co-founder of PayPal. And he really does have a vision, so he gets the last word on the people who make up the ninth link in the chain that leads from the mines in Congo to the phones in our pockets: "There are no sidelines in the struggle for dignity and freedom. Those who know what goes on in the world cannot sit back and expect government or some other abstract organization to handle it. . . . When you recognize that a principle, like liberty, is important, you should strive to promote it in all areas of your life: your work, investments, speeches, writing and philanthropy. The more you engage, the more effective you'll become."

The tenth link in the chain is where the corporations meet the consumers—in the store. Electronics are sold everywhere, and some companies like RadioShack or Best Buy, or giant retailers like Walmart and Target, sell truly vast amounts of goods, not just phones and computers, that *might* include conflict minerals. I would assume that these big retailers, understanding that consumers generally prefer not to buy goods tainted with slavery, would want to make their positions clear. Sadly, that doesn't seem to be the case. While it is possible that each of these companies does have a policy against selling electronics containing slave-harvested conflict minerals, you wouldn't know it from their websites. I used the search option on the main websites for RadioShack, Target, Walmart, Best

Buy, Costco, and the big UK electronic retailers Currys and Dixons, and found that "conflict minerals" always brought the same answer: "Unfortunately we could not find anything matching your request." So how is the average consumer going to know? To be fair, if one reads the fine print at the bottom of these websites, there's normally a little "corporate" link that will take you to a "global responsibility link," which will take you to an "ethical sourcing" link, which will lead you to a "suppliers and sourcing standards" link, and so on. So maybe they *are* being responsible, they just don't want anyone to know about it, and that's because none of them want to put their head above the parapet and admit they might have a problem. Their marketing department tells them that putting sad stories about conflict minerals on the front page of the website will just confuse and drive away customers. Their lawyers don't want anything on the website that might be interpreted as an admission of liability. And their market researchers point out that the number of consumers who know and care about slavery and minerals is so small as to be trivial. So the minimum gets done.

Of course, the supply chain doesn't end with the people running the big stores or the brand-name companies that make computers and phones; it ends with you and me. We're the last link. Thiel's words are a challenge to us as well. And we need that challenge. It is a sad truth that many of us think the supply chain ends in the shop where we buy things instead of in our homes where things get used. Everyone in the supply chain is responsible for making it slave-free and ecocide-free, and that includes us. So, what can *we* do? As it turns out, some of things you and I can do are pretty easy: You can send an email to Dell or Apple or IBM or Nokia and tell them it's important to you that your phone and laptop are free of slavery. You can dig through the fine print on their websites to see who has effective policies against slavery and environmental destruction when you choose a phone or computer. You can get behind one of the organizations that are pushing hard on this issue. And before you buy, you can have a look at the Enough Project's rankings and report—they give specific numbers rating each individual company's commitment to using conflict-free materials. And luckily in the United States, we've got some help with a new law on the books.

In 2009 Congressmen Jim McDermott (D-WA) and Frank Wolf (R-VA) co-sponsored the Conflict Minerals Trade Act. It didn't pass in Congress, but it came back in the next session as part of the much larger Dodd-Frank bill on financial reform of Wall Street; the Dodd-Frank Wall Street Reform and Consumer Protection Act passed in July 2010 and came into effect in 2011. Among other things, this law requires US companies that import products containing certain minerals to report whether they get their minerals from Congo or one of the surrounding countries. If a company reports that its supply chain passes through the region, they then have to report what they are doing to trace the minerals and prevent their purchases from funding the armed groups. The law doesn't make it illegal to import slave-mined minerals (there's already a law against that), but it does require companies to report on their websites exactly what they are doing (or not doing) so that consumers can choose companies they want to buy from. On the Apple website, for example, a search for "conflict minerals" takes you to a section devoted to "Supplier Responsibility—Labor and Human Rights." There among the reports on factory conditions and hiring practices, is a report on conflict minerals, and some reassuring news: "In January 2014, we confirmed that all active, identified tantalum smelters in Apple's supply chain were validated as conflict-free by third-party auditors, and we will continue to require all suppliers to use only verified tantalum sources. We know supply chains fluctuate, and we'll maintain ongoing monitoring of our suppliers' smelters." Then they report how far along they are in policing their supplies of tin, tungsten, and gold. Quarterly reports are provided for all smelters they work with, as well as a list of their NGO and industry partners in the work to clean things up. This is exactly what a consumer should be looking for, and other companies could be compared to Apple's level of compliance, or, even better, to Intel's.

The Dodd-Frank law has been something of a shock for a number of companies that use one of the listed conflict minerals—gold. The Senior Counsel at the U.S. Jewelers Vigilance Committee, speaking at the World Jewellery Confederation annual conference, said the new law has "caused great confusion—and expense." The confederation also wrote to the U.S. Securities and Exchange Commission to complain that gold was "very difficult to trace given the lack of a linear supply chain and the ease with which valuable yet small amounts of gold can be smuggled."

That's the thing about criminals that commit slavery and ecocide, they hide what they do and make things hard to trace. But if you're making your living dealing in metals, whether in the form of jewelry or cellphones, you have a responsibility to not hurt other people while you make profits. The supply chain may be complicated; the morals are not.

．　　■　　．

Back in Walikale the sun eases down and people are laughing at me. Waiting outside a low building I see a cloud of butterflies swarming some bushes near the road. These aren't your little Northern Hemisphere butterflies, but several different kinds of big equatorial forest butterflies. Their colors are astounding, their numbers vast, and my gawky leaping from bush to bush to get a closer look is cracking up a small crowd. The children, especially, are practically rolling in the dirt with laughter. After a few moments a couple of police come over, fix the scene with a stern look, and then lay down their weapons and start to chase butterflies. Slapping cupped hands together, one young soldier, with a shy grin, brings me an iridescent blue and white butterfly. I take it gently for a moment, admiring the wonder of it in the warm sunshine, then lift my hands and let it fly.

The situation in Eastern Congo is about as bad as it gets. War, random violence and rape, environmental destruction, chaos, and corruption seem to be locked in a constant vicious cycle, but there is also a chance the place is about to turn a corner. Whether it does and whether the people of Eastern Congo can begin to live without fear and slavery will depend, in part, on what you and I do over the next few years. In late 2010 things began to crack. First, President Kabila announced a ban on exports from the Walikale region, including the Bisie mine. He followed this up with a ban on exports from both North and South Kivu. We can hope Kabila was doing this for the right reasons, but upcoming elections in Congo and the passage of the Dodd-Frank law were also pushing him. At about the same time many of the largest companies in the electronics industry announced that they would no longer source from Eastern Congo, and the Congolese government announced it was backing the ITRI tracing project for clean minerals. It was a triple whammy—an export ban, the new US law on conflict minerals, and a de facto boycott by the main players in the electronics world. No one knows how much is still being smuggled out illegally, but some of the blatant offenders have been sidelined.

There was no better indication of progress than the spring 2011 withdrawal of the Congolese Army brigade that had been running the Bisie mine. Over a six-week period the troops were moved and the site was handed over to the North Kivu Provincial Mining Concessions Authority. In the hiatus, a local armed group, the Mai Mai Sheka, temporarily occupied the Bisie mine, stealing ore and whatever local property or money the local diggers had. Then like the bandits they are, the Mai Mai fled. The director of the state-run licensing body for mines stated, "The government's intention is to end artisanal mining in the East." At the same time, Alphamin Resources Corp., a mining company based in Vancouver, Canada, announced that they had acquired a 70 percent stake in the Bisie mine. By 2014, Alphamin had not just taken control of the site, but were carrying out an extensive geological survey to determine the extent of the mineral deposits. The armed gangs were literally just scratching the surface; it turns out there are rich deposits deep underground and the mine looks to be a great producer well into the future. At the same time, Alphamin has begun training programs for local people who will be employed as the mine develops, and has established a charitable foundation that allocates 4 percent of the local budget to projects chosen to aid the local communities. More mundane, but potentially more important for local development, the mining company has started construction of a road to link Bisie with the main road. When that is completed, the mine and the communities around it will no longer be isolated and vulnerable.

All this sounds good in the long run, but big changes are rarely easy or comfortable in the short run, and never in Eastern Congo. In the ongoing governmental shake-up, renegade Congolese soldiers attacked villages in South Kivu in late June 2011, raping and beating some 170 women. A mobile court in Baraka had earlier sentenced Lieutenant Colonel Kibibi Mutware to twenty years' imprisonment for mass rapes committed by his soldiers in apparent reprisal for the earlier lynching of a soldier from their unit. When the sentences were handed down, Kibibi and his officers fled an army training center with 150 men and attacked the local villages. Other mining sites were scenes of intense struggle as thugs worked furiously to get ore out before the US Dodd-Frank law came into effect.

Uncertainty still rules in the Kivus, and the fate of local people, those who have been enslaved and those whose precarious lives depend on the little they can make from small-scale mining, is unclear. While the Congolese army has driven armed groups out of some of the mining areas, rebel groups continue to control hundreds of the more remote mining sites and to pillage mineral markets, traders, and transporters.

And with the armed groups fading, there is the inevitable aftermath that follows a hot war. Jeffrey McNeely, a respected scientist specializing in tropical forests, put it this way: "While war is bad for biodiversity, peace can be even worse." He points to the civil wars and border wars in Borneo, Indonesia, Nicaragua, Laos, and Viet Nam that, once ended, started a race among the ex-combatants to illegally cut and sell timber. It will be a challenge to reassert control over the protected forests, and that will need help from the outside.

If peace comes to Eastern Congo it will increase the demand for land, fuel, building materials, minerals, and livelihoods. The people of North and South Kivu have been waiting to rebuild, to relaunch their farms and businesses, and all of that will require natural and financial resources. Ultimately, that's a good thing, and should bring in its wake more stability and infrastructure. With the factors that create slavery enclaves receding, slavery will likely diminish. Of course, slavery is unlikely to disappear completely. The large-scale enslavement of people as miners and porters may diminish, the children and young people forced to be soldiers may fade, but the enslavement of girls and women for commercial sexual use, and the use of boys and girls as domestic slaves could well increase as people have more money and some people choose to spend it on acquiring sex or enslaved servants.

That's why the problems of slavery and ecocide can't just be handled à la carte. If you solve only one piece of the problem, it may well exacerbate other parts of the issue. There has to be a holistic solution. The demand for desirable new consumer products didn't cause the horrors in Eastern Congo, but it helped create a context in which the mineral riches of the region became a curse. As the rule of law collapsed, thugs ruled and black markets thrived. As criminal smash-and-grab exploitation expanded, slavery and ecocide inevitably followed. To come back from slavery and ecocide, all of these must be reversed. We don't have to give up our cool consumer electronics, the key is to reinstate the rule of law, and rebuild a society that accepts the law. That way the vicious cycle of slavery and environmental destruction can be reversed to a virtuous cycle of sustainable development and responsible environmental stewardship. One local conservationist, who helped protect the gorillas, told me: "If it is sustainable and environmentally appropriate, then the mining is acceptable *outside the preserve*. We can't keep the whole forest isolated, but we can't allow the destruction of the forest until nothing is left. That is the problem! There has to be a balance, so local communities benefit. These [nature] reserves used to be protected by the traditional chiefs and tribes, but then the outsiders [the armed groups] came, they said 'Just close your eyes while we take the mahogany' and they began to strip the forest until it is ruined. If you resisted, you were shot." The armed groups have left behind a chaotic and dismembered society; somehow it has to be rebuilt.

■   ■   ■

I set out to understand how ecocide and slavery walk hand in hand. But learning about the human and environmental wreckage left behind, I also learned about my own shortsightedness. If we are the beneficiaries of the work of slaves and the devastation of the environment, our responsibility goes far beyond ensuring that we have clean laptops. If others paid for our favorite tools and toys with their bodies and minds, we owe them relief, care, and restitution. Without that their damage will roll like a hereditary disease down through the generations.

The psychological impact alone is daunting. For instance, the women in the Panzi Hospital in Bukavu in the Eastern Congo have become known around the world both for their horrific injuries and for their strength. More than 25,000 operations have been performed there, most to repair the terrible damage done to women's genitals by repeated rape and other sexual violence. These rapes have not been the actions of rogue soldiers breaking discipline, but a calculated weapon of war, smashing families and communities. The psychological impact of just under half of all women and nearly a quarter of men *in the entire population* of Eastern Congo suffering rape and sexual violence is hard to comprehend.

The shock of sexual assault is often the beginning of slavery, followed by grinding abuse and dangerous and degrading work that destroys the natural world. Rape is used to break the spirit and make the new slave more pliable, and that slave is then used as a tool against nature, crushing it to fund more violence and more slavery. This cycle of rape, slavery, and ecocide is not the work of lone criminals, but a vicious policy from the very top that brings new meaning to the term "total war."

It is a truth that human beings survive what so often seems to be un-survivable. At the same time, survivors are changed. William Faulkner, writing of his own Mississippi, understood this when he wrote, "The past is never dead. It's not even past." For the survivors of this total war, the past will be a long time dying—but their deliverance can be hastened if we help.

How do we—and the men and women in the electronics companies who share our responsibility—make this right? The first step is just to admit what we've done and stop thinking *we're* some kind of victim because conflict minerals have been foisted upon us. Yes, criminals tried hard to conceal what they were doing, but we created the market, rushing headlong into the wonders of our new electronics and demanding that they be cheap and plentiful. The corporations responded to our demand, and we've done well out of it, but we were heedless of where all this great stuff was coming from. It's time to accept our responsibility. Then we can start to clean up the mess we helped to create.

The next steps involve focusing on two areas. This first is to get behind the people and groups that are making a difference in Eastern Congo. At the end of this book you can find a list of solid, honest organizations working in Eastern Congo that would really appreciate your help. The second is to let our politicians know we care about this. Eastern Congo has about the same population as the state of Connecticut. What would our response be if half the women and a quarter of the men in Connecticut were suffering rape and sexual violence? And what would we feel if this violence was being carried out, in part, to provide components for our phones and computers? Connecticut is also one of the most wooded states in America—60 percent of the land is forested. How would we feel about the wholesale destruction of these Appalachian woodlands in order to fuel even greater violence in the state? Righting a vast wrong, one in which we've had a hand, is more important than partisan politics and ideological wrangling. Calling on governments, whether in the United States or Europe, is important because the widespread corruption of the Congolese state is the fertile ground where violence, slavery, and ecocide grow. It is almost impossible for individuals to confront that corruption from afar, but governments bring more weight and leverage. The bottom line is this: cleaning up our supply chain is just step one; cleaning up the mess left behind by the corruption and violence of the supply chain, healing the damage done to the innocent and to the natural world is also our responsibility and is going to take a while. How long it takes will depend on how quickly and how fully we choose to make things right.

· · ·

In the Congo, the sheer scale of human and ecological suffering boggled me. Was this the result of a particularly vicious war? When the Rwandan genocide spilled over into Congo and exploded into civil war, did the force of that whirlwind create a situation of unique violence and destruction? Clearly, slavery and ecocide can go hand in hand in the chaos of war, especially when ripping the environment to pieces can bring in millions of dollars. But what if a country is at peace? I'd heard of similar destruction and slavery in Asia, of a great forest falling to the slaveholders. If the link between slavery and ecocide is not just a tragic anomaly rooted in war, then I needed to show that it could grow anywhere. In Bangladesh I found a watery maze where children may not have to flee rape and kidnap by armed thugs, but once captured and sent to fell trees they are pushed into a different kind of conflict. This time with an adversary that doesn't care to enslave them, only to kill and consume them—the Bengal tiger.

4

SHRIMP COCKTAIL

Shumir is about nineteen years old, with a young man's thin mustache and light soft stubble on his cheeks. His thick black hair is combed back and his reddish brown skin is marked with small scars—between his eyebrows, above his left eye, and on his right cheek. His forehead is high and his eyes are peppery, showing uncertainty but no fear. He wears his pale blue long-sleeved shirt buttoned loosely over a gray and black T-shirt, which is over another T-shirt, a yellow one. He needs the layers, it's a chilly day. We're sitting together in a schoolroom, a simple pole frame building, the walls and floor covered in woven palm mats under a tin roof. There are no windows, but open palm-leaf shutters let in the morning light. No furniture except a single desk for the teacher.

We're in a small river village far down the Rupsa River at the bottom of the country of Bangladesh. It's accessible only by boat, and about thirty miles farther downriver is the island of Dublar Char. Surrounding us are the Sundarbans, hundreds of islands that hold the largest mangrove forest in the world. As we sit cross-legged on the floor Shumir tells me his story.

"When I was sixteen," Shumir says, "my father sent me to Dublar Char. My family, my parents, were very poor, and the economy was so bad, my parents sent me there. A recruiter came to our house. He

told my parents he would give them 2,000 taka [$29] if they'd let me
come and work. He promised to pay them more later when I had
earned more. He said the work was easy, you just cut fish and hang
them on racks to dry, and there was plenty of food to eat. My parents needed the money and I wanted to help, so it was agreed and I
left with the recruiter.

"We traveled all night on a boat, it was cold but all right, and they
gave me some rice. There were some other boys on the boat as well.
In the morning we reached the island and the recruiter handed us
over to a boss. Right away the boss began to shout at us, he told us
we had to make our own shelter. He gave us tools and we began to
cut poles and palm leaves. As we worked, one of the trees fell on one
boy breaking his hand. The bones were pushing out, the skin all
lumpy, the boss just sent him to a boat and told them to take him
back.

"Before we could finish the shelter, boats came to the island with
the fish they'd caught that day. Now the work really started. As long
as the boats came we had to keep working. First we'd wade into the
water and carry baskets of fish to shore. Once several basket loads
were spilled out on a mat some of us would begin to cut open the
fish and clean them. Some fish had to be cut a certain way, others
had to be split just right. As the cleaned and split fish piled up, other
boys would run them over to the racks and hang them to dry. The
racks were just poles tied together, some were one level, maybe four
feet high, but others were built up and up and you had to climb up
eight, ten, twelve feet or more to put fish on the different levels.

"It was cold. We were always cold and wet. My clothes would be
soaked from wading into the water to the boats, and the fish guts
were everywhere, splashing onto us as we cut them open. We sat on
the wet ground all night. If we slowed down or stopped the boss
would hit us, if we weren't moving fast when we hung the fish on the
racks he'd hit us with a long stick he carried. All the time he'd yell at
us, calling us filthy names. Some boats brought their catch at night,
others just at dawn. Often we'd have to work twenty-four hours

straight. Maybe we'd be able to snatch a little sleep. The boss made us keep going as long as there were fish to clean and hang on the racks. The longer I worked, I'd get exhausted and clumsy. Sometimes I'd cut myself with the gutting knife or slip and fall from the drying rack. If you were cut or hurt, you had to keep working. Whenever I made a mistake, the boss would hit me.

"About twelve of us slept in the same shelter, and we got one meal a day. The recruiter lied about the food. The boss would give us 250 grams of old dried lentils [9 ounces, about a cup and a half] for the whole group, and we'd make a thin soup. There were bits of fish around but we couldn't eat them. There were fish guts everywhere, everything stank of fish, we didn't want to eat fish, we were sick of fish. Sometimes, if we got really hungry, we'd eat a small handful of fish. With the lentils the boss sometimes gave us two or three potatoes to split between all of us, or maybe some old cauliflower to put in the soup. We'd put a lot of chili peppers in the soup to cover up the rank old lentils. We were hungry all the time.

"I got sick. Once I had a fever, I was too sick to work. The boss came and beat me till I got up and went back to work. It was always this way, fevers and diarrhea. While I was there, seven or eight people in the fishing camp died of diarrhea. The guard would just take their bodies into the forest and leave them.

"There were two small boys in our hut. The guard was sexually abusing them. He would come and get one or the other of them from the shelter at night. They were really hurt. I felt so guilty that I couldn't protect them. The guard would come at night and take a boy, and we'd want to stop him but we couldn't. If we said anything, the guards would beat us. Finally, after two and a half months a boat came from my village to buy dried fish. I knew someone on the boat. I talked to the people on the boat and told them what was happening. That night, as we were loading fish, we sneaked the two boys onto the boat. They were hidden behind the baskets of dried fish when the boat left. The people on the boat were frightened, they knew they'd be hurt if they were caught.

"That night we were very frightened too. I knew the guard would kill us if he found out, but I had an idea. So early the next morning *we* went to the guard and said, 'Where are those boys? What did you do with them? We can't find them!' We knew the guard would kill us if he knew the truth. The guard was confused, he just said, 'Oh, maybe they ran into the forest and a tiger ate them . . . ' He never suspected what had happened. He probably thought they had run away into the forest.

"I was on Dublar Char six months, the whole winter when the fish are coming. When the season came to an end, the boss let me get on a boat with some of the last fish sold. I was sick and weak, but the boat left me near my village and I was able to get home. I was never paid, my parents never got anything beyond the 2,000 taka the recruiter gave them. Now it is winter again and my father wants me to go because he wants the money, but I said 'no'—now there is a training project and I am learning carpentry. I am making chairs and tables. I make them according to order. I'm doing okay."

Shumir doesn't seem nervous now, we've been talking for nearly an hour and his gaze is steady and slightly inquisitive. I thank him and dearly wish I could order some chairs from him to help him get started. What he's told me confirms what I've been hearing and seeing. This whole region has been transformed by the demand for fish and shrimp. And Shumir's fish camp is just one part of a much larger picture.

.   .   .

There are thousands of children enslaved on Dublar Char and other islands in Sundarbans as well as the wider Bay of Bengal. Some process fish like Shumir, others work the shrimp farms or process shrimp in makeshift factories. Fifty years ago there were no shrimp farms or camps like his carved out of the protected forest. In the past local fishermen worked the waters and took their catch to the markets in nearby river towns. At that time, the Sundarban islands, already a UNESCO World Heritage Site, and the great mangrove forest, the largest carbon sink in Southeast Asia, was protected more by its wild remoteness than by the laws setting it aside as a national park.

All that changed when seafood went global.

In America and Europe it was a slow, barely noticeable change. In the 1950s a fancy meal might start with shrimp cocktail, four or five shrimp arranged around the rim of a cocktail glass filled with sauce. It was country club food, it cost more than steak, and you turned up your pinkie as you ate it and got to think of yourself as sophisticated in the bargain. Unless you happened to be near the Gulf of Mexico, those fresh little shrimp would have been rushed over a long distance at enormous cost. Adjusted for inflation, those five little shrimp around a cocktail glass in 1950 cost over a dollar *each*. Today three dollars will buy you a whole pound of shrimp brought all the way from Bangladesh to your refrigerator.

No labor costs

In the USA and Europe shrimp and frozen fish are everywhere, big bags in the freezer, popcorn shrimp by the bucket, cheap, convenient, and maybe even healthy. When cargo ships were turned into floating freezers the size of office buildings, shrimp and fish became freight. And unlike the declining stocks of wild deepwater fish like cod or tuna, shrimp can be farmed. All you need is a flat and floodable coastline that can be turned into pools like giant rice paddies.

True worth is Bio?

As demand for cheap fish and shrimp ramped up, a gold rush began in Bangladesh, Southern India, Indonesia, Thailand, Burma, and Sri Lanka. "Worthless" swamp was converted into monoculture shrimp farms, fish processing camps sprang up, and the great freezer ships were always hungry for more. Hearing of work, poor families flooded into the Sundarban wilderness. Some people were able to make a fresh start, and some landowners working in fish and shrimp were honest and treated their workers well. But criminals were already using child slaves on fishing platforms out in the ocean, and for them it was an easy step to enslave more workers to rip out mangrove forests and farm the little wrigglers that would make such a fine profit.

From a camp like Shumir's, dried fish flow mainly into local markets, for pet food and livestock feed and human food, such as fish
stock cubes. You don't think of organized crime being involved in
stock cubes, but a wilderness island like Dublar Char makes a perfect slave-based processing site.

Not all seafood is touched by slavery, of course, but across the
region children are enslaved to catch, clean, pack, and sometimes
dry, fish and shrimp. Americans import around 2.4 billion pounds of
seafood a year, which makes up about 85 percent of the seafood
Americans eat. And when it comes to shrimp, the United States imports significantly more than other countries. Americans love
shrimp, and almost half of all US seafood imports are shrimp.
Ninety percent of this shrimp comes from Southeast Asia. Asian
shrimp is also the second-largest imported seafood to Great Britain
(after cod) and is increasing every year. The amount of shrimp imported from Bangladesh and the Sundarbans was down in 2009 after
Cyclone Aila crashed into the area, but the trend in 2011 and 2012
was up sharply as farms recovered.

The cyclone reminded everyone that the border between ocean
and wilderness can be a dangerous place. Aila brought a storm surge
ten to twenty-five feet high that swept over low clay dikes, washed
away villages, and destroyed some 6,000 shrimp farms in the area
just above the Sundarbans. The surge generated by Hurricane Katrina in 2005 was about the same size, but unlike New Orleans, the
Sundarbans had no large-scale levees or concrete sea walls. For enslaved children on fishing platforms or in fishing camps along the
shoreline, there was no warning or protection. A shrimp farm
worker many miles upriver from the ocean told me, "When the
surge reached all the way to us, we only had a few minutes to climb
as high as we could. I stood on the roof of a house that was up on
stilts and it still flooded above its windows. The incoming flood
water was full of floating bodies."

．　．　．

Up close, the Sundarbans look, feel, and smell like the world was created last week. Nothing seems to have settled down, life oozes up from the mud, and earth and water keep struggling for dominance. Yet for thousands of years the "Holy River" Ganges and other rivers of South Asia have come here to meet the sea. Most of the country of Bangladesh is simply the vast delta of these rivers, a delta growing infinitesimally higher with their silt deposits, even as global warming causes sea levels to rise ever faster. Sediment, soil, vegetation, and all the floaty dead from insects to elephants have washed down these rivers for millennia, slowed their journey in the flatness of the delta, and settled into the mud. Mote by mote the mud and soil pile up. Where mud nears the surface, colonies of mangrove take root. Wrapped in mist and fog, this is a world of water and earth in constant dance, but water is the leading partner. The mangrove forests thrive on this rhythm, branches in the sky, trunks awash with the nutrients of regular, sometimes daily floods. More than one hundred species live in this special place where river meets sea, their biologies specially adapted to the tidal interplay of fresh and salty water.

Two vibrant ecosystems rub shoulders here. On the ocean side the nutrient-rich waters of the sandy coastal shelf are home to crabs, fish, sea birds, urchins, turtles, clams, mollusks, and all the life that roils and grows where the ocean meets the land. On the other side, fresh water running down to the sea sustains the mangroves, trees that spread wide roots in the slosh and muck of the coastal flats. At the interface between the two, nature really goes wild—monkeys, birds of all descriptions, flowering plants, parasitic orchids, marsh irises, fruit and bush, vine and creeper, and below them frogs, more turtles, snakes, fish, and sometimes the sleek flash of an otter. The water here is brackish; sometimes the seawater pushes in, sometimes the fresh water presses back into the sea—an invigorating cycle for the fauna of this rich swamp. Vegetation falls and rots and feeds the fish and crustaceans of the coastal waters, the waves push in from the sea and flush out food for sea birds and scavengers. Intertwined

like the fingers of two hands, the wet and dry worlds are locked in
balance, transmuting the struggle of sea and earth, of salt and fresh,
into life. *love* ♡

But to settle here people need to separate the wet and dry. Dikes
are built, the swamps drained and trees cut. The easiest way to kill a
tree is to girdle it, carving away a strip of bark in a circle all the way
around the trunk. This stops the flow of nutrients coming up from
the roots and the tree starves to death. You can kill a forest in the
same way. Dikes girdle a mangrove jungle, cutting the supply of
water to the roots. As the ground dries, the trees and brush die back
and are chopped down and hauled away, driving off the birds and
animals that live there. To grow shrimp the cleared land is plowed
and treated with manure. When the mudflat is stripped clean and
ready, the water is let back in. What was a living forest is now a
shrimp farm, a lake two to three feet deep covering hundreds of
acres.

Some of the earth dug out for shrimp farms is piled up for camps
and villages. In the settlements the exposed muddy clay has a smooth
gray-yellow consistency. It is thick, sticky, viscous, and malleable
when wet, but left in the sun and air it dries hard. For the people
who come here mud is the universal construction material. Damp
mud is sliced into blocks and loaded into baskets. Carried on shoulders, millions of basket loads are stacked up to make the dikes. As
dry land appears on one side of the dike, walks, more dams, walls,
platforms, foundations, houses, animal pens, pump stands, outdoor
workspaces, and ledges for stacking goods are all built up from the
mud blocks. More blocks are packed tightly to make raised walkways from one house or workplace to the next.

On a mud-block foundation huts are framed up with poles, then
walled in with woven mats plastered with stucco made of mud and
cow manure. The walls are decorated with grooved finger stripes
and the prints of the hands that have kneaded, pressed, and smoothed
it into place. Thatch mixes haphazardly with clay tiles or a sheet of
corrugated tin to form the roof. Inside the hut, raised platforms of

hardened mud hold pots and pans. Even the stove is made of the same clay mud, baked hard by the fire within, a round hole on top neatly cupping a cooking pot.

Where enough of the clay has been removed water claims a permanent space—creating channels, ponds, boat landings, lakes, watering holes for livestock, and shrimp and fish pools. The channels and dikes tame the river and tide, moving them from pond to pond to grow or harvest the fish or shrimp. The biggest and highest dikes face the rivers, and little villages are strung along the top of the dikes connected by footpaths. The dikes and their paths stretch for miles, enclosing thousands of acres of wetland, cleared of trees, flooded, shallow, and flat.

Walking the circumference of one dike I was boggled by the sheer human effort that went into it. Basically a broad hardened mud wall with a path three or four feet wide on top, it stretched for miles and raised me ten or more feet above the water. How many people labored to make this wall and path, built up by hand, one basket load of mud at a time? How many of the children at play along the path were born in the huts that cling to the top of this wall? Every few hundred yards a little village, maybe four or five families, hung like a barnacle on the edge of the dike. The path on the top of the dike is Main Street for these families, and I passed within inches of women cooking, children playing near their beds, men mending nets or chopping wood. Where the dike faced the broad river it grew another ten to twenty feet. It had to, this is a mighty stream, up to a mile wide and rising and falling many feet each day with the tide.

Very little grows in the hardened clay. Grass can sometimes take root, and in the villages some trees and bushes are planted and cared for. A few trees are also left standing along the riverbank to keep the dike from being undercut through erosion, or along the path for shade. Otherwise the space around the huts is bare and dusty, a sharp contrast to the deep green of the forest nearby.

One afternoon, after walking past all the villages, I reached a point where the dike bordered the mangrove jungle, virgin land still untouched. After the sterility of the sunbaked and barren dike, I felt drawn to the woods. There was life here, I could smell it. The air seemed lighter, fresher, more complex. I caught the scent of blossoms, and underneath that was something dark and musky. Flocks of birds flitted along the water's edge, swallows twisting and turning as they took insects on the wing. Enjoying the lively show, I eased down the bank toward the forest. But as I did a man walking behind me began to shout, "No! No! Get away, get on the other side, away from the forest! Don't walk by the jungle!" I was baffled, this quiet, almost meditative walk was suddenly shot through with panic. Then he screamed: "Tigers! There are tigers there, they will take you!"

Tigers? The man was agitated but I wasn't convinced. When I had first arrived at the shrimp camp I was given a palm hut to sleep in. It was set on poles seven feet off the ground as protection against floods. There was no electricity and the outhouse on the edge of camp was just a hole in the ground. Four sticks set in the ground around it were draped with old rice sacks, just enough to preserve modesty. An old fisherman at the camp showed me the outhouse, but said, "Never go out to pee at night, never!"

"What? Why?"

"Because of the tigers!"

At the moment he said this I was looking across a little bridge to a village jammed against the side of a dike, people working and talking, children playing. There were boats and rectangular pools of water where the tide brings in the shrimp. The forest was nearly a mile away. Tigers? I didn't think so. I knew what this warning was: country people telling tall tales to scare a foreigner. I'd done the same back home, spinning stories to spook the city folk when they came down South. And for the next two nights I didn't worry about slipping out to watch the moon on the water, listen to the quiet and the birds, and marvel at the noisy silence of the wilderness.

Now standing in the blazing sunlight, I felt sure no tiger would strike at the top of a dike with three noisy humans clomping and shouting. But the man wouldn't be quiet and shouted and gestured again and again. As I wondered what to do, his son climbed down to me and pointed to the fresh mud at my feet. There, among leaves and twigs, was the fresh paw print of a cat. It was as clear as if a housecat had stepped in water and walked across dry concrete pavement. But this print was big, very big, and when I scrambled down the bank to measure it, I saw it was nearly the size of my hand. The cat that went with this print was much bigger than me.

A chill went through me in spite of the heat, and for a moment I wondered, "What's a tiger doing *here?*" But then I realized that I was the one out of place, not the tiger. Bengal tigers have been here for thousands of years, lords of the food chain, perfectly at home in both the trees and the water. They are made for it; this ecosystem is their evolutionary niche. Tigers live alone and aggressively scent-mark large territories to keep their rivals away. How much of this tiger's territory had been walled off and decimated by this dike? Were these shrimp farms and little villages inside his boundary? When population pressure and desperation drive people into the wilderness, the tigers feel pressure too. Female tigers give birth to two to six cubs every few years. Around age two the young tigers spread out to claim their own territory. Was this tiger looking for living space just where the jungle is being chewed away for shrimp farms? Was I just one more addition to the menu now that his feeding range had been reduced?

[handwritten margin note: strain on nature]

■ ■ ■

While the natural ebb and flow of tide and water are stopped when the dikes are built and the forest is removed, the shrimp farms echo this rhythm but manipulate it. This is not fishing, it is a factory farm for crustaceans. Just like the factory farms that provide our pigs or turkeys, bacon or veal, there is no normal breeding, egg laying, or raising of babies; disease, pollution, and mistreated workers are the norm. I had come to this shrimp camp to learn how shrimp are farmed. This operation was a well-established but still rather primi-

tive camp owned by an absentee landlord and the workers living
here were free to come and go. Enclosing and clearing this piece of
forest had made a pool about three hundred acres in size.

Every month the men who live and work at the camp throw
around 150,000 baby shrimp, called fry, into the shallow water.
They buy these fry from families that fish for them in the deepest
parts of the tidal river. Going out on the river, I pulled alongside
three wooden boats that were seining for fry to supply the farms.
From a distance it had looked as if one boat, about twelve feet long,
was inflating a giant hot air balloon, a vast bubble rising electric blue
from the surface of the river. In fact, they were using the wind to fill,
straighten, and smooth the super-fine mesh net used to catch fry.
Two women wrestled with the net as it filled, determined to keep it
under control. As we drew near I could see children gently scraping
a residue of fine pinkish lint from the net, and carefully placing it in
a small pan of water. Climbing into their boat and looking into the
pan I could make out the tiny fry. They looked like short thin red
lines in the water, as if drawn with a fine pen. Smaller than an eye-
lash, they would jerk and float awhile, then jerk and float again.
Some of the longer wrigglers had a tiny bump at one end, like microscopic protozoa. The net was very large, swelling to the size of a
proper living room when filled with the wind, but when pulled out
of the river it held only two handfuls of the tiny fry. "You have to go
deep for fry," said the woman, "these are from about thirty feet
down."

Once collected, the fry are spread into the three hundred acres of
the shrimp farm pond and left to grow. The pond is connected to
the river by a single channel with a sluice gate cut into the dike next
to the camp. This channel is the business end of the farm. About
twenty yards long, a tightly woven fence of sticks and reeds crosses
it, with a second, smaller dike at the far end facing the shrimp pool.
Where the pond enters the channel there's a V-shaped weir, an ancient type of fish trap dating back to the Bronze Age. Most of the

time nothing happens in the channel, and life at the camp is pretty relaxed. There are nets, tools, and huts to be mended, daily prayers, meals to be cooked and eaten, and some fishing in the pond. It's a good idea to catch the crabs and fish that will eat the growing shrimp, and they can be sold or eaten right away. But when the moon is new or waxes toward full, the work increases.

"When the moon is full, the shrimp get crazy," I was told. Crazy they may be, but normal shrimp behavior makes them easy to catch. Shrimp tend to be active at night, swimming and looking for food, and they are most lively shortly after sunset and in the hour or two before sunrise. They are also stimulated by water movement and, as they grow larger, will swim against any current they find, following an urge to migrate into deeper offshore water. Duplicate the natural currents of the sea and the shrimp will deliver themselves into the channel for harvest.

When night falls and both the tide and full moon rise, the river sluice gate is opened and water pours through the channel and into the pond. The larger shrimp can "smell" the new water, feel the current, and begin to swim toward the river and, they hope, the deeper ocean. Soon shrimp enter the channel and congregate as they swim to the small gap at the point of the V-shaped weir. The weir is a gate of no return, once they pass through, it is nearly impossible to go back the other way, and, anyway, they're yearning for the wide-open spaces. A few yards farther down the channel they can feel and smell the river but now they are pressed against the tightly woven fence of reeds and sticks—the current flows through and draws them, but the shrimp are stuck.

In the morning, the sluice gate is closed and the flow of river water stops. With daylight the shrimp settle to the bottom as the water level in the channel rapidly falls, draining into the pond. As the sun comes over the horizon, boys with nets wade up to their knees in mud and sweep up the shrimp, crabs, and fish, dragging them onto the grass and separating them into baskets. From the direction of the river, as if they too are drawn by the full moon, merchants run their boats aground next to the camp. Nearby, on a concrete slab, the sorting and bartering begin.

The merchants are buying. Big "tiger" shrimp are selling for about $4 a pound and medium shrimp for $3. Fish are the real bargain: tilapia and other big fish like bass are going for fifty cents a pound. Really big crabs get a premium, selling for almost as much as the shrimp, but small crabs go cheaply. As the buyers rake up their purchases, the man in charge of the shrimp camp talks to me about the buyers. "Most of these men are honest," he says, "but that man there, he's not." When I ask if the dishonest man tries to cheat him, he replies, "Not me, he cheats his customers, and the exporters. He'll take these big shrimp and then inject them with water that has been used for boiling rice. It's heavy and starchy, with the extra weight he doubles the price he gets. Sometimes the export buyers notice and reject his shrimp, but mostly they don't, so it's worth the risk." So, if its flavor seems a little exotic, it could be because that plump shrimp on your barbeque was pumped up with the leftover rice water from a Bangladeshi family's dinner.

Many of the shrimp farms are not as laid-back as the one where I stayed, where the workers are paid. On many farms the profits are higher because the workers are enslaved. It takes only a simple bait-and-switch with wages and debt, plus investment in a weapon or a thug, and profits rise dramatically. No one knows how many of the shrimp farms have been constructed with slave labor and now use enslaved men, women, and children to cultivate and harvest the shrimp. Children like Shumir, who was trapped on the island of Dublar Char, are also sucked into slavery in the dispersed shrimp ponds. The most that can be said is that by the time they are harvested, *some* shrimp are tainted by slavery. But the story doesn't end at harvest.

The shrimp camp where I stayed had no slavery, but that didn't affect the environmental cost. Sure, some of the shrimp will be injected with rice water, but most arrive in the city of Khulna within hours of harvest. Khulna, Bangladesh, is a key port for shipping frozen shrimp to America and Europe, the water there is deep enough to take the big freighters, and processing factories line the docks ready to turn tons of fresh raw shrimp into cleaned, packaged, and frozen food ready for shipment. In the heart of Khulna, where the main streets are lined with fancy hotels, the city fathers have erected a statue to their most illustrious benefactor. Standing on a broad pedestal at the intersection of the city's three most important avenues, and rearing up another fifteen feet, is a giant shrimp sculpted of golden metal. The crustacean is far more imposing and dignified than the life-sized bronze of a politician a couple of blocks away, relegated to the edge of a dusty park. In Khulna they know who pays the bills.

The huge demand for shrimp in Europe and North America means that money pours into this city. It is a city of "shrimp magnates," men who own the grand hotels and mansions, the big farms on the edge of town, fancy cars, and who party in the flashy clubs and restaurants that are far beyond the reach of the average Bangladeshi family. These magnates are factory owners who hold foreign export licenses and deal directly with North American and European companies. Their factories process the shrimp and freeze them, but long ago the factory owners learned that, paradoxically, you make more money by having a smaller factory. This is because many of their American and European customers want to inspect their factories, checking on cleanliness and looking into the health and safety of the workers. The foreigners want to see gloves and protective clothing on the employees, hard hats and blade guards so that a sliced-off finger doesn't end up in a package of frozen shrimp. Some even want to label the shrimp they bought as "slavery free." They want to be able to tell their customers that the women cleaning and packing their shrimp are working normal hours and getting enough pay to support their families. So the factory owners make sure the little factory their company owns is safe and clean and ready for inspection.

Of course, this small factory is window dressing. It is too small to handle more than a fraction of the shrimp the magnate processes. While it does prepare, pack, and freeze shrimp for export, even making a small profit, the bulk of what the exporter sells will come from subcontractors. Nine out of ten workers processing shrimp in Khulna work for these subcontractors, and almost all the workers are women. The subcontractors don't worry about inspections, protective clothing, hard hats, or blade guards. Their mostly female employees work sixty, seventy, even eighty hours a week, but they don't have a regular job. In spite of the law that any operation with more than five workers is to be treated as a factory and covered by labor regulations, these women are hired as "day laborers." They're not paid by the day, however, but by the amount of shrimp they process, and may have to wait weeks for their pay to be handed over. As one lawyer told me: "They have no rights, no set working hours, no fixed wages, no contract or appointment letter, and no employment record book. In Khulna this complete negation of the labor laws has existed for at least thirty years, so today there is no sense that this is anything but normal."

Poor women are drawn into the work by recruiters who promise good wages and regular employment. Once on the job they discover the truth, but stay because they feel it is the only work they can get, and they need their wages to feed their children. I'll let Amrita explain how this happens. She is one of a group of women "day laborers" I met one afternoon in a secret spot in Khulna. It was their afternoon off, which comes only once every two weeks, precious time I was very grateful they shared with me. Women who spoke to journalists or researchers in the past have been badly beaten, so they were worried that no one could identify them. "Amrita" is a name I've chosen from a list of popular Bengali girls' names I found on the Web. That cool morning Amrita was wearing an orange sweater and had covered her head with a pretty patterned scarf of orange, black, and yellow. She sat forward in her chair, clearly worried, her shoulders tight and her arms crossed rigidly in front. A woman in her thirties, her face was clear and determined, but more than a little grim—she knew she was taking a big risk by talking to me. As we talked, her dark brown eyes would sometimes flash with anger.

"I didn't really have a choice about working in shrimp," said Amrita. "There was no food for my children, my husband was not working, it was the only job available. If I had some education, maybe I could have found a different job, but it's hard to get a job when you don't have any education. [Two thirds of women in Bangladesh are illiterate.] When I started work, my job was head removal. I didn't get an advance, just 3 taka [less than 5 cents] for every kilogram of shrimp I processed. Every time I'd turn in a basket of shrimp I'd be given a receipt. This gave the weight of what I had done, but I think they were writing down less than I actually did. You have to hold on to these little slips of paper, because you can get paid only once a week, and you are paid only for the slips of paper you have. If you lose a receipt, or if it gets wet and can't be read, then you don't get paid for that work. Once a girl lost all her receipts for that week—the contractor got all that work for nothing. This is how the contractors keep you there, how you always have to do what they say, otherwise they just throw you out and you lose what they owe you. Delayed payments are another way to keep you tied and dependent on the contractor. Sometimes they say they don't have enough money and then they give food instead of money. This is a kind of side business for him. The contractor will give me 15 taka worth of rice, but then he deducts 20 taka from my pay later. What can I do? My children need food. The contractor does this with everything we need—oil, rice, lentils, and soap.

"But the worst part is how we're treated. The contractors are rough, they behave like animals, they even beat me. One woman I was working with was older, about forty. The contractor wanted to get rid of her, so one of his men threw a basket of shrimp on the floor and blamed her. They took her to another room and beat her. They beat her so much she wet herself, then threw her out on the street. I slipped away and called the woman's daughter, who came and got her. Later the contractor tried to bribe her to keep her quiet, but the woman said, 'No! You've destroyed my body and now I can't work anymore,' and she contacted a lawyer with a rights organization. The case has been going for three years but nothing happens, I'm keeping quiet, but if there is ever a trial, I'll be a witness for her.

"At work we're forbidden to talk to each other. And if you say anything, complain about anything, you're punished. Sometimes they just won't pay you. When it comes time to be paid, you give them your receipts, and they just say, 'No, no pay for you.' What can you do? You can't refuse any order, always they are shouting and talking very rough to you. Always watching you, the contractor won't allow you to say 'no' to anything. If you say you won't do something, they just grab you by the neck and throw you in the street.

"If a buyer does come to where we are working, the contractor tells us to lie about how much we are paid and how much we work. He says that if we don't lie, we'll be fired. In fact, in the high season he makes us work all night as well. If a lot of shrimp come in, he'll keep us there and we'll be working for twenty-four hours. If we get sick, they just push us and shout at us to keep working. When a big shipment has to go out in high season we'll have to do other jobs after the shrimp are packed, like stack the boxes and load the trucks, everything to get the shipment out on time. We'll be working until two A.M. Then in the low season we're laid off, there's very little work and we go hungry. In the low season we live hand to mouth, trying to find food for the children.

"There are a lot of problems, but I can't find an alternative. I don't have any ID card, and there is nothing to prove I even work for the contractor. If anything goes wrong, he just says we don't work there and then there's no pay and if you complain they hit you. This happens. Anyway, we're women, so even if we only work twelve hours, there is still more work. We go home and we have to work there, cooking and taking care of the children. I barely see my children! On one Friday we have to work a double shift, twenty-four hours, then we get the next Friday off. If you have to stay home because your child is sick, then there is no pay, nothing to buy food.

"All I want is for my children to get an education, to be able to live a life that is better than mine. Maybe if I could get a better job this could happen. It would be so good to live peacefully, that would be so much better for my family. And, well, I would like to have an ID card, so I could get better pay. Maybe you could tell the people in other countries about this. Tell them that we are working very hard here but we are not getting our rights, how the contractors are sucking the life out of us, no proper salary, and everything else. Maybe then things will change." After saying all this Amrita looked at me with the same determined look. Her eyes were a little softer on me now, but she is realistic, she knows if change does come it will be slow and hard, and may not be in time for her and her family.

A human rights worker told me how hard it can be to bring change. A young lawyer, with a Clark Gable smile and impossibly long eyelashes, he has been working in Khulna for six years. Many of his cases concern violence against women, such as women whose faces have been burned with acid in conflicts over dowry money. When he started pressing cases on back pay and sexual harassment for women like Amrita he began to get threats. When he kept up the cases, he was assaulted. When he filed a case asking that a woman be given the legal maternity leave, he had a call from a senior government official in the nation's capital ordering him to drop the case (he didn't). When he publicly reported illegal child labor, more pressure came from the national government. He was told by one high-level bureaucrat, "You are an enemy of the nation."

This government pressure is all about money and corruption. All along the supply chain bribes are being paid. There is an official fee for an export license, but a much, much larger bribe, plus regular monthly payments, is needed to actually get and keep the license. These bribes and payments flow to government officials in the capital who help the exporters and contractors—and themselves—by making sure that labor laws are not enforced. A local gang controls the docks, they sell "insurance" that all shipments will go out on time and that workers will stay in line. They share the proceeds with local police and politicians. The gang, the politicians, the contractors, the exporters, and the slaveholders are all part of a big machine that delivers shrimp to your local supermarket. We know how much legal money this industry generates each year, about $13 billion; what hasn't been counted is the illegal funds and the human and environmental cost. The women who process, pack, and freeze the shrimp are very small cogs in a big shrimp machine. Their lives are tough, they feel trapped, they suffer sexual assault, but they're not slaves. They still have choices. They can choose to walk away from their job, go hungry, and watch their children go hungry. When slavery and consumer demand meet, the damage spreads out in all directions, to exploited workers like Amrita, to enslaved boys like Shumir, and to the natural environment we all hope to preserve.

. . .

I was waiting through the late afternoon and early evening to take a boat down the river into the Sundarban forest. A kind family gave me tea, serving it with four jars of local honey, each one a different flavor. The beehives had been kept in different fields, drawing the nectar from cumin, coriander, lychee, and mustard plants. To my American taste buds, honey with a strong taste of mustard or cumin was a shock. I felt as if a new room had opened in the tasting part of my brain, but I wasn't sure I was glad about it. Honey is supposed to be sweet—mustard honey breaks every rule your tongue ever learned.

After night had fallen we climbed into an open wooden boat, about thirty feet long, and headed down the river. I sat in the bow as far as I could get from the loud blat-blat-blat of the old diesel engine in the stern. After the first curve in the river there were no more lights on the shore, and a deep but starlit blackness covered everything. I watched the constellation Orion swing back and forth overhead as the river curved again and again. Low sweeping wings would whisper by, ripples in the liquid darkness. Suddenly crisscrossing spotlights and flashing lights from the shore illuminated us. It was frightening at first, but I realized no one else seemed to be bothered. "It's the Indian military base," someone said, "we're just on top of the border." Soon we were curving away from the lights and one by one they winked out.

In pitch darkness we reached the shrimp camp where we would stay, flashlights wriggling like glow-worms along the riverbanks and the mud boat landing. We stumbled into a small compound fenced with thorn bushes and up into a hut raised high on stilts. Stretching out on bamboo mats I drifted in and out of sleep, listening to the night sounds. Two dogs raised a lonely and musical lament. Sensing something, one would softly bark, just yip quietly once or twice, then immediately bend the note of the yip into a soft howl. This was the other dog's cue, and it would join the song, his note wavering in and out of harmony and discord. All this was dirgelike; barked, yipped, and howled with deep resignation, the fatalism born of being a small watchdog in a land of tigers.

At dawn I surfaced from sleep with the faint recorded call to prayer of a muezzin drifting in from the left, then from the right another recording joined the first, chanting a different tune, layering and weaving the sounds. They were so like the dogs in the night, I had to stifle my laughter to keep from waking the others sleeping in the hut.

I've come here after the Congo and it seems heavenly. There are no weapons in sight, no sense of threat or watchfulness. The infrastructure may be simple, but it works. Building and cultivation are everywhere. Bangladesh may be crippled by corruption, but it is limping ahead vigorously. In many ways the cultivation of this vast delta is beautiful—a careful, gentle preparation of soil and plants. The result is rice, vegetables, chickens, goats, and fish, a potentially rich diet.

■ ■ ■

Out to meet the day, I watch as huge white herons stitch the sky. We've reached a place where five rivers come together and the stream widens to an open space miles across. India is a line of trees in the misty far distance. From the level of the river, the dikes are just low mud walls along the shore, punctuated with the occasional channel or sluice gate. Where the mangrove forest is still intact, their roots show thousands of knobs, many more than a foot high, rising from the mudflats. The roots are spiderlike, twisting in the water. The current is so strong, the water so wide, that the world of mud dikes and villages suddenly seems very fragile. As I am thinking this, a white-breasted sea eagle lifts haughtily from a riverside branch, his seven-foot wingspan leaving no doubt about which of us is at home here and which is fragile.

Back on the river, as we leave the dikes and little villages behind, the forest fills all sides and the streams begin to split and split again. The Sundarbans are a maze of inlets, streams, rivers, low islands awash with water, higher islands with some dry land, and never a rocky shore or beach. Everywhere the mangroves push out into the water, their lower trunks submerged. Behind them I see trees like magnolias and flowering bushes that look like rhododendrons, and farther still from the water stand palms and tall deciduous trees swaying above the rest. The low forest near the riverbank is a dense tangle. The soil is so rich, the water so abundant, that limbs and roots and trunks, grasses, vines, and flowers are intertwined. A person could not penetrate here without chopping their way inch by inch.

Deep into the unmarked twisty streams, the boatman wants to turn back because of the "rovers." What? "It's the rovers," he says in his strong Bengali accent. "If we go deeper, we may meet them." "What are rovers?" I ask, confused. "Ah, yes," he explains, "rovers are like thieves, er, Vikings, but smaller." The idea of being set upon by miniature Vikings makes me laugh, but I know what he means, there are river pirates here and any police are far away. We turn back and from the bow of the boat I watch as the forest and its many side streams and eddies slide by.

In the streams and inlets we see the water people, families living on two or three boats. Sometimes they tie all the boats together, making a home against the shore, other times they are separated, traveling, fishing, or hauling goods. These families, watery pioneers nibbling at the edge of the forest, cutting timber for sale, are the sign that soon more people will follow. Washing down toward the sea, an ocean of people is threatening to drown this forest and, without knowing it, condemn themselves to misery.

Put simply, without the mangroves, people die. Old maps and satellite images taken over time show how true this is. In the 1950s, villages in the region had, on average, five miles of mangroves between themselves and the waters of the delta and ocean. By the late 1990s that had been reduced to less than a mile, and often none at all, as rice fields reaching toward the sea met the shrimp farms crawling up the shore. Today villages encrust the tops of the clay dikes, the water lapping at their toes.

Like hurricanes in the Gulf of Mexico, the cyclones of the Bay of Bengal come every year. The question is not if there is going to be a cyclone, but how big will it be? In 1991 a major cyclone plowed into southern Bangladesh, the storm surge was about twenty feet high, comparable to Hurricane Katrina, but in this low-lying land with the mangroves stripped away, the death toll was an astounding 138,000 people killed by the storm. The highest mortality was among children and the elderly. As many as 10 million were made homeless. By comparison, Hurricane Katrina was responsible for 1,836 deaths. In 1999, another major cyclone passed near, but did not collide with the Sundarbans. When it made landfall in India, the death toll was around 15,000, but the distribution of death was geographically uneven. Researchers from Duke University explained that there was: "a clear inverse relationship between the number of deaths per village and the width of the mangroves located between those villages and the coast . . . villages with wider mangroves suffered significantly fewer deaths than ones with narrower or no mangroves." They added, "This is a measure of the life-saving impact of the mangroves that remained in 1999 . . . they cut the death toll by about two-thirds." When the tsunami struck in 2004, the same effect was seen to the south in Burma and Thailand, where more than 80 percent of coastal mangrove forests had been removed and slave-based shrimp farming is common; around 250,000 were killed in the region.

As the mangroves disappear each storm sets off a cycle of flight and further forest destruction. Without the mangrove belt the cyclones flood the shore, killing crops with salty seawater and washing away the shrimp farms along with the villages. After Cyclone Aila in 2009, 400,000 people, having lost everything to the storm surge, pushed into the protected forests. As the people push in more trees are cut, more islands are taken over, and more children and adults are enslaved to do the work. Some act in desperation, others from greed, but the cycle means that more and more of the forests that protect both people and the rich ecosystem are destroyed.

The loss to nature is profound. Nearly half of the amphibians, reptiles, mammals, and birds living in mangrove forests are threatened with extinction. These animals, for the most part, aren't found anywhere else: their range is restricted to the mangrove forests of Asia and Australia. At the current rate of forest loss, the forests and all they hold will all be extinct in one hundred years.

■   ■   ■

I love forests, especially the rich Southern forests of America with their understory redbud and dogwood trees, and the English forests with their towering oaks, ash, and beech trees. Whenever I can, I walk in the woods—it rests me and heals me.

In forests the number of species of trees and other plants, the diversity of birds and animals, usually reflects the depth and duration of the local winter. Forty or fifty types of tree might grow in a Mississippi forest. But in northern Canada or Siberia, larch, spruce, fir, and pine pretty much does it. In the astounding fecundity of the Amazon basin some 12,500 species of trees grow. The warm and wet parts of our world are the great storehouses of life.

But a mangrove forest is different. While there's no bitter winter, there is the ocean. Salt, normally the enemy of plants, is everywhere and life must adapt. There are fifty-four kinds of mangrove trees around the world, and what they all have in common is the ability to live in salty water. They do this in ways that are unique: filtering out salt at the roots, exuding salt crystals from their leaves, and sending up root knobs or straws that act as snorkels and keep the tree breathing even when under water. They create a forest world that is also a sea world. Vast, complicated, and interlocking root systems anchor into the soft mud to hold the trees against the winds and tides. On land, mice or squirrels run over tree trunks and roots. On the underwater "floor" of the mangrove forest, fish, crabs, and mollusks live and feed, and provide prey for the hawks and eagles striking from the branches above. Of course, like all trees, mangroves also sweep carbon dioxide (CO_2) from the air, but even the way they do that is special.

In 2013 the amount of carbon in the atmosphere reached 400 parts per million (ppm), while most scientists agree that 350 ppm is the safe limit for our planet. Anything above that and the world starts to heat up in ways that are dangerous. The great challenge of global warming is how to both reduce the CO_2 we pump into the air and remove the CO_2 that is already in the atmosphere. That is why mangrove forests are so important. Like all plants, mangroves take CO_2 out of the air, but because they are constantly washed by waves and tides much of the carbon from mangroves moves into the oceans in a form that doesn't break down easily. Because of that, mangrove forests are known as a "carbon sink," a place where the CO_2 is literally scrubbed out of the air and deposited in the oceans in a way that

GMO plants w/ mangrove salt filters...?

keeps it locked away. Healthy mangroves help reduce global warming, and the Sundarban forest is the largest carbon sink in South Asia.

Locking away atmospheric carbon is called "sequestration." We know precisely how much carbon is locked away by the one fifth of the Sundarban forest that lies inside India. That part of the forest still covers thousands of square miles and provides a clear picture of the importance of the mangroves. About 21 million tons of CO_2 is locked away in the trees of this forest, and another 5.5 million tons of CO_2 is locked in the soil around the tree roots. Every year about 3 million more tons are scrubbed from the air and locked away. What's crucial here is that in spite of being less diverse than the Amazon forest, these mangroves do a better job of scrubbing and locking carbon. While there is a smaller amount of biomass (the total weight of all the plants per acre) in a mangrove forest, these water-dwelling trees scrub carbon from the air up to four times faster than a forest on land. Every mangrove tree is a protection against the impact of global warming.

Cut these trees down and the result is much worse than simply losing their ability to scrub carbon. They are, in fact, keystones of the natural world. Cut them down and everything begins to go to pieces. Hurricane Katrina and the deadly cyclones of the Bay of Bengal show one part of this breakdown. Scientists at both the US National Oceanic and Atmospheric Administration and the UN expert team on climate change and tropical cyclones have said that the number of very intense tropical storms (like Katrina) will increase this century because of global warming. In addition to the storms, sea levels rise, and here is the special conundrum of the Sundarban forest.

The country of Bangladesh is one of the flattest places on earth, and the most susceptible to sea level rise. If the sea level increases three feet, the Sundarbans are gone, the entire 12,000 square miles are underwater, and 20 million people are refugees. Add to that the increased ferocity of cyclones and a thirty-foot storm surge and what happened to large parts of the city of New Orleans can happen to almost the entire country of Bangladesh. Americans' energy-rich lifestyle, and the by-products of livestock farming contribute the most to global warming, but every slaveholder cutting down mangroves for shrimp or fish camps in the protected forest is increasing the likelihood of that catastrophe as well.

Slavery and environmental destruction are doing a deadly dance. The scale of their joint disaster is so great that it has simply been too big to see, until now. It is also subtle, a creeping erosion of life wrought by the hands of millions of slaves compelled to destroy their own livelihoods even as they destroy any chance of arresting global warming. Yet, it is precisely the role slaves play in this ecological catastrophe that opens a new solution, one that unleashes the power of abolition to save and preserve the natural world.

5

THE RUNAWAY TRAIN

The day I saw the tiger's paw print in the sand, I ignored the shouted warnings and began to creep down the earthen dike separating the river and the forest. The shouting man—my guide—scrambled down the bank holding a wooden club and his companion scanned the edge of the wood. They knew this cat. Pushed into a smaller and smaller range by the encroaching shrimp farms, he was hungry. Late at night he would prowl into the nearby village, and any domestic animal not locked away might be taken. Yet for all his power, this big cat was at a loss, unable to fight back against the rolling changes that threatened not just him but his whole species.

Our human species is wandering along a different path, seemingly oblivious to the warnings echoing around us. The crisis of global warming is much bigger than that tiger, the Sundarban forest, Bangladesh, global slavery, or any single one of us. It's a runaway train and we're all standing right in its path—unaware that we have in our hands a way to reduce global warming immediately and effectively. End slavery. One of the key causes of global warming is the destruction of the world's forests, a process enabled by slave labor.

. . .

To understand how this phenomenon works, we have to start with the special role of forests in holding the global climate steady. Five million years ago our world was pretty hot, and has been slowly cooling. In the last 800,000 years the temperatures have swung back and forth between warm periods and "ice ages" about twelve times. The fact that there has been a narrow range of temperature for millions of years reflects what is called the planet's *energy balance*. The Earth absorbs energy from sunlight and radiates a lot of that energy back into space. When there is a balance between incoming and outgoing energy, then the climate is stable and temperature highs and lows tend to fall within a narrow range.

That regular fluctuation began to change when the industrial revolution got under way in the eighteenth century. At an ever-increasing rate wood and fossil fuels were burned to support an immense transformation in human societies—in just 150 years or so, the industrial revolution dramatically altered the way people had lived for thousands of years. In terms of the natural world, 150 years is the blink of an eye. Yet, in that time the global population shot from fewer than 2 billion to the 7 billion people alive today, per capita energy consumption increased one hundred times, urban life overtook rural life, and incredible inequalities arose as some parts of the world accrued unprecedented wealth and luxury while other parts remained trapped in conditions of privation, disease, and insecurity.

These vast changes were driven by energy. As the world transformed, gases from the burning of fossil fuels and the destruction of forests were being released into the atmosphere. These gases are called "greenhouse gases" because they function like the glass panes that trap the sun's heat in a greenhouse. We've all experienced this effect when we get into a car that has been standing in the sun with its windows closed—the sunlight comes in the car's windows and heats the confined air inside the vehicle until it is much hotter than the air outside the car. These gases essentially do the same to the earth's atmosphere, creating a barrier that traps heat that would normally radiate back into space. Once trapped, the heat builds up and up and glaciers melt, storms brew, crops fail, and tropical diseases move north.

A good way to understand the full impact of this burning of fossil fuels and forests is to compare it to volcanoes. Volcanoes have an immediate and literally chilling impact on climate, followed by a slower warming effect. Benjamin Franklin first linked volcanoes and climate change in 1784. He noted that the summer of 1783 was abnormally harsh in both North America and Europe; the winter came earlier, stayed longer, and was very cold. He wrote that there seemed to be "a constant fog over all Europe, and [a] great part of North America." This super-chill was the result of an eruption of the Laki volcanoes in Iceland. In Iceland the impact was much worse. A quarter of the people living there, and three quarters of the animals, died of starvation or poisoning by volcanic gases. Other major volcanic eruptions—by Mount Tambora (1815), Krakatoa (1883), Mount St. Helens (1980), El Chichon (1982), and Mount Pinatubo (1991)— have had a similar if not greater effect on the global climate, filling the sky with dust and ash that reflects warming sunlight back into space.

This impact of volcanoes is obvious, visible, and drastic, but it's also essentially fleeting and ephemeral. In contrast, the greenhouse gases emitted by burning fossil fuels and the cutting and burning of forests is, in the words of Terrence Gerlach, a retired volcanologist formerly with the Cascades Volcano Observatory, "comparatively unspectacular, commonplace, and familiar, and in addition they are ubiquitous, ceaseless, and relentless." Instead of a single volcano, today billions of little fires are burning and emitting greenhouse gases into the air every second. The sources of these fires run the gamut from the internal combustion of our car engines to the acrid fumes of slave-tended charcoal ovens. These human sources of global warming gases are also much, much larger, between 100 and 150 times bigger, than anything belched out by volcanoes, ultimately overpowering any cooling effect of volcanic dust and ash. Put another way, to match the CO_2 and other greenhouse gases that people are pouring into the atmosphere, Mount St. Helens would have to erupt every two and a half hours, every day, forever.

. . .

Understanding the human contribution to global warming is important because human activity is something people can change if they choose to, and that's where slavery comes in. Deforestation accounts for somewhere between 17 percent and 25 percent of the world's emissions of greenhouse gases. In other words, on the day you are reading this, deforestation will release as much CO_2 into the air as if eight million people were flying from New York to London. A lot of emphasis is put on the fact that forests scrub CO_2 from the air and lock it away, but the other side of the coin is that when forests are cut, and especially when they are burned, they release all that stored CO_2 back into the atmosphere. The cutting of forests, whether mangroves or tropical jungles or even Siberian forests, releases an estimated two billion tons of CO_2 every year. If the world's forests were a country, their greenhouse gas emissions would be greater than those of India or Russia, and would be exceeded in CO_2 emissions only by the United States. Or compare the two billion tons of CO_2 released through deforestation to the little over three billion tons of CO_2 from all the oil burned in the world in a year.

When you add the loss of a tree's ability to soak up CO_2 into the greenhouse gas balance sheet, deforestation becomes one of the top causes of global warming. If deforestation were slowed or stopped, we might reverse what James Hansen, probably the world's most respected climate change expert, described as: "climate impact that literally produces a different planet than the one on which civilization developed." Hansen goes on to explain that without action "the consequences for young people, future generations, and other species would continue to mount over years and centuries. Ice sheet disintegration would cause continual shoreline adjustments with massive civil engineering cost implications as well as widespread heritage loss in the nearly uncountable number of coastal cities. Shifting of climatic zones and repeated climate disruptions would have enormous economic and social costs, especially in the developing world."

Now it is important to make clear that trees aren't magical. When leaves fall, when trees die, the stored carbon is released back into the atmosphere. For the most part trees are only temporary repositories of carbon. At the same time the more living trees there are, the more carbon is being swept up and held, and the better we can maintain our *energy balance*.

Much of our understanding of how trees store carbon has been focused on the Amazon rain forest because that's the biggest forest we've got—but it probably isn't the *best* forest we've got when it comes to storing carbon. A tree in the Amazon has an average expected life of around fifteen years, and its stored carbon is then slowly released as it rots away. But let's look once more at the Sundarban *mangrove* forest. Although it's much smaller and the trees aren't nearly so tall, it is far and away better at locking down carbon.

The key difference is that, unlike forests on land, mangrove roots and soil are washed by tides, and the carbon emitted by mangrove trees goes into the ocean instead of the air. Mangroves release carbon into the ocean in large molecules (such as carbonates) that don't easily break down. This carbon is truly locked away, held in the ocean for decades instead of being immediately returned to the atmosphere as carbon dioxide. Coastal mangroves, like those of the Sundarbans, are so good at this that even though they cover only 0.1 percent of the world's surface, they contribute 10 percent of the ocean's dissolved carbon. The oceans are the world's best carbon bank, but as global warming heats them up, they also release carbon into the air. And that takes us back to the runaway train of global warming.

There are two key facts that we are just beginning to comprehend. One is the extremely powerful role of mangroves in storing carbon. The full story on this wasn't made clear until 2011 when an international research team discovered that mangroves store four times more carbon than other forests. The lead researcher also explained, "When we did the math, we were surprised to see just how much carbon is likely being released from mangrove clearing." Cutting mangrove forests quickly makes the global situation worse, and potentially catastrophic. The researchers speculated that a rapid decline in mangroves could shut off the cycle of carbon being transferred from the land and stored in the ocean. If that happens the world can quickly reach a tipping point, a dramatic increase in greenhouse gases that raises temperature and brings severe and permanent flooding, millions of refugees, and unprecedented species loss. Avoiding that worst-case scenario leads to the second important fact we are just beginning to understand—how slavery plays a major role in deforestation.

The destruction of the great tropical forests has been a focus of environmental campaigning for decades. "Save the Amazon!" would be a cliché if it wasn't still so crucial. Over the past forty years the public understanding of environmental issues and the nature of those issues has been growing, dynamic, and changeable. Thirty years ago deforestation was accomplished primarily by commercial interests holding the legal right to cut forests. This was true in North America, where clear-cutting was seen as perfectly legal—as well as in governments throughout Africa, Asia, and South America who handed out timbering leases and logging rights, though often through favoritism and bribery. As the environmental movement grew, it sought to change the laws that allowed this destruction.

As a result, legal deforestation has slowed dramatically. Every other year the United Nations publishes a report on the state of the world's forests, and in the 2009 and 2011 reports they expressed special concern over the increase in *illegal* logging. In Brazil, Congo, and other countries, large tracts of forest have now come under government protection. They may not be permanently set aside as preserves, but they are controlled so that they can be sustainably managed. At least, that is the intention. But what has happened instead is the continuation of the same destruction, but accomplished with slave labor.

． ． ．

In the late 1990s I was investigating slavery in charcoal production in the state of Mato Grosso do Sul in western Brazil. At the time I thought the deforestation by slavery I was observing was unique. This is how I described the situation then: "Between twenty and thirty years ago nearly one million acres in just three counties of Mato Grosso do Sul were stripped of their forests (mato grosso means 'thick wood') and replaced with eucalyptus [to feed a boondoggle government paper mill that was never built]. The native forests here were not the vast rain forests of the Amazon basin, but the shorter, tangled *cerrado* or scrub forests of the South American central plateau. The destruction of these forests was the first major impact of humans on this part of Brazil. It was, and still is, the edge, the frontier of 'civilization.'

"Slavery flourishes where old rules, old ways of life break down. Environmental destruction also creates chaos for the people who live and work in the environment. Much of the slavery in Brazil grows out of this social chaos. Think of the way serious flooding or an earthquake can destroy sanitation and spread disease. In even the most modern countries, when natural or man-made disaster demolishes a city's water system and sewers, killer diseases like dysentery or cholera can erupt and infect the population. In the same way environmental destruction and economic disaster can cause an existing society to collapse and the disease of slavery can grow up in the wreckage.

"But destruction is never stable, no place or people ever slide into chaos and remain there forever. Economically driven destruction sweeps like a tidal wave across Brazil. Before it is the *cerrado* or the Amazonian forest, behind it are the eucalyptus plantations and the new cattle ranches, planted with alien grasses, emptied of native animals, and serving the meat markets of the cities. Where the wave is passing is turmoil. The space between the old forests and 'civilization' is a battle zone where the old rules are dead and the new rules are yet to come into force. As the native ecosystem and peoples are uprooted, displaced workers, even the urban unemployed, become vulnerable to enslavement.

"The frontier can be swept by several waves of exploitation, the first which sweeps away the old forest, another which is the leading edge of the alien planting, a third rolls through when the alien forests are cut. Inside the wave of destruction laws disappear. Once trapped within one of these waves a person is beyond social norms and protection. The only road in is an isolated dirt track. This track stops at the line where old forest ends and new destruction begins. It is the first tentacle of change, moving ahead with the wave. The people caught up and forced to carry out the destruction of the forests live without electricity, running water, or communication with the outside world. They are completely under the control of their masters. As the wave passes, it carries slavery with it. The land ahead is still exploitable, the land behind is stripped, and when all the land is stripped the slaves will be dumped.

"We tend to think of environmental destruction as huge bulldozers gouging their way through pristine forests, crushing life under their steel tracks, scraping away nature in order to cover the land with concrete. In fact the process is more insidious. The people who live in the forest and rely on it are usually forced to destroy it. Tree by tree, the hands of slaves wrench the life out of their own land and prepare it for a new kind of exploitation. The slavery of Brazil is a temporary slavery because environmental destruction is temporary: you only get to ruin a forest once and it doesn't take that long.

"Sometimes when a forest is destroyed something of value is taken out, at other times the destruction is total. In Mato Grosso both have happened. In the 1970s when the *cerrado* was cleared to make way for the eucalyptus, the wood was just dragged into great piles and burnt. Today as the final wave of destruction sweeps across the Mato Grosso, the *cerrado* and the eucalyptus are still being burned, but this time it turns them into money. The wood is made into charcoal, just like the kind you use in your barbecue. This is a special kind of charcoal because it is hand-made, by slaves."

Since the 1990s, with an increasing amount of forest placed under protection, fewer legitimate loggers are involved and more and more criminal slaveholders are cutting trees. We see this in the Eastern Congo where the armed gangs slash and burn in the protected Virunga Park. We see it in the UNESCO World Heritage Site of the Sundarbans mangrove forest, and we see this pillage by slavery being repeated around the world. Across Africa, forests are cut illegally using slave labor, and the same is true of the equatorial countries of South America—Colombia, Peru, Venezuela, Guyana, Suriname, French Guiana, and up into the forests of Central America. In Southeast Asia the illegal cutting is well documented, as is the use of slave labor—in Burma, Laos, Thailand, Viet Nam, and Malaysia. The speed of forest loss in Indonesia and the Philippines is severe. Not every logging outfit is using slaves, and certainly the poor who cut for fuel are not slaveholders, but enough of the loss involves slave labor that we are coming to understand how suppressing slavery is essential if we are to protect the environment.

And this is not just about the lush forests that ring the world at the equator. As I write this I am looking at two photos taken recently in the state of Uttar Pradesh in northern India. This part of India is a long way from the equator, at the same latitude as the US state of Georgia, and can be very cold in winter since it rests on the high plateau that edges up into the Himalayas. In the first photo is an open quarry where men, women, and children are breaking stone with primitive hammers and steel bars. In the second picture, standing on the top edge of the quarry is their slaveholder sweeping his arm over the broken land and slaves below him, tricked by an undercover anti-slavery worker into talking about how much land he controls (see photo on page 5). Beyond the slaveholder the land is flat and bare with only a few rare, stunted trees. It is not an unusual picture in this region. Here is a village whose inhabitants are trapped in hereditary debt bondage slavery, children as young as three or four working in the pit, and a violent slaveholder who controls them all and sexually assaults the women and girls with impunity. But all of this is happening within the boundaries of a *protected national forest*. The only thing missing is the forest, long gone now through the machinations of the slaveholders.

. . .

Slavery is being used to rip away the world's forests just when we need them most, but we have to understand that other slave-based enterprises also feed into global warming. To be sure, the sheer volume of energy use in America and China produces more greenhouse gases than other sources, but the brick kilns, charcoal camps, mines, and factories worked by slaves are adding CO_2 and pollutants to the air at a ferocious rate.

All around the equatorial belt of the planet, slave-cut forests feed ovens making charcoal. In Africa and Asia this charcoal is sold as fuel for cooking and heating. In Brazil, the charcoal is sold to iron smelters that bolster the steel industry. These charcoal camps can be very large, easily seen from space, with hundreds of primitive clay ovens each running constantly and reducing freshly cut wood into charcoal. Spend a little time on Google Maps in western Brazil and you will find the telltale signature of a charcoal camp. From the air you see a line of clay-covered bumps, which are the ovens; above and around them is a pall of permanent smoke, and radiating out from the camp is an ever-increasing wasteland stripped of trees. When the extent of the cutting means trees have to be dragged a long way to the camp, then the camp is moved deeper into the forest and the cancerous clear-cutting begins again. Not every charcoal camp uses slaves, but in Mato Grosso do Sul about a third did. Since then, the number of illegal camps has increased, and from talking with anti-slavery workers on the ground I understand the proportion using slaves is now over half.

Parallel to the charcoal camps, but away from the forests is another slave-based industry that spews out toxic greenhouse gases in large amounts—brick making. The dirty, onerous, repetitive, simple, and extremely lucrative work of brick making has been the work of slaves for thousands of years. From the beginning of human history, slaves have been used to make bricks. Stories in the Bible attest to Hebrew slaves making bricks for their Egyptian masters. Egyptian tomb paintings from 2000 B.C. show slaves at work in brick kilns. When hundreds of thousands of African-Americans were re-enslaved after the Civil War in the peonage system, many were consumed by brick kilns. Pulitzer Prize–winner Douglas Blackmon described one such operation owned by James W. English, the mayor of Atlanta, Georgia: "Gangs of prisoners sold from the pestilential city stockade on Bryan Street dug wet clay with shovels and picks in nearby riverbank pits for transport to the plant. There, a squad of men pushed clay that had been cured in the open air into tens of thousands of rectangular molds. Once dried, the bricks were carried at a double-time pace by two dozen laborers running back and forth—under almost continual lashing by English's overseer, Capt. James T. Casey—to move bricks to one of nearly a dozen huge coal-fired kilns, also called 'clamps.' At each kiln, one worker stood atop a barrel, in the withering heat radiating from the fires, furiously tossing the bricks into the top of the ten-foot-high oven." The scale of the operation was mind-boggling: in the twelve months ending in May 1907, these slaves produced nearly 33 million bricks, and Mayor James W. English pocketed the equivalent of $1.9 million in today's money.

Today, slaves still make bricks. In a wide belt that spans areas of Pakistan, India, and Nepal and then crosses into China, illegal brick kilns use slaves and generate intense pollution. The ancient methods of brick-making described in the Bible or implemented in Atlanta in 1907 continue unchanged. Enslaved men, women, and children dig mud, pack it into molds, dry the formed bricks and then stack them into kilns to fire and harden. In the Asian brick-belt, however, the kilns dwarf the ten-foot-high barrel ovens of nineteenth-century Atlanta. In Pakistan, where I spent weeks studying slavery in brick-making, the kilns were ten- to fifteen-foot-high hollow ovals, roughly the size and shape of a football field. The oval shape meant that the fire burned constantly, working its way round and round the track. In front of the fire, slaves hurriedly stack bricks for baking, behind the fire other slaves unstack the hardened bricks and load them onto carts for sale. Between these two crews more slaves, often children, are feeding the fire, clambering over the top and around the kiln in the intense heat. The air temperature here is well over 130 degrees, and the workers, including the children, wear sandals with thick wooden soles against the heat of the kiln. For all their heavy footgear, the workers tread lightly, and the smaller children have an advantage, for as the fires rage in the kiln below them sometimes the top level of bricks gives way. When this happens a person can fall through. If they fall completely into the kiln there is no hope for them: the temperature inside is more than 1,500 degrees and they are instantly incinerated. If only a leg or a foot pushes through, there may be hope depending on how quickly they are pulled up and out. But their burns will be serious and life-changing.

To fire the bricks, to keep the kilns at 1,500 degrees for months at a time, takes a lot of fuel. When they can get it the slaveholders use coal, but since coal can be expensive or unavailable, they'll burn anything they can get their hands on. The result is a toxic soup and a greenhouse gas nightmare. There are two key ingredients that keep the fires burning in slave-driving brick kilns: old tires and used motor oil. Some North American industrial plants have shown that it is just about possible to burn a car tire without creating severe pollution if you build in a lot of high-technology scrubbers, filters, smoke recyclers, and particulate-capturing screens. Slave-using brick kilns have none of these. So the roiling black smoke from burning tires carries polycyclic aromatic hydrocarbons: dioxin, benzene, styrene, phenols; as well as heavy metals, and butadiene into the air. If you're not familiar with these chemicals, the key thing you need to know is that they make you sick, give you cancer, and once in the water or soil are almost impossible to get rid of. In addition to the smoke, when you burn a tire, about two gallons of oil melts and drains away, carrying the same mixture of toxic compounds into the soil and groundwater. In the United States a tire fire is officially classified as an environmental crisis, and tire fire sites end up so poisoned they qualify for Superfund cleanup status. All these poisons are *in addition* to the CO_2 and other greenhouse gases produced—after all, a tire is just a ring of concentrated fossil fuel.

To get a bunch of tires really burning well, you stack scrap wood all around them and drench the lot with used motor oil. In the kilns, used motor oil provides an extra kick to keep temperatures high and the fire moving quickly, and you'll often see children perched on top of the kiln pouring the thick black oil into fire holes. The problem with used motor oil is that it carries the by-products of engine wear and combustion. When you burn it, toxic metals such as barium, lead, chromium, nickel, cadmium, and zinc, as well as the chemicals dioxin, PCB, and benzene, go into the air and contaminate the environment and harm people. This is nasty stuff. For example, cadmium causes kidney cancer, and according to the US Environmental Protection Agency there is no safe level of cadmium in the air. And, again, you get this deadly cocktail *along with* the high levels of greenhouses gases that come from burning oil.

In the brick belt of Pakistan, India, and Nepal the kilns run twenty-four hours a day for two "seasons," each four to five months in length. In Pakistan there are about 7,000 brick kilns. A kiln produces between 500,000 and 2 million bricks each time the fire goes round the circuit. This means an annual production of some 65 *billion* bricks. Each one of those bricks is shaped and formed by hand by the families who are enslaved or do piece-rate work of molding raw bricks. With 15 to 35 families at each kiln, there are something like 150,000 to 200,000 families at work in the kilns. Given the average family size of 5.3 people, and the fact that children often work along with their parents, the total workforce is around 750,000 people, just in Pakistan. There are at least that number and possibly more kilns and workers in India, and a smaller number in Nepal. No one knows how many slave-using brick kilns there are in China, only that they exist in numbers large enough to have brought on a rare government crackdown. All this suggests that there may be around 20,000 of these hyper-polluting kilns in the South Asian brick belt. In other parts of Asia, in Africa, and in South America there are more, but again, no one is sure how many.

But it's fair to ask if all these slaves were set free wouldn't the kilns keep running and polluting with free workers? In a word, no. You can make a profit making bricks using thousand-year-old, Bible-era "technology" if you use slaves, but *not* if you have to pay the workers. Small, efficient, mechanical brick molders and kilns are readily available, and are ultimately more profitable than slave-based brick-making. Slaveholders, however, don't see the need to invest in new machines when they have slaves. So once again—stop the slavery and the pollution and CO_2 will drop dramatically.

．　．　．

Because slavery is illegal in every country, it is hard to be precise about how many slaves are caught up in different types of work. On top of that, the criminals using slaves are slippery and always finding new ways to duck and dodge exposure while exploiting the people they control. But while it is difficult to measure the amount of greenhouses gases that can be traced to slavery, it *is* possible to make an estimate.

Let's start with deforestation. In 2010 and 2011, CO_2 emissions increased as the global economy began to rebound from the 2009 financial meltdown. In 2010 emissions increased almost 8 percent to a global total of 33.16 billion tons of carbon sent into the air. Driven by surging oil, coal, and gas consumption, China's greenhouse gas emissions reached 8.33 billion tons. At the same time, deforestation accounted for even more of the atmospheric carbon than China's emissions, some 10.7 billion tons. This increase is alarming, but a study published in 2011 balances this with the finding that existing and new growth forests in the tropics absorb nearly 15 billion tons of CO_2,—about half of the global total spewed into the atmosphere from all sources. There's a lot of adding and subtracting going on here, but the important upshot is this: while deforestation accounts for almost a third of greenhouse gases entering the atmosphere, the remaining living forests manage to scrub nearly half of the world's greenhouse gases from the air. In other words, if we stopped deforestation and replanted forests we'd be on our way to absorbing as much CO_2 as gets sent into the atmosphere each year. Reaching that step takes you to the edge of redemption, the *energy balance*—a world where more CO_2 is being scrubbed than produced, and global warming can be slowed or stopped. That's a tall order, but understanding slavery's environmental impact is important if we want to reach that redemption point. It is important for four distinct, but interrelated, reasons.

The first reason is that initiatives like the United Nations Collaborative Programme on Reducing Emissions from Deforestation and Forest Degradation (the UN-REDD program) are based on governments forging agreements about forestry policy and carrying them out. These agreements usually reduce the amount of forest available for logging, set controls on what types of trees can be cut, and require sustainable practice and replanting. The problem is that criminal slaveholders don't pay any attention to international agreements. Treaties mean nothing to them, and the enacted policies rarely include slavery-busting law enforcement provisions or protecting forest reserves against criminal assault. So, the deforestation continues.

Second, new agreements rarely reach into *existing* protected areas like UNESCO World Heritage Sites. After all, why should they? Aren't these forests already locked away? But we already know the answer to that—slavery thrives in protected areas because they *are* protected. Slaveholders have no competition from commercial loggers here, and there's no active law enforcement except a handful of forest rangers. Protected forests, with their big old trees and valuable tropical hardwoods, are the perfect setting for smash-and-grab cutting and burning. With sufficient tactical intelligence and law enforcement resources such preserves can be made safe—but that is not the current situation and the deforestation continues.

Third, we know that slavery and environmental destruction grow and thrive where the rule of law doesn't reach: in war zones, on frontiers, along disputed borders, and when countries collapse in civil unrest and ethnic conflict. International treaties don't reach into these areas of conflict and chaos either, and the concerns of local populations are fixed on their own safety and rarely stretch to the natural world around them. Criminal slaveholders understand this and take advantage, raping the land and reaping fat profits, and the deforestation continues.

So, international agreements are very important, but they won't reach the forests most at risk from criminals that use slaves to cut their timber. Of course, if slavery were just a small part of the problem, then it would be right to concentrate on forging treaties to lock up forest reserves, but that's not the case. The fourth key reason why understanding slavery is important to reducing greenhouse gases and getting global warming under control is the sheer scale of the destruction carried out with slave labor.

Paradoxically, the protections for forests that came with environmental treaties have actually put them under greater threat from slave-using criminals. In Africa, Asia, and South America, criminals step in as commercial loggers retreat because of new laws and treaties. It is impossible to make a precise measurement of global deforestation by slavery, but the evidence is clear that it is pervasive and growing. In the Congo, we've seen how armed thugs enslave people and loot forests. Calculations for that country point to severe woodland loss and estimate that by 2050 forest clearance in the Congo will spew up to 34.4 billion tons of CO_2 into the atmosphere, roughly equivalent to Great Britain's CO_2 emissions over the last sixty years.

As one environmental group put it: "The impact of logging infrastructure on the climate is significant but does not figure in global calculations."

So, how much logging is illegal, and how much is slave based? Again, there is no solid global estimate, but if you dig deeply you find facts like these: the World Bank estimates that 80 percent of logging operations are illegal in Bolivia and Peru and 42 percent in Colombia. Meanwhile, research carried out by the Worldwide Fund for Nature (WWF) in 2002 states that in Africa rates of illegal logging vary from 50 percent for Cameroon and Equatorial Guinea to 70 percent in Gabon and 80 percent in Liberia—where revenues from timbering also fueled the civil war (as they continue to do in Congo). Recent estimates suggest that 88 percent of logging in Indonesia is illegal in some way, and 80 percent of logging in the Amazon violates government controls. For what it's worth, I have seen with my own eyes slave-based illegal logging, or spoken with reliable witnesses to it, in five of the nine countries just listed—and that's in addition to the slave-based logging I've observed in Bangladesh, Ghana, India, and Burma.

All this suggests the practice is pervasive, but still doesn't get us to an estimate for slave-based deforestation. In a situation like this, it is right to be cautious and conservative. Even if the rates of illegal logging range from 40 percent to almost 90 percent, I'm going to assume that not all illegal cutting uses slaves and lean toward the low end of the estimates. So let's assume that only 40 percent of deforestation is accomplished with slavery, which is a lower rate than in any of the countries I've studied over the last fifteen years. What does that mean in terms of CO_2 emissions?

To answer that question we have to determine how much deforestation adds to the total CO_2 emissions each year, but on that point there isn't clear agreement. The amount of CO_2 scientists say comes from deforestation runs from 17 percent to 20 percent to 25 percent to "almost 30 percent." I'm going to go with the 20 percent estimate because that number is supported by more of the scientific research institutes around the world. So, if 40 percent of deforestation is slave-based, then slavery is responsible for 2.54 billion tons of CO_2 per year, not counting the scrubbing capacity that is lost when the trees are cut. For 2010 that amount of greenhouse gas is also greater than the emissions of all the countries in the world *except* China and the United States (the world's largest emitters). That's worth saying another way. If slavery were a country, it would have the third largest CO_2 emissions on the planet. But we're not done yet.

Slavery also figures into those other greenhouse gas engines like brick-making and charcoal-burning. In 2009 two researchers analyzed data suggesting that the 4,000 brick kilns in the Punjab region of Pakistan released 525,440 tons of CO_2 every year. If we multiply that by the estimated 20,000 kilns across the brick belt that adds another 2.6 million tons of CO_2 produced with slave labor. Brick kilns also account for an additional increase in global warming by the type of smoke they produce. This is not surprising if you've seen what pours out of brick kiln chimneys. This particularly damaging type of smoke is called black soot, or sometimes "black carbon." As Elisabeth Rosenthal explained in *The New York Times*: "While carbon dioxide may be the No. 1 contributor to rising global temperatures, scientists say black carbon has emerged as an important No. 2, with recent studies estimating that it is responsible for 18 percent of the planet's warming, compared with 40 percent for carbon dioxide." The most important way to reduce black soot is to get families in the developing world to cook and heat with more efficient stoves, but the dense black smoke pouring out of brick kilns and charcoal ovens is also significant. Though with charcoal-making there is a twist in the tale.

The curious thing about charcoal-making is that it is basically a process designed to make carbon more portable. When you burn wood to make charcoal you don't release all of its energy or CO_2 into the air. About 52 percent of the carbon in the fuel wood is converted into charcoal (which can be burned later) and about 25 percent is sent into the air as CO_2. The fact that charcoal holds on to carbon and can be stored or even buried has led some scientists and environmentalists to see charcoal as a way to store away huge amounts of carbon and get it out of the atmosphere. These scientists are pointing to a special kind of charcoal, usually called "biochar," made from plant waste rather than solid wood. Biochar can hold on to its carbon for hundreds, even thousands, of years. Plowing it into farmland increases soil fertility and is a great way to store the carbon. It looks like there is important potential in biochar, but at the moment there is no widespread support for producing it, and deforestation for plain old cooking charcoal continues unabated. So at the moment, it looks like slave-based deforestation, plus dirty slave-using businesses like brick-making and charcoal production are making a significant contribution to both greenhouse gases and global warming.

·   ·   ·

Wouldn't it be wonderful if bringing slavery to an end also stopped the global warming that threatens the lives of our children and their children? After all, we know that slavery *can* be brought to an end. The 35 million slaves in the world today make up the smallest fraction of the global population to ever be in slavery, and the $150 billion in slave production each year is the tiniest proportion of the global economy ever represented by slavery. Slavery is illegal in every country and rejected by all religions and political groups. It has been pushed to the very edges of our global society, where it hides and hurts the poor and vulnerable. We know how much it would cost to bring slavery to an end—about $11 billion over a period of twenty to thirty years. And it is worth remembering that in the scale of the world economy $11 billion is chicken feed. In fact, it is *less* than the amount that Great Britain alone will spend on chicken feed over the same period. Eleven billion dollars is also the amount that the World Bank says is lost to the global market every year because of illegal logging. Like smallpox, with commitment and resources, slavery can be eradicated—reduced from millions in bondage to just a few isolated cases.

We also know that getting people out of slavery unleashes immediate economic growth as they finally get the chance to work for their own families and to build better lives. This "freedom dividend" pays off in better healthcare, more education, and more respect for the environment. When liberation and freedom came to the village I described earlier that was enslaved in the rock quarry in India, one of their first projects was replanting the forest around them. People in slavery understand that they are being forced to ruin the environment. They don't like it, and they don't want to destroy the forests, pollute the air in brick kilns and charcoal camps, or devastate and poison the earth through mining. Given the chance, they want lives that are sustainable and whole, and they'll protect the environment that makes that possible.

Going back to the tally sheet of CO_2 production and capture, we can assert this: pushing hard to end the illegal logging that uses slaves could bring global CO_2 output down from 31.8 billion tons to just over 29 billion tons. Add in the atmospheric scrubbing effect of the forests saved in the process (especially those mangroves) and the global total falls to something over 28 billion tons. Then remove the carbon disgorged by brick kilns and charcoal camps, and you get closer to 27 billion. A key fact here is that "the world's forests have a net effect on atmospheric CO_2 equivalent to the removal of 1.1 billion tons of carbon every year," according to a study in 2011. The forests are still scrubbing more CO_2 than is being lost through deforestation, but every felled tree takes us closer to the tipping point, the day when so much forest is gone that the natural scrubbing effect can't keep up. At the same time every tree planted or replanted puts one more scrubber to work saving our bacon. Involve freed slaves in the important work of replanting decimated forests and CO_2 levels drop even faster. Ending slavery can't end global warming, but based on these figures it can get us a long way down the road in the right direction.

The fact is, we already know how to end global warming, we know how to get the carbon in the air back to 350 ppm. It involves all of us doing things like using eco-friendly lightbulbs, weaning ourselves off fossil fuels, recycling, eating less meat, and getting over the idea that we need a Mac-Mansion to have a full life. But here's the thing: criminal slaveholders don't care. They don't care about global warming, they don't care about people, and they don't care about laws or environmental protection treaties. They're not the only big hidden polluters, but they are the ones that everyone agrees should be shut down *immediately*, no negotiation and no car-bon trading. They are criminals according to the laws of every country on the planet. There can be no special pleading for the slave industry. Closing down slave-based logging, brick-making, or char-coal production won't hurt our lifestyles or the economy. What it will do is get people out of slavery and slow global warming. It is a classic win-win situation.

. . .

There are some great mysteries in life, but how to end slavery and how to fix global warming are not all that mysterious. On one hand it is great news that the link between slavery and global warming opens a way that will help end both. But it raises another question: Who is going to do this work? Where are the workers who will take this on and be physically present where slavery and ecocide are actu-ally happening? To tackle the problem of slavery in our shrimp and fish in Bangladesh (or any other product), and the impact that has on global warming, requires more than just an informed choice at the supermarket.

Of course, solving these interlinked problems *should* fall to law enforcement agencies, since slavery and environmental destruction are both against the law. But for a number of reasons the Bangla-deshi police are not up to the task. If this were a local violation, like littering, and it only affected local people, we might say, "Fine, if they're not willing to deal with it, then that's their problem." But we can't say that, this is slavery, this is illegal environmental destruction—these are crimes against humanity and against the planet. We cannot allow them anywhere for any reason. It's true that there are a handful of groups in Bangladesh that work against slavery and environmental destruction, but they are obstructed at every turn by both the shrimp industry and corrupt members of their own government. The only thing that will get us within reach of helping children enslaved in the fish camps is getting behind anyone in Bangladesh who cares enough to wade in and do the work.

I know this from my own experience. Some years ago a very brave Bangladeshi photographer penetrated one of the largest islands covered with fish processing camps and enslaved children. Bluffing his way along, he took pictures of amazing power, photos that showed small children scrambling along the high fish-drying racks while a slave driver whipped their legs and backs. Back in the coastal city he took his photographs to the authorities. Their response was to threaten him with arrest and violence. These local police were corrupt and being paid off by the slaveholders. Going to the capital, climbing higher up the rungs of government, going to the offices that should have been protecting human rights, he was threatened again. For his own safety he left the country and came to the United States, bringing the photographs with him.

I met this brave man at a Midwestern university where his wife was studying. A little while after we met, he asked if he could show me some photos. The images were astounding and heartbreaking. The photographer and his wife, fearful of the threats they'd received, were at a loss as to how to take action to rescue these children. I was shocked by what I saw, but I had one idea about what might be done.

I took the photos to Ambassador John Miller, at that time the director of the US State Department's Office to Monitor and Combat Trafficking in Persons. Miller promised to do what he could and that gave me hope, for John is both a man of his word and a man who knows a moral imperative when he meets one. At the top level of government a quiet but firm push began. The power of the US administration called in ambassadors and government ministers, and pressed them to take action. Finally, under orders from their own top politicians, an independent force from the Bangladeshi army raided the island, freeing hundreds of children. It was a wonderful outcome—or was it? Most children were taken from the island to a coastal city and just dumped, many far from their homes. Today, local anti-slavery activists tell me the island is going full steam again, the slave operations have even expanded. Some of the children I interviewed for this book were enslaved on that very island.

Corruption is the strongest support for slavery, so how can we break this cycle? The answer is through long and careful work by the Bangladeshis themselves, with any support that we can muster. At least it is true that we don't have to bring corruption to an end to get children out of slavery, that can be done right away by honest law enforcement agents and the local groups who are risking their lives to liberate others. Our job is to support them in the ways that they need, and to keep the pressure up on the government to enforce their own laws, dismiss and jail corrupt officials, and guard the precious mangrove forests that are both protecting Bangladesh from flooding and protecting the rest of us from global warming.

■ ■ ■

For most of the Obama presidency, Ambassador Luis C. deBaca led the State Department's Office to Monitor and Combat Trafficking in Persons—the US government's lead post on modern slavery. He knows about slavery in shrimp and fish and how it plays out in Bangladesh. Research supported by the State Department found the majority of shrimp imported to the United States comes from processing centers similar to the type I found in Khulna, or from even worse situations, like the fish camps of Dublar Char that use small children. Out at sea it can be just as bad. "Bodies wash up routinely on the shores of Malaysia, Thailand, and Cambodia, where they have been tossed overboard," deBaca said, describing the slavery on fishing boats in the region. "And usually it's for asking for a fair wage, talking back to the boss, asking to be taken back to shore." The demand for shrimp and fish is driving a stinking slave-based industry that spreads beyond Bangladesh throughout Southeast Asia.

It's an industry that feeds a global market that stretches into our supermarkets and hammers American shrimp fishermen in the process. Paul Willis is an independent businessman who makes his living fishing for shrimp out of New Orleans. He loves his work, but he doesn't think he can compete with slave labor. "We are trying to make a living," he explained, "but because these foreign countries are using cheap labor, slave labor—call it whatever you want—we can't compete, we just can't compete." The shrimp get active at night and come nearer to the surface of the water, and Willis remembers when there might have been three hundred boats off the Louisiana coast in an evening. Since the advent of cheap Asian shrimp, he says, "You are going to see eight tonight, that's what's happened to this industry." Shrimpers like Willis have faced a fatal triple whammy. Many fishermen survived the impact of Hurricane Katrina even though many shrimp boats were destroyed, and some of these survivors have been able to wait out the effects of the Deepwater Horizon oil spill that began in April 2010. But when the low cost of slave-produced and -processed shrimp pushes prices down to the rock bottom, American shrimpers have to sell their catch at a loss. That's just economic suicide. And, of course, it has nothing to do with fair trade or free trade: we have laws against the importation of slave-made goods. Capitalism is about competition in a free market—slavery is the opposite of freedom both in life and in the market.

Ambassador deBaca was one of the first to understand the links between slavery in the things we buy and issues like global warming. As he put it, "We talk now a lot about the carbon footprint, and rightly so. We ask, 'What decisions do I make that add to global warming?' I think it's time to ask the next question, which is 'what decisions have I made today that contribute to slavery?'" And he admits that this is tough, even in his job as the government's lead abolitionist: "Even with me, based on what I do for a living, I can't guarantee you that I'm slavery free." Our challenge as well as our opportunity is the fact that these two questions are inextricably tied together. The decisions we make that contribute to slavery are also increasing environmental destruction and global warming. Our life choices that increase global warming feed slavery and help it grow. But we can make other choices—we can choose life and freedom.

. . .

The big picture of global warming, environmental destruction, and shrimp and fish production is both right next door and a million miles away from Shankar's world. He's another lad who was offered work on the island of Dublar Char in the protected Sundarban forest, but he's much smaller than Shumir, the boy we met at the beginning of the last chapter. Shankar's only twelve and can't weigh more than about fifty pounds. It's as if all his nutrition has gone into growing his huge mahogany eyes and the long gorgeous eyelashes that frame them. You hardly notice his crooked yellow teeth and chapped lips. More obvious is his slight twitchiness; something seems to be eating at him. I wonder if he is cold; it's a chilly morning and he's only wearing a loose button-up cotton shirt, green with white flowers, over his cotton trousers. His thick black hair is cropped short around his large noble ears—but it's his eyes that are arresting, both for their beauty and for the strange blankness that seems to see everything and nothing.

"The man who recruited me," explains Shankar, "said nothing about the hard work, but it was bad. As soon as we got to the island, the smell was terrible, I'll never forget it. Then the man said, 'You'll clean fish, and dry and pack fish, and if you don't work, well, we'll be very angry.' So I followed the other boys when the fishing boats would come close to the shore and we'd walk out into the water and carry baskets of fish back to the camp. The baskets were heavy, but you had to carry them, if I couldn't carry one or if I dropped it, I'd be beaten. I'd watch the sea, because I knew when the tide came, the fishing boats would come with their fish.

"In the middle of the camp was a big space for cleaning fish, this is where I'd take a basket and dump it on palm-leaf mats spread on the ground. First, everyone dumps their fish, then everyone starts sorting the fish. Each type of fish had to be sorted into its own pile. Then we'd tie the fish together by their mouths, unless they were knife-fish, then we'd attach their tails together. When they were tied together they were ready to hang on the drying frames. Some fish you cut a little bit to make it dry more quickly, others you made cuts so it could be hung on the rack. There are a lot of different types of fish, but the worst kind is shark. Cutting and cleaning the sharks was the hardest part for me because they are so big, you have to cut out their stomachs and wash them inside. They were heavy. Then you had to cut them in half lengthwise in order to put them to dry.

"When you're cutting fish, you cut yourself too; it happens all the time. There were fifteen or twenty other boys there with me. Some were little like me, some were aged fifteen or sixteen, and some were smaller, maybe eight or ten years old. When one load of fish was done, you'd start another. If there wasn't another load, then I'd just sit, but we'd also have to use that time to make food, or repair nets, or collect the dried fish from the racks and pack them into big burlap bags.

"We got to sleep if there were no fish to clean, but that might be for only an hour between loads. I felt confused all the time because I had no sleep. Sometimes when I was cutting fish my head would start nodding and I would fall asleep, then the boss would hit me. See, there's a guard there all the time with a stick. He was a big man, a fat man. He would shout or hit me. If I worked really hard he would be happy, but if I didn't he would swear at me—'son-of-a-bitch,' he called me, or 'pig's-son,' or worse things. I felt so bad when that happened.

"Whenever I was tired he'd hit me; basically this was every day. Sometimes I got sick, like with a fever, other boys did too. There was someone who sold medicine, but no money, no medicine, so we never got medicine. One boy had terrible diarrhea and died. And headaches, I had horrible headaches, maybe from carrying the baskets on my head. But this wasn't the worst. The worst thing was the tigers.

"Tigers live on the island and in the forest by the camp. At night we'd hear the tigers. When they roar you can hear them from a long way away. We'd never know how close they were. One day a boy was sent into the forest next to the camp to gather wood for cooking. A tiger took him, a couple of days later we found him. He had been eaten. This was the most frightening thing."

Shankar stopped dead when he said that. His eyes went flat and focused somewhere far away. I kept silent, trying to imagine what it would mean to find your friend dismembered, knowing tigers were prowling nearby, hearing them in the night. After a little while, Shankar came back from wherever his mind had taken him. I changed the subject, asking about what he was doing now.

"Well, after I escaped [he stowed away on a boat], I got back here and started catching crabs with my father. I like being back here and working here. Of course, this is my home. I don't want to go to school anymore, I want to work. I want to work with my dad on his boat. My mom died in childbirth a while back, that was when I went to the island, so it is hard. But I just want to stay here." Shankar paused again, another wave passed over his face, then he looked up at me and said in a small voice, "There are still a lot of children there. . . ."

6

GOLD RINGS

As the demand and the price of gold spiral upward, our *irrationality* about gold also spreads like a pandemic. This is, after all, a mineral that human beings can easily live without. Its practical uses are few, and for most of those it could be easily replaced. Its appeal is all on the surface: a warm color like sunlight and a shine that doesn't rust or fade. This luster makes it ideal for decoration, especially since it is easy to work. It is just right for shaping and cutting and making into rings or chains or thin leaf. The same durability we want in a ring also makes gold ideal to serve as money. Today, of course, the world's gold supply could never support the value or variation in the global economy—as John Maynard Keynes said, gold is nothing more than a "barbarous relic." At the same time the tailspin of national economies after 2009, as in past periods of hyperinflation, sent many people running for the stability of this "relic." Whenever an economy is in shambles, gold rules.

Chaos, war, ethnic conflict, economic collapse, and corruption all destroy the value of paper money by destroying the governments that stand behind it. Every crisis increases reliance on objects that have (or are thought to have) inherent value: food, tools, fuel, gold, and slaves. The long-lasting historical link between gold and slaves is no accident. The same destructive forces that unleash slavery, like civil war and ethnic conflict, create a greater and greater demand for gold. And when the gold itself is produced by slaves, then a perpetual motion machine of greed, suffering, and profit is set running. Today that machine is running in Ghana, fueled once again by demand from Europe, India, and North America. In a feverish and vacillating global economy, brought on by the crash caused by unregulated European and North American speculation, gold and slaves provide a rock-solid foundation for financial security.

There's gold at my fingertips. That sounds like I'm rich, but there is almost certainly gold near your fingertips too, just under the keyboard of your phone or laptop, a ring on your finger, or perhaps there's a little bit of gold in your earlobe or one of your teeth. Jewelry gold, dental gold, electronic gold, it's all the same: super-stable, non-rusting, and easily worked. Your dentist, the company that made your computer or phone, the jeweler where you bought your ring, they all tend to buy their gold from dealers, who in turn are buying from wholesalers, who are buying from "bullion banks." These bullion banks aren't like the banks we use for our checking accounts, but private companies that buy and sell on the global exchange. The largest trading space is the London bullion market. This is where the big boys play, where the minimum trade is a thousand ounces of gold. But gold is also the ultimate recyclable mineral, so a chain of jewelry shops, or the dental supply company, is more likely to be buying in "scrap" gold and melting it down for reuse. Almost half of all the gold in the supply chain is thought to be recycled, but is it?

There's another, rapidly growing, bullion bank in Dubai that serves as the back door to global markets. *Time* magazine says a "stroll through the dazzling Gold *Souk* [Arabic for 'open air market'] is a must" for any tourist in Dubai. Apparently, visiting the Gold Souk is also a "must" for any ambitious gold smuggler with conflict minerals to sell. There are some 250 dealers in the souk, and many are willing to buy undocumented gold at a 10 percent discount from shady dealers arriving from the world's war zones. Once in the hands of Dubai-based gold traders, the gold is "clean" and sold on to refineries or directly to firms making jewelry. One of the big refiners, Emirates Gold, processes around 450 tons of gold a year. The firm is known as a "major refiner of scrap gold from the Middle East and India," but analysts think this is also the route from the slave-based mines to our fingertips. Of the gold that comes out of the ground each year, most comes from China, the USA, Canada, Australia, and Peru, where big industrial mining is the rule. But around the world miners are still doing it the hard way—swinging a pick and shovel, or panning for gold in a stream. Some of these miners are working for themselves, but far too many are slaves.

■   ■   ■

Ibrahim is a small man who carries a heavy load. He limps as he walks. An injury to his foot went untreated and never healed right. His face is a light brown and well-formed, even handsome, but too thin, the cheekbones protruding. His eyes are a rich dark brown, almost black, but there seems to be a film over them that dulls their light. He is tired and he is hungry. Insect bites speckle his arms and his forehead. His clothes are faded and stained, and his plastic flip-flops are worn and cracked. A warm, complex smell comes from Ibrahim, not foul but the scent of muscles and earth, old tools and dust. He is a man who earns his bread by his own sweat. Or rather someone is earning bread from his sweat, for as Abraham Lincoln said, slaveholders "have been wringing their bread from the sweat of other men's faces," and Ibrahim is a slave. His bondage is hard, and anxiety about his family is an additional weight on his shoulders. He worries about his wife, brother, and children. He wants to care for them and protect them even as he feels powerless against the forces of debt and coercion and exhaustion.

It's late at night and we are sitting and talking at a tree-shaded table on the edge of a town called Obuasi in the gold-mining region of southern Ghana. I've ordered some simple food—soft deep-fried slices of yam, but Ibrahim is just picking at his plate, nervous to be with strangers, fearful that what he tells me might rebound and hurt his family. Still he is determined to tell the truth.

"I come from a little village in the north of the country, up near the border with Burkina Faso," he says. "It is very poor there, the land is poor, there is little water. Hot winds come down from the Sahara. There are lots of people, but not much work.

"When I was six years old, my father died. I don't know how or why. My mother tried to hold us together, but it was hard, we didn't have much to eat. Then, when I was nine, she died too. She just got weaker and weaker and died. My brothers and sisters were given to other families, I don't know what has happened to them. My uncle took me, he wasn't married, so it was just the two of us. By that time I had done two years of school, but when my mother died I had to stop going to school and start working. After a while my uncle decided to leave our village and come south and find work. That was how I came here."

Ibrahim and his uncle were following a trail of words, stories of the golden south where there was plenty of food and good jobs. They joined an exodus so great that the population of northern Ghana fell by a third over the space of ten years. Ibrahim and his uncle tracked the rumors south to the gold mines in Ashanti state— believing that any work involving gold would have to pay well. They'd heard wonderful stories about the jobs in the big company mines: training, equipment, sometimes even housing was provided, and a whopping regular salary. There was even medical care if you needed it. But when Ibrahim and his uncle reached the mining town of Obuasi, there were no jobs for them. To get a job you needed education and recommendations, and they were just two more Northerners in a flood of desperate migrants. The mining companies turned them away. Ibrahim explained what happened next:

"We'd run out of money and we knew no one in the south. We didn't have a place to stay and we were hungry. My uncle was looking everywhere for work, we just wanted to earn a little so we could live. But there were no jobs. Then we met a man who said he could get us a job in a gold mine. He said there would be food and plenty of work, and that the more gold we mined, the more money we could make. So my uncle agreed to join an eight-man crew that would be working together. The man gave us some money to buy food before we went to the mine. He said we would work for three months and then we would be paid according to the amount of gold we had mined.

"We had to walk a long way into the forest where the mining camp was hidden. When we got to the mine, we realized this wasn't a legal mine being run by one of the big companies. We were told not to tell anyone about the mine, and there were guards to warn if anyone came near, but also to keep us from leaving. It was a big camp spread around the entrance to a deep shaft mine, more than four hundred people were working there.

"My uncle became the co-leader of the eight-man work gang. At first they were just carriers, hauling the ore on their backs from deep in the mine to the surface and then carrying it on a path out to the road. This is the lowest job; you only get paid a little according to the amount of ore that you carry. Then, after a while, my uncle began to work with a hammer and chisel at the rock face, this was a better job, but also more dangerous. I was still small, so I did whatever I could to earn and help out. Sometimes I would carry ore, fetch tools, or run errands, I had to do anything anyone ordered me to do.

"My uncle was able to protect me, but only a little. He kept me from having to work at the rock face, or deep in the mine, but it was still very hard. I was beaten pretty often. Some men would bully me, one would hit me on the back with the flat side of his machete. Anything I did wrong, any kind of mistake, would bring on a beating. If I overslept I would be beaten. This happened all the time. Sometimes it was the gang leader, sometimes other men in the gang, sometimes it was my uncle who hit me. It was bad, but my uncle and the rest of the gang were working flat out to earn as much as they could in the three months they had to work. They wanted to make a lot so they could send money to their families.

"After three months the man who had brought us to the mine—we found out he was also the local gold buyer—came to settle up with my uncle and the work gang. We were expecting to be paid, but he told us that we hadn't earned enough. He said that the gold ore we had mined and carried wasn't worth enough to cover the advance he had given us to buy food plus the cost of tools and food we'd had over the three months at the mine. We didn't make anything! In fact now we *owed* even more money. It was a big sum and he said we would have to repay that with interest before we could leave the mine. The interest rate was fifty percent. We were shocked, but the boss wasn't angry, he said he would help us and told us not to worry. 'You'll get lucky with some rich ore soon,' he said, 'and make plenty to pay me back. Meanwhile, I'll advance you a little more money so you'll have the food to keep working.'"

.   .   .

You could call it bad luck, or bait and switch, or fraud, but the debt trap is one of the most common ways to trick people into slavery. It has many advantages for the slaveholders: no need for kidnapping or violence, the slaves are motivated and work hard, and the cost of getting slaves is very, very low. It takes little more than slick promises and some food to get desperate people like Ibrahim and his uncle to surrender, unknowingly, into slavery. And once they're enslaved, the debt trap has a powerful force that locks them in bondage—honesty. Dishonesty feeds on honesty. The very rules of trust and honesty that guided Ibrahim and his uncle in their dealings with other people were a tool used against them. They were poor, but they were honest and religious people. They had a very strong sense that debts *must* be repaid, and that a person who did not pay their debts was a thief and a sinner.

The abuse of this fundamental belief by the gold buyer was very clever, since it was in his interest to string the slaves along with lies as long as possible. If a slaveholder resorts to violence too soon or too arbitrarily, the workers will realize that they can never work their way out of debt and their pride and honesty can no longer be used to manipulate them. When it becomes clear that the boss is lying, that they are being cheated, then a different set of rules applies. For that reason, the boss will keep appealing to their sense of "fair play." The workers are told they just have to try a little harder, that the boss is trying to help them. The workers are caught in a situation where they believe trust *might* pay off but running away will pay nothing. To increase his psychological control, the slaveholder boss may choose to actually pay some of the workers occasionally, though late and usually below the agreed rate. The fact that they *might* get paid (or are paid even a little) gives them hope and keeps them working, especially since the alternative is no work, no money, nothing to support their families, and no way to get home. The crucial truth that workers like Ibrahim and his uncle don't know is that when they realize the truth of their situation and try to get away, violence will fall on them like a hammer.

For Ibrahim these first months at the mine were the passage into a new life. He told me: "For three years we worked there, until I was twelve. My uncle tried to prepare me for what was happening. He told me I needed to be hardened, and that if I didn't get hardened then others would do worse to me. I had believed that when my uncle brought me south I would get to go to school, but that never happened."

They were stuck, but they assumed it was their own fault. They thought they must not have worked hard enough while they were learning the job, or maybe, this time, the ore was just low quality. Given that they hadn't made enough to pay their debt, some of the gang even felt lucky that the gold buyer was willing to keep them on. In any event, Ibrahim, his uncle, and the other workers believed a person should keep their word and pay their debts, and, in spite of the rough treatment, they still thought the gold buyer was honest. So they began again, working even harder, stretching their food until there was just a single meal per day. Just after his tenth birth-day the jaws of the debt trap snapped shut and Ibrahim became a slave. There was no ceremony or clear marker as he lost his free-dom, but hemmed in by hunger and exhaustion, accepting the "fact" of his crippling debt, and knowing that resistance brought violence, he was just swallowed by slavery. He didn't know it but he was join-ing the hundreds of thousands of others who, over the centuries, had been enslaved in this very same place as gold fed greed and greed spawned bondage.

■ ■ ■

Ghana's Atlantic coast has been plagued by riches and greed for at least five hundred years, driven by having two extremely desirable and fabulously profitable commodities—gold and slaves—in seem-ingly endless supply. By the 1490s Portuguese traders were dealing in both, sometimes bringing slaves from other parts of Africa to exchange for gold, selling them for more than the slaves would fetch in Europe. The amount of available gold was so great that across Europe and into the New World, this part of Africa came to be known by the name it would carry into the twentieth century—the Gold Coast.

The Europeans' insatiable thirst for gold pulled more and more Africans away from agriculture and into the slash-and-dig hunt for the mineral. At first the Europeans were more interested in gold than slaves, but with rising demand in the New World the trickle of slaves soon grew into a steady flow. Every ship that loaded a cargo of slaves along the coast generated a rippling call into the interior for more, and a vicious and destructive cycle began. Coastal chiefs found that their gold bought foreign goods, including weapons, which then increased their power to reach further into the country-side to capture more slaves. One inland ethnic group, the Ashanti, abandoned their traditional ways of farming, grazing, hunting, and trading. Profiting from both gold and slaves, they adopted firearms and rapidly dominated and enslaved their neighbors. Soon the

Ashanti made slavery an industry, dramatically expanded the trade, and exported thousands of men, women, and children each year. The Gold Coast, according to one European trader, was "changing completely into a slave coast, and the natives no longer concentrate on the search for gold, but make war on each other to acquire slaves."

For nearly three hundred years the Europeans clustered along the beaches of the Gold Coast, feeding on its riches, and left the interior to the Ashanti and other groups who did the dirty work of capturing and delivering new slaves. The lucrative slave forts Europeans built on the coast were both conduits of gold and holding pens and processing centers for the transatlantic slave trade; they changed hands several times as the Portuguese, English, Dutch, Swedes, Danes, and Prussians jockeyed for control. By the nineteenth century, when the slave trade was retreating in the face of abolition, the growing global power of the British Empire placed them firmly in charge. Claiming the Gold Coast as a colony, the British sent their troops inland, defeating the Ashanti and other groups, and took the lucrative gold fields for themselves. At the same time the British were developing new techniques of steam-powered industrial mining, and were quick to bring these new technologies to Africa. In 1897 Queen Victoria granted more than one hundred square miles of land to a new British company, the Ashanti Goldfields Corporation (AGC). The royal grant included much more than land, awarding an *imperium in imperio* (the power of a state within a state) giving the company the right to establish towns, trade, extract timber, and control waterways, as well as mining. Annual payments were promised to the two local ethnic communities and fixed forever at a paltry £100.

It had taken seventy-three years and four wars to shatter Ashanti control, but now the British could bring their industrial strength to gold. Where the Ashanti had used the simple methods of surface digging and washing to extract gold, much like the prospectors of the California gold rush, the AGC brought in huge steam-powered shovels and began to dig and process ore at an enormous rate, cutting out the locals and exporting it directly to Europe. Today the area is still fabulously rich in gold, and in spite of the end of British colonial power in 1957, the AGC is still there. After more than a century of mining, producing billions and billions of dollars' worth of gold, the estimated amount still to be mined, under just the AGC land, is 20 million ounces, worth at least another $18 billion. European companies still have large stakes, but now the government of Ghana also has some control over the flow of gold.

. . .

Around this great feast of gold skitter the parasite slaveholders. Under the table set for the big legal mining companies, they nibble away at every step in the mining process, until the gold from illegal mines is turned into bundles of cash, cash they use to live high and expand their control over more illegal mines and more slaves. Taking gold from the earth and turning it into cash is remarkably simple for the slaveholders. Slave mines are extremely primitive, from the open pits and pounding and washing camps, through to the blacksmiths who extract the pure gold. Clustered near great industrial mines, with their safety gear, modern equipment, pneumatic drills, and enormous trucks carrying ore, the slaveholders use mining techniques and technology straight out of the Middle Ages or ancient Rome. In the hidden illegal mines disposable slaves replace every machine with muscle and primitive hand tools.

Turning sweat into gold works like this: first, a site is selected where a vein or "reef" of gold-bearing quartzite might be found below the surface. Since the geology of the region is shot through and through with these veins of quartzite, this is not much of a gamble, and there are clues to follow: gold flecks in nearby streams, a legal mine nearby, or even a point where quartzite pushes up to the surface. Once a spot is selected, the slaves begin to dig straight down, jamming trimmed tree branches into the sides of the shaft as they go. The result is an irregular ladder of short poles running along the walls of the square dirt shaft and helping keep the sides from caving in.

The shafts are deep; the miners measure them in "telephone poles," a rough gauge perhaps sixteen to eighteen feet in length. "This shaft is six telephone poles deep," I was told at one site, "that one is eight poles deep." That's the height of a ten-story building and every inch is dug by hand, every ounce of soil and rock carried to the surface on someone's back. Some are deep and some less so, since the digging continues until a reef of quartzite is found and the real work begins.

Imagine cutting into a chocolate marble cake, the veins of white cake and chocolate cake swirling around each other, twisting and turning, tapering off then swelling again. Deep in the earth the veins of quartzite, granite, shale, and other minerals twist and swirl around each other like that marble cake. Forget about clean, flat layers of sedimentary rock, gold is found in metamorphic minerals, born of volcanoes and incredible pressure and heat, stirred by earthquakes and the grinding of tectonic plates. When the vein of gold is found, the diggers become chiselers. The quartzite ore that holds the flecks of gold is very hard; geologists rank it equal to hardened steel.

The chiselers attack the reef with their own sharpened bars of steel and crude hammers. The seam of ore may go straight or curve gently for ten, twenty, or even a hundred feet, then turn abruptly or just end. Deep in the earth, crouching, lying flat, cramped into corners, they follow the twists, the sharp downturns, the narrowing and widening of the ore, chiseling away until they hit soil or other rock, then turn to chase the dirty white quartzite wherever it leads.

Outside the mining town of Obuasi I go down a mine to see for myself. It's not a particularly deep mine, the shaft only about two telephone poles deep. There is no electricity in the mines; instead a battered flashlight is strapped to the side of your head with fat rubber bands. The flashlight is by far the most modern piece of equipment on site. There are no helmets, no gloves, and rarely shoes, just hard bodies, crude tools, and jagged rock. Darkness closes in on me as I climb down the irregular poles and foot holes dug into the dirt sides of the shaft; a deep darkness and silence grows with every step. At the bottom of the shaft I see in my flashlight's weak yellow beam the white vein of ore over my head where the chiselers have stood and hammered away, the stone and dust falling in their faces and filling the stale air. Crawling or walking stooped through the mine for thirty or forty feet I see the reef suddenly drop, and a new shaft runs along it, straight down for another twenty feet. Climbing down this shaft and creeping along for another ten or fifteen feet I reach the bottom of the mine. Here there is a small turnaround hole, a little over a yard on each side, a place to put the sacks of broken ore before they are carried to the surface. To one side is a small opening at floor level, about eighteen inches tall and two feet wide, I crawl on my belly through this gap as it opens into a space the size of a small closet and meets the rock face. Here the walls slope, the roof is loose irregular rock, and the floor is covered in mud and rubble. Two chiselers stand here, shoulder to shoulder, pounding away at the rock with their pointed steel rods and hammers, praying the roof doesn't come down all at once. Every few minutes one stops and shovels the rubble out the crawl hole to another man who scrapes and shovels it into a thick plastic rice bag and stacks it in the turnaround hole to the side. Within moments a carrier comes down and reaches the turnaround, takes a bag of ore on his back and heads for the surface. Each bag weighs just over fifty pounds, and he holds it on his shoulder with one hand as he begins the long climb to the surface. The stream of haulers is constant, like ants, up and down the shaft in a river of faint yellow headlamps, drizzling dirt, broken rock, and sweat.

At the bottom of the mine the air is hot and stale. A small plastic pipe is supposed to bring air down from the surface, but the day I descend, it is not working. Human lungs take in half a gallon to a gallon of air with every breath; in a normal day more than two thousand gallons are inhaled and exhaled. In this small space there could not be more than two hundred gallons of air to use and three men are working and breathing hard. Within a few minutes I can feel the oxygen being used up. I begin to suck hard, but no matter how big a breath I take in, my body can't seem to get the oxygen it craves. A little seed of panic blossoms in my stomach; it is the fear that comes with suffocation. Knowing what it is, controlling it, I find my heart still races, making me breathe even faster, gasping with no relief and so the little blossom grows. Standing still, willing myself calm, my breathing becomes ragged and I know it is time to go, to climb for the surface and air. As I climb I hold back the urge to scramble, knowing the precarious sticks and muddy footholds could easily tumble me back to the bottom of the shaft. Men pass me, going down for more sacks of ore, behind me others climb carefully, the bags of stone balanced on their shoulders and backs.

At the top, in the daylight and the hot and humid fresh air, I keep pulling deep breaths into my lungs, trying to ease past the fear oxygen depletion brings. I find my hair is full of dust and pebbles from the gentle rain of dirt that falls constantly down the shaft and in the mine. Digging the dirty white stones from my scalp, I look at the young haulers. Worked like devils, for all the dust and dirt, they look like angels. They have remarkably muscular physiques; like weightlifters, their bodies are bulging and hard and perfectly defined. It must be an ideal muscle-building routine—put fifty pounds of rock on your back and climb an irregular ladder nearly a hundred feet high, then repeat just as quickly as you can for eight to ten hours a day. While they look like bodybuilders now, they will soon be just good-looking corpses. As they climb up and down, their lungs are filling with quartz dust that chokes their breathing. This is a deadly dust that brings the disease of silicosis and as it worsens their hearts will fail from the strain.

. . .

While some chisel, others haul the bags of ore to the top. Once on the surface, the fifty-pound bags of ore are combined into larger 150-pound bags, the standard measure of ore as it starts down the road to becoming pure gold. From the mine to the nearest road, or possibly to a nearby pounding site, more men hump the heavy bags down forest trails, moving at a trot, hurried along with blows and shouts from the gang boss or his thugs. Soon the bags reach the next stage in the process where the jagged rocks and rubble of quartzite ore will be pounded into a fine powder.

Whether carried to a pounding site by truck or worker, the ore is dumped around a rough open pole shelter with no walls and a ragged thatched roof. The earth under the thatch is bare and strangely lunar—covered with small round craters in the hardened dark red dirt. When the bags of ore arrive, the craters disappear as twenty to twenty-five men, each squatting on a small can or stool, place between their knees a heavy steel bucket that fits neatly into one of the craters. The bucket is smooth sided with a rounded bottom, less than a foot across. Sitting or squatting, the men scoop handfuls of ore into the bucket and begin to pound it with a steel bar. The bar weighs about fifteen pounds and is smooth and flattened on the end. Bucket and bar together make a primitive mortar and pestle, and to crack and crush the hard stone takes a mighty swing, the whole body flexing as the steel rod crashes down again and again. When the ore pounders are all going at once the noise is terrific, each steel bucket singing its individual note. Sometimes the rhythms come together in peals of ringing like church bells, and then break apart again into earsplitting cacophony.

As long as there is ore the work goes nonstop. The day starts at three A.M., and the pounding goes on for a minimum of twelve hours, but normally much longer. After hours of pounding, a bucket of rocks and rubble is reduced to a fine powder that is measured out into "helmets," old plastic hard hats with the straps and lining gone. It's odd to see these old hard hats used only as measuring cups, when they could literally save lives if worn down in the mines. Each 150-pound bag of ore yields six or eight helmets; each helmet holds two or three cups of a dark gray powder.

This work is deadly. It is not the backbreaking exertion, but the dark gray powder that kills the young men. As they hunch over the buckets every blow of their steel bars sends a cloud of fine dust into the faces of the workers. The sides of the shelter are open to the air, but with ten to thirty men all pounding away together a dust cloud thickens and hangs over them. The men know something is wrong with this, but what has been concealed from them is that they are committing suicide by silicosis. No one has told these young men that there could be no quicker way to die from this irreversible, incurable, and fatal disease.

We've known about silicosis for a long time; hundreds of years ago it was known to kill stonecutters and grinders. And a shocking demonstration of its destructive power occurred in 1930 when the US government dug the three-mile-long Hawk's Nest tunnel in West Virginia. Using pneumatic drills and dynamite, the workers created clouds of rock dust, digging and hauling, glad to have a job in the Great Depression. When the diggers hit veins of silica they were told to mine it for sale, but were never given masks or any other protective equipment. The poor local whites and black migrant workers kept going as long as they could, but many died on the job within a year. Other workers were fired when they got sick and then just tried to get home to die. No one is sure, but it is thought that silicosis killed a thousand men out of the Hawk's Nest workforce of three thousand. It remains America's worst industrial disaster.

Silicosis can begin with the first deep breath of quartzite dust. The particles embed themselves in the tiny alveolar sacs and ducts in the lungs. The body responds with coughing and by producing mucus, but because of the particles' sharp angular edges the normal action of the lungs can't dislodge them. Irritating the lungs, the sharp particles cause fibroids and tumors, and infections become more likely. When the exposure is high, as at the ore-pounding site, acute silicosis occurs. Within a few months the body is desperately trying to dislodge the particles, pouring in white blood cells and fluid. As their lungs fill with fluid, the young men suffer severe and

disabling shortness of breath, weakness, and weight loss. At one
pounding site I talked to the men about their constant coughs. The
site was a large one, with nearly one hundred workers involved in
different jobs. They told me fifteen men had died in the last year,
the oldest aged forty, the youngest aged eighteen. "Sometimes
someone begins to cough, and they can't stop," one man told me,
"they complain of pain in their sides, then they begin to vomit
blood, and then, sometimes, they just fall down dead." The enslaved
workers are drowning on dry land as their lungs fill with fluid and
gold dust. And at the same time they are dying of silicosis, the men
are being forced to poison themselves and the forest around them
with mercury.

■ ■ ■

To go from ore dust to gold requires another ancient mining technique, one familiar to the forty-niners of the California gold rush,
the innocent-sounding work of "washing." Near the pounding site,
close to a stream, rickety sticks and boards are assembled into long,
narrow sloping tables. Like a dinner table, two or three feet wide
and six to eight feet long, the washing tables slope slightly downward to ease the flow of water. The tables are covered with towels or
sometimes a bit of thin nylon carpet. Once pounded to a very fine
powder, the ore dust is mixed with water, stirred, and then slowly
poured out at the top of the table. As the mixture ripples down the
slope, the heavier gold particles begin to fall out of the water and are
caught in the toweling or carpet. The quartzite dust is lighter and
washes past and into a bucket at the bottom. Whatever ends up in
the bucket is mixed and poured over the slope again for a second
wash, and sometimes a third time as well. In time a sludgy black
mud collects in the toweling, called simply "the black." In yet another bucket "the black" is gently washed out of the toweling, making another batch of dark dirty water, but one with a difference.

Left to sink to the bottom, the thick "black" sludge is scooped
into a smaller pail or maybe one of the helmets. The worker doing

this job moves carefully and thoughtfully, almost reverently, for this is the moment when the gold appears. From a safe place a tiny flask of mercury is produced, and some of it is dribbled into the fine dark mud. Watching intently, the miner carefully churns the mercury through the "black" with his fingers, finding the shining silver droplets and smearing them around. Now the magic begins, and beads of an off-white waxy paste appear, beads that can be pressed together into lumps. They are small and nondescript, but excitement grows as they form tiny waxy pebbles. These waxy nodules occur when mercury and gold bond together, the mercury absorbing two or three times its own weight in gold particles. Placed on a cotton handkerchief the waxy blobs are squeezed hard and most of the mercury passes through the cloth back into the bucket for more stirring and gathering of gold. The hard waxy ball left behind is set aside to be joined to others as they too are squeezed free of most of their mercury. More water is scooped into the bucket to further spread the mercury through the mud until no more waxy beads form. Then the bucket is emptied into the stream or spilled one more time over the washing table.

The water that splashes into the stream is laced with mercury. It is easy to see how the mercury begins to flow into the bodies of the workers and the environment poisoning anyone and anything nearby. At one pounding and washing site I watched the mercury runoff flow into a rippling stream, and then I walked along the brook to see where it went. In just a quarter mile the forest opened and I found myself among a loose cluster of houses. On both sides of the stream were vegetable gardens that families watered from the stream. Goats and chickens, whose meat and eggs would be eaten by these families, nibbled and pecked in the grass and weeds and drank from the stream. Near the brook was a long yellow building of battered clapboard with shuttered windows and a wobbly tin roof, a hand-lettered sign above the door reading "Christ Apostolic Church International." Children played in the churchyard and I wondered if they had been baptized in this stream as well. For the people living in this little village, and especially for the children, the poisoning would be slow but unstoppable.

. . .

Even a tiny amount of mercury is dangerous. Exposure damages the brain, kidneys, and lungs, impairs vision, hearing, and speech, and generates nerve damage, high blood pressure, and a host of other symptoms, including having your skin die and peel off in layers. In the womb, the unborn exposed to mercury can suffer serious birth defects; and exposed children suffer permanent nerve damage. If mercury is in water or food and heated while cooking it can release a vapor. Inhaling mercury vapor is the most dangerous type of exposure. In March 2008, for example, a man in Oklahoma breathed in mercury vapor while trying to extract gold from old computer parts. He died ten days later and his home had to be gutted because of the contamination. In the countryside of Ghana where municipal water systems are unknown, the streams and creeks, the shallow wells, the standing pools are easily poisoned wherever gold is mined and processed. Normally there is no other water source and no warning when the pollution occurs, so the mercury-laced water is used for washing, watering gardens, cooking, and drinking. Boiling may kill germs, but it doesn't remove the mercury and may release it into the air.

The next step in gold processing also brings the danger for mercury poisoning. Once all the gold has been extracted from the "black" the man who runs the pounding site takes the large waxy ball of mercury-gold amalgam to a blacksmith. The local smithy is just a rough shed with a small clay furnace and bellows, a range of tools hanging on pegs on the wall. The floor is hard-packed dirt, scattered with charcoal, metal filings, and pebbles. In one corner is a hearth made from the steel rim of a truck wheel.

The blacksmith takes the waxy ball and mixes it with acid in a small bowl. The acid eats away the mercury and everyone stands back from the rising cloud of acrid gases. Then the acid mixture is heated and deadly mercury fumes spiral up into the air and out the open spaces in the walls. Anyone standing too close, or even passing by outside, risks breathing these fatal fumes. The mercury disappears from the waxy ball, but it is not truly gone, just converted into a gas that will attack the environment in a new way, drifting and spreading into foliage, insects, birds, and animals. Back at the blacksmith's, the thumb-sized gray residue that is left is carefully brushed into a small ceramic pot and nestled into glowing charcoal. Another chunk of burning charcoal is placed on top and then more is heaped all around the pot. A blower is switched on and the fire begins to rage and throw sparks and embers across the room. To melt the gold and remove the impurities, the temperature in the ceramic pot has to reach nearly 2,000 degrees Fahrenheit. Within minutes the dross is burned away and pure molten gold, glowing and shining like a tiny sun in the ceramic pot, is carefully lifted out. Dropped into water, the gold cools and hardens until a warm, sparkly droplet of gold is turned out onto the blacksmith's palm. Days of chiseling at the rock face, thousands of pounds of ore hauled up mine shafts and along forest trails, twenty men pounding ore to powder, and other men washing and blending the "black" with mercury, have produced a small lozenge of gold, the size of a bite-size chocolate candy.

■ ■ ■

Just next to the blacksmith's shop is the gold buyer's office, a small shop with a long counter running across the room. It is rare that the gold buyer is there, and the day I stepped into the shop was no exception. Only his workers, some armed with rifles, were there to meet me. I explained I was interested in understanding the local ways of measuring gold, and though suspicious and cagey, they tried to answer my questions. Then a man came in from the blacksmith with gold to sell. On the long counter were scales for weighing gold and the clerk who would weigh and pay for the gold. Sliding over to the side of the room to watch, I saw something that amazed me: behind the counter, all along the back wall, were stacks and stacks of bundled banknotes, a good two feet high and three wide. It was enough cash to fill two or three suitcases. It was a staggering amount of money to see in a small rural village. In 2007 Ghana adjusted their currency, the cedi, to equal the US dollar, so the cash I saw behind the desk in this little shack in a run-down neighborhood in a poor rural area would have been worth hundreds of thousands of dollars. A few minutes later another worker linked to the gold buyer came into the shop and ordered us out. Someone had reported our presence and the boss sent word to the armed guards to make us leave. Grabbing a few last surreptitious photographs, we obeyed and strolled back to our car.

■　■　■

Behind the little shop and up a hill is the one nice house in the area, a vast two-storied stone and stucco house with a tile roof. Workers were enlarging it as I passed by, and more rooms were shooting up from the roof and off from the side. Brand-new four-wheel-drive SUVs were parked outside. This was the home of the gold buyer, where he sits spiderlike at the center of a web that ties him to the slaves in the mines, the haulers, the ore pounders and washers, the truck drivers that move ore, the blacksmith, the gold-buying shop, and upward through the government's Precious Minerals Marketing Company to the global gold market and your local jeweler. It is a web that leads, ultimately, to the ring on your finger.

The gold buyer is a very modern slave master. Satellites bring him up-to-date information on the price of gold, his collection of cellphones keep him in constant touch with the thugs controlling the work gangs in different illegal mines, and, most importantly, he keeps himself completely insulated from the slavery that makes him rich.

If you ask, the gold buyer spins the story that he is just a simple businessman who provides two essential services to the poor workers. On one hand he loans money to people no bank would touch, to help them get started in mining, and then he gives them a place nearby where the gold can be sold. "Of course," he would say, "I make a little money when I buy the gold and I charge interest on the loans I make—but that is normal business!" And it is true that in the most visible part of his business, gold buying, his profit margin is reasonable, the price paid for raw gold (set by the government) is normally around 90 percent of that day's world market price. This gives him a profit of $80 to $110 on every ounce of gold he buys from other mine operators. But this profit is just the icing on the cake, the real money is in the cycle of debt bondage he creates and the gold his own mines produce, the mines where Ibrahim and thousands of others are trapped.

■　■　■

Enslaved through his uncle's debt at age ten, Ibrahim grew to manhood in bondage. From the time he was twelve he began to carry sacks of ore, and at seventeen he began to chisel at the rock face deep in the mine. One day his chiseling dislodged a large rock that fell and smashed into his forehead. Ibrahim lay unconscious in the mud on the floor of the mine for four hours. When he came to and was helped to the surface he was confused and disoriented. A lump the size of an orange had swollen on his head. Over the next weeks he found he couldn't remember things, and would often lose his balance and topple over. "Even today," he told me, "whenever I get hot, I get headaches." To get medical treatment, Ibrahim's uncle went to the gold buyer's overseer at the mine and asked to borrow money. A loan of $300 was added to their existing debt.

Accidents like this help lock workers into slavery. At first their debt seems manageable, just the cost of their food and tools as they mine for three months. The fact that they never seem able to pay off the debt is discouraging, but they want to be honest. Still trying to see it as an opportunity, they want to hold up their end of the bargain. Meanwhile they hope and pray for that one big break, perhaps finding a rare nugget of solid gold that will pay off everything and set them free.

Injury changes all that. Not able to work, no ore is produced to earn money, and the medical costs increase the debt until it equals several years' income. When it is time to settle up, the debt for living expenses, tools, and the medical costs is reduced by any amount earned for the ore they have managed to mine, but then the remaining debt swells with added interest. Injury leaves workers owing sums far beyond their ability to pay. Of course, if it were only debt, there might be another way out, but the debt is just a mask for slavery. It gives the mine owner a ready explanation for how he is using his workers, and it works, at least for a little while, to cloud the minds of the workers to their real situation. It is a powerful ambiguity, an uncertainty that leaves the new slave constantly in doubt about what is really happening. Even the armed guards patrolling the mines and keeping the slaves under control are rationalized as being there to protect the mine and the workers against thieves or police raids. For migrants like Ibrahim and his uncle, unclear about the customs and work in the mines, it can all seem reasonable at first. And when they begin to realize their true situation, the guards are there and waiting.

After the accident and what must have been a severe concussion, Ibrahim and his uncle were suddenly carrying more than $1,000 in debt, between two and four times what they might earn in a good year. But the truth is that there is *never* a good year because the system is rigged at every turn to keep them in bondage. As an adult, Ibrahim chisels more than a ton of ore from the rock face every day. On the surface, a boss oversees the loading of the stone into larger bags and their movement to a pounding or crushing site. This boss, as well as any truck driver that carries the ore, gets to take some of the bags as their "fee" for managing and moving the ore. The boss that oversees the pounding site also gets to take some of the ore, which he will wash and remove the gold dust from for himself. Sometimes the ore will be taken to a mechanical crushing machine. If so, the man who owns the machine gets to keep a portion of the ore for himself. Each of these men kicks some of their profit up to the gold buyer. Then the blacksmith gets another fee, and then the gold buyer takes his 10 percent of the value of the gold. Along the way there can be other payments, to corrupt police, to local chiefs for "permission" to mine on tribal land, to defray the cost of mercury, to anyone who might betray the location of the illegal mine, or to local criminals who have enough clout to take a cut of the money as it flows past. The ton of ore Ibrahim mines in a day yields, on average, about ten dollars' worth of gold, but by the time all the "fees" are paid, his share will barely cover the one or two dollars a day needed to pay for that day's food, and goes nowhere toward clearing his existing debt.

Over time it becomes clear to the workers that they are trapped. It's fair to ask why they don't just run away. The answer is simple, as simple as slavery has been throughout history—if you try to leave you'll be hunted down and beaten. The boss at each mine keeps an eye on the enslaved haulers and chiselers, encouraging them to work harder with blows and abuse. He forces the sick back to work, and if someone tries to slip off, he drags them back and beats them in front of everyone else. If a worker does manage to escape, corrupt local police know they will be paid to track him down. Once caught, after the police have beaten him, he'll be returned to the mine or taken before a judge where another bribe will secure his conviction for defrauding the gold buyer (in his role of moneylender). The cost of the trial and bribe are then added to the worker's debt. The miners learn they can't win, or as one miner told me: "I know this is a crime, but there is nothing I can do about it. If I tried anything my children would go hungry." Not even death provides an escape. When a miner dies the debt passes to his next of kin, and the gold buyer's thugs make sure the brother, wife, or child know that they now carry the load.

. . .

A few days later, at an open-pit mine, I saw this load descending on families. When a river has been diverted and the open sandy pits gouged out of the streambed, there is a strict division of labor by sex. Men search out likely spots in the mud and muck and go to work with shovels, hoping to find flakes of gold. This is lowly, bent-back work, hard and sweaty labor scooping the sludge, mud, and gravel into wide and shallow aluminum bowls, the sort you might use to make a big salad for twenty guests. Hauling these bowls to the washing table is the "women's work," carrying them anywhere up to half a mile. All day long the women loop between the open pits and up a low hill to where the mud is washed and the gold is extracted. They carry the bowls full of mud and rock on the tops of their heads,

resting them on a cloth "donut" they wedge between their skull and the hot metal. Incongruously, many of the women wear brightly patterned skirts or dresses, unlike the muddy and ragged T-shirts worn by the men. As they balance the broad bowls on their heads, one hand often reaches down to hike up the skirt edge from the mud. They are the only splash of bright color in a blighted and drab landscape.

Standing to the side making notes, I glanced up to see a tiny girl, not much older than two, in a blue and yellow patterned shift dutifully trudging along with a plate of stones on her head. Intrigued, I followed as she wove her way through pits and sloughs and among other children who were playing in the polluted water. Reaching the washing table, she turned and started the walk back without dropping off her load. Getting closer, I saw that her "bowl" was just the plastic lid from a gallon can, and that her load was a selection of sandstones and pebbles. It was a game. She was pretending to be a mommy, doing what her own mother was doing, proud to be taking part.

The little girl was proud to be helping, but how does a mother feel, watching her daughter happily pretending to be a slave? How will she feel when her daughter's pretend work blurs into real work, real exploitation, and real abuse? Slavery steals so much from a person. Free will, movement, having your own money and charting your own way, they are all lost. For an adult who has come to slavery by making bad choices or just by being tricked, this loss is deeply painful. But what of the little child who is enslaved, and grows up to know nothing but bondage? Their loss is the greatest of all, for they lose the chance to construct from their memories that most precious of mysterious creations: a self.

7

THE MASSACRE OF MEMORY

It was two days before Christmas, and President George W. Bush was melting down right in front of us. Called to the Oval Office to witness the signing of a new anti-slavery law, I was still reeling from my time in the gold mines and the devastating illness that hit me late on the night of my last interview with Ibrahim. For the first time in all my years in the field, I lost days in fever and violent sickness. Now back in the United States, I was medicated and recovering. Perhaps it was the medication that lent a hallucinatory glow to the sullen cabinet members, shocked anti-slavery workers, and an agitated, lame-duck president rationalizing his time in power.

We formed a broad semicircle behind the president as he sat at his desk, preparing for the photographers to capture this special moment. But just before the presidential pen touched the bill, President Bush seemed to change his mind about signing the bill. Coming around in front of his desk to face us, he began to talk. It was sad and surreal. Rambling, he grasped at straws of justification, and went on about the challenge of decision making, whether it involved declaring war or choosing the color of the Oval Office carpet. Smiles frozen, we waited, and in time he ran out of energy and, blinking, seemed to wake up as to why we were all there. Minutes later, a good but not great anti-slavery bill was signed into law and we stumbled out into the cold, bemused by our brush with history. Standing outside the White House, I stared at the commemorative gift the president had given each man at the signing—a gold tie clasp engraved with his signature.

The slavery feeding into a stream of gold baubles that we might give to our loved ones (or receive from the president) is so immediately heartbreaking that it is hard to see beyond it. It is a crime and an affront to any sense of decency. But there is more to this crime than just slavery. The silicosis, the mercury poisoning, and the environmental destruction mean that families who are not enslaved also suffer, that communities that don't have anything to do with gold can end up slowly dying of poison and disease. That damage is a widening gyre encompassing all of us, a circle that soon overlaps other circles of slavery and destruction. But that damage also reaches from the physical world and into the special realm of memory.

■ ■ ■

Scattered in the lush forests of the gold mining region, covered over with vines and wildflowers, are great ruins. These are not the crumbled walls of ancient cities or ruined temples, but the enormous stone, iron, and concrete remains of nineteenth-century steam-powered gold mines. Walking through these ruins I watched enslaved workers scramble over what had once been the foundations or supporting braces for huge machines. They have no knowledge of what these crumbling obstacles were or how they worked. The rusting hulks of steam engines as big as city buses are now criss-crossed with root tendrils that seem to be pulling the wrecks into the earth. Bounded by shattered walls, trees sprout through one-hundred-year-old stone floors now exposed to the sun and rain. The footpaths used by the haulers with their bags of ore simply detour around the ruined machines and structures. In the twenty-first century, slavery has brought a dark age of ignorance to the gold region.

The enslaved workers know no history and no future. There are virtually no machines, but plenty of constant, mindless toil. As so many times before, memory is a casualty of slavery.

It is hard to measure this loss of memory. How do you fathom what is not there; how do you gauge a void? Most of us are replete with memories, and surrounded by *aide-mémoires*. We don't just hold a mind full of experiences, we keep photos, letters, videos, cards, gifts, drawings, seashells, feathers, a gold ring perhaps— anything that stores precious or crucial or even frivolous memories for us. It is difficult for those of us who live in freedom, who are so glutted with memory, to imagine a mind that cannot store away the meaningful or the simply enjoyable. Yet, one way that slavery steals life in its essence is by never allowing memories to form.

When I first met people who had been enslaved I didn't understand slavery's power to deny and destroy memory. I arrived in their lives with a rich set of misconceptions and assumptions about what it was like to be a slave. Freed slaves gently disabused me of my arrogance and ignorance and led me to a better understanding, including a realization of the power of slavery to prevent and erase memory. Seba, a young woman who had been enslaved in Paris, first opened my eyes. Seba had been sent from her native Mali to France as a small girl, supposedly to live with a family to learn French and get an education. The reality was brutal slavery as a domestic servant, torture, and sexual assault that lasted from the time she was eight or nine until she was twenty-two.

When I met her Seba had recently been freed and was living with a volunteer foster family. She was receiving counseling and learning to read and write. As we talked, I plied her with questions, based on my assumptions about what slavery must be like, about her life and views and memories, and I soon realized that we weren't really communicating. Trying a new tack, I pointed to a nearby round lampshade printed to look like a globe of the world, using it to ask some questions about where she was from. Within seconds it was clear— she did not know the world. There was no recognition that this ball represented our earth; that it was anything but a paper lampshade marked with blue and green splotches. I stepped back and started again, asking this bright and verbal young woman about the simplest of things. Yes, she had heard that the world was round. At the same time I found she had no concept of weeks, months, or years, and I came to understand that for Seba her only memory, her only understanding, was an endless round of work and sleep. Denied the knowledge of time, her memories were strangely amorphous. She knew that there were hot days and cold days, but didn't know that the seasons follow a pattern. If she ever knew her birthday she had forgotten it, and did not know her age. And she was baffled by the idea of "choice." She told me she knew she was supposed to like these things called "choices," that everyone seemed excited about her having this thing called a "choice," but that no one had ever shown her one, so she just played along. It was in these moments that I got my first inkling of the lived reality of slavery. I learned slavery is much more than the loss of freedom, more than not having any choices. The brutality of slavery extends to the theft of our common knowledge, and the denial and destruction of our memories.

We tend to see our memories as who we are, the very stuff of our beings. Without memory we might not cease to exist, but we would cease to be who we are. The denial and destruction of memory is the special crime of slavery. The law might say that slavery occurs when one person has the rights of ownership over another person, but that is simply control, not the denial and destruction of a personality that is the less visible outcome of slavery. And as this is done to a single slave, it can be perpetrated on whole populations, whole generations of slaves. In the same way slavery denies individual memory, it also massacres the common memory. The millions of slaves taken to the Americas from the Gold Coast and other parts of Africa were pressed hard to forget, worked into a stupor of exhaustion, separated from kin, and stripped of any physical remnant—clothing, charm, or comb—of their past. Often the only survival was a story, a song, or a seed, things that were intangible or seemingly unimportant. Brought together they might form a precious relic, a stew of okra cooked to a chant of words that still carried the rhythm and tone of memories if not their meaning.

In India I've met families with no memory of how they came into slavery, stating only that "our family has always belonged to this man's family." In the Congo, where millions were enslaved at the end of the nineteenth century, I was surrounded by the descendants of those slaves, but I met only one man who knew of it, and he had learned it as a university student in France. It is only when modern victims of human trafficking are enslaved in young adulthood that memories survive even though clouded by violence. The first generation to be enslaved remembers freedom, after that the acid of slavery eats away at memory. In Ghana, for Ibrahim and his family, the extermination of memory is well advanced. Ibrahim still holds to his mosque and the memory of his village in the north, but his children have no sense of where they come from, only that a debt hangs over them that is like a god—all powerful, irresistible, and expecting complete obedience.

When memory is lost, so is a sense of place. The slave has no home that is a refuge or a comfort. When your body is a disposable commodity, it is not hard to see everything reduced to the base valuation of greed. This is how slavery perniciously extends its devastation in new ways. This is how enslavement crushes Ibrahim's family and also consumes the natural world that could sustain them in freedom. The destruction of a single mind in slavery is multiplied out, to other people, and across species, space, and time to the natural world beyond.

. . .

The natural world has a memory too; it is the complete record of life written in our genes and the genes of every living thing. Every plant and animal, every bird and fish and germ holds in its genetic material a record stretching back millions of years. Each unique species, including our own, is a distinct volume of that story, chapters in a great, never-finished work. But slavery's acid eats away at nature's memory as well. As slaves are used to destroy the environment, annihilating people and the earth, whole species are also wiped out. Sometimes complete ecosystems, comprising whole libraries of nature's memory, will be smashed, burned, and destroyed all at once. Open-pit, "dig and wash" gold mining is especially effective at this.

To reach an illegal open-pit mine means taking a narrow footpath through relatively untouched forest. Along these paths, yellow hibiscus-like flowers sparkle in the undergrowth, with little blue irises growing from the soil below. Nearby bushes sport clusters of small star-shaped flowers, and gentle light-green ferns grow from the wrinkled bark of old trees. Sometimes a curtain of flowering vines hang from rock; holding still, I can hear the chittering little things that live behind the vines. Banana trees, pawpaw trees, and palms fill the forest understory, clustering around the massive trunks of teak trees that rise high to the canopy to spread their leaves. More than three hundred species of trees live here. It is a rich, complex, and diverse ecosystem: in Ghana there are thousands of plant species, and many hundreds of species of fish, birds, mammals, amphibians, and reptiles, not to mention twenty-three species of butterflies. Mining threatens them all, and the forest-dwelling chimpanzees, and colobus and Diana monkeys are especially endangered.

In Ghana, where sunshine, warm wet weather, and fertile soil make for deep and beautiful forests, the open-pit gold mines are spreading like cancerous sores. While the deep shafts are especially dangerous to people, the open "dig and wash" mines do the most damage to the environment. To open this type of mine slaves are made to strip away the earth to a depth anywhere from two to twenty feet, as deep as a two-story house. With bare hands and crude tools, all plants, bushes, and trees are ripped out to get at the sand and gravel beneath. With the topsoil gone, nothing grows, and only the twisted and battered remains of dead trees rise from the sand and clay. These open mines resemble a battlefield. Gouges and holes appear randomly as if blasted out, some filled with stinking water. Like a battlefield, there is trash everywhere: broken tools, smashed buckets, pieces of clothing, plastic bags and bottles, splintered wood, sometimes in piles but more often just scattered as if by explosion.

Climbing down into one of these pits, I gag on the acrid stench, a mix between that of a latrine and an oil refinery. At the bottom of one hole, as wide and deep as a house, is a small pool of water, fed from the trickling stream used to wash the gold on the long sloping tables. It is the *color* of this pool of water that stops me in my tracks. Beneath a patchy layer of scum it is magenta, fading to a dull metallic blue at the edges. Putting my face down to the pool's surface I see that even the ubiquitous mosquitoes aren't breeding here, and after a single sniff I jerk back from a coppery reek of sour metal.

On one edge of the abandoned site and surrounded by forest is another pit. The floor of this pit is wide and flat; time and weather have left the surface windswept, a soft and smooth layer of mud and fine sand. I carefully climb down because this is a perfect place to record animal, bird, and insect life. Testing the surface with my fingertips, it is clear that anything that might crawl, walk, or land here would leave a trace as clear as ink on paper. But searching the pit, I find nothing—no bird's footprint or animal track, not the weaving line of a snake, or even the tiny skittering trail of a beetle. After covering a large area, I found a single track, the hoofprints of three small deer crossing one far edge of the pit, not running, but stepping carefully across six feet of sand from one arm of the forest to another. In the midst of lush and fertile highland jungle, this is a dead zone.

This destruction of all forms of life is no surprise, given the pernicious nature of mercury and the other chemicals that flush through an open-pit mine. The nervous system and organ damage that affect humans occur in all mammals and most other animals exposed to mercury. Poisoned birds become too weak to walk or fly and have kidney failure. Mercury builds up in the body becoming concentrated, for example, in the flesh of fish. This is the reason pregnant women in North America and Europe are warned against eating predator fish such as shark, swordfish, or mackerel that have high concentrations of mercury. Birds that eat fish also get high doses, as do birds that eat insects. Even spiders pile up big doses of mercury from the insects they eat, a load of poison they pass on to any bird that eats them. Scientists call this *biomagnification*—the increasing concentration of a substance as it travels up the food chain. One ecologist explained, "Anything that lengthens the food chain pushes the mercury up, and it is biomagnified by about a factor of 10 with each step. . . . Mercury is a particularly slippery customer."

You can see this slavery-based destruction in a mercury-laced beetle, and you can see it from the window of an airplane as well. The last time someone tried to measure the deforestation due to gold mining in Ghana was 1995, estimating 30,000 acres had been lost. Since then illegal mining has increased dramatically. The best estimates are that between 1990 and 2010, Ghana lost 33.7 percent of its forest and woodland habitat, or around six million acres. The impact of such rapid deforestation is serious, costing the country about 4 percent of its gross domestic product. It has also increased the rate that land is lost to deserts or grasslands, some of this new savannah extending well into what had been rain forests. And the effect extends beyond the country's borders. *National Geographic*, under a headline reading "Forest Holocaust," described how "destruction of rain forests in such West African countries as Nigeria, Ghana, and Côte d'Ivoire may have caused two decades of droughts in the interior of Africa, with attendant hardship and famine." Or as Robert D. Mann, a British tropical agriculturist, has warned, "There will be further disintegration of the local climate, deterioration of soil fertility and reduced food-crop production, if the present trend of denudation by felling trees and uncontrolled bush fires is not halted and reversed."

Given the pressure of global warming, all deforestation is bad, but this kind of forest loss might be the worst kind short of nuclear attack. To understand this it helps to compare Ghana's open-pit mines to what is happening in the Amazon. In Brazil millions of acres of forest are being lost, but after the trees are cut down some topsoil remains and the land is converted into cattle grazing. It is an incredibly shortsighted, and frankly stupid, thing to do, but at least life, though pale and infinitely less diverse, continues on the land.

When a "dig and wash" open-pit mine begins, clear-cutting the trees is just the *overture* of a four-act environmental tragedy. Act One is the removal of all life, plant and animal, to expose the sandy clay or stone below. Act Two is digging out great pits and trenches, and land near streams and rivers is especially sought after. Some riverbanks are excavated to a depth of one hundred feet with the pits extending into the surrounding forest for another two hundred feet. This converts a living river into a stagnant, dead pond writhing along the bottom of a barren ditch. Act Three is the poisoning, the leeching and seeping of mercury, and the spread of death to the animals, birds, reptiles, amphibians, fish, and insects in the sur-rounding forest. Act Four of this tragedy is the abandonment. When the gold peters out, the slaveholders take their slaves and walk away. Piles of rubbish and mineral tailings are left where they sit. Soil, pushed to one side when the pits are opened, is never spread back over the scarred land. Streams and rivers, wrenched from their nat-ural banks, are left trapped in pools or diverted in ways that further erode the forest. If the land *can* recover, which is often not possible, it will take decades, if not centuries.

Still, wherever it is left to grow, the forest is a lively and beautiful place even when it presses up against a gold mine. Walking along a forest trail to a mine or pounding site, I would sometimes stop dead, transfixed by the honey-scent of flowers or speckled light through the canopy dancing across glowing light-green ferns along the path. My Ghanaian co-workers, used to this natural beauty, would hurry on and then stop and stare at me, asking if something was wrong. "No," I would say and get moving again, but something *was* terribly wrong, and I was just beginning to comprehend the size of the wrong that fed on gold and how high it reached into governments, the economy, and our lives.

. . .

Gold flows out of Ghana at an amazing rate. Global sales of Ghanaian gold were more than $5.5 billion in 2012, and hit $6 billion in 2013. The rush to gold has boomed as the global economic recession that began in 2008 pushed up its price more than 250 percent. It is believed that nearly one third of the entire country of Ghana is now leased out to mining firms, and legal production is expected to rise by more than 6.5 percent each year through 2014. No one knows how quickly illegal production is growing and increasing its appetite for slaves, but small-scale mining that doesn't bother with legal permits responds much more quickly to market forces so the expansion is likely to be very rapid indeed.

The result, in a country like Ghana, is a situation moving rapidly just outside, yet also inside, the control of the government. Gold exports bring vast sums into government coffers, while the rapid expansion of gold mining greatly disrupts the lives of whole communities of the rural poor. Meanwhile, illegal mining and enslavement work like a sponge, soaking up some of these displaced families. Whether migrating from the depressed north of the country or displaced when their family farms are lost to international mining companies in the south, the minimum number of illegal miners in Ghana is thought to be two hundred thousand, or up to one million if their dependents are included. That's a lot of people, and they are easy to see. Mining towns and some of the large illegal mines are not hidden away. Even small slave-using mines are not hard to find with a little time and effort. Illegal mining, slavery, and the accompanying environmental devastation continue so blatantly because while the rich and powerful of Ghana might want to put an end to these crimes, they'd rather not do it *just now*.

Clearly, the government of Ghana has a responsibility to protect its citizens from slavery and its environment from destruction, but it also has a responsibility to honor contracts signed with mining companies and to safeguard revenue flowing into the national treasury (and the pockets of some politicians) from gold exports. As in many countries, the government of Ghana is the main buyer and seller of gold. According to law, all gold from small-scale mines, meaning concessions under twenty-five acres, must be sold to the government's Precious Minerals Marketing Company (PMMC). To buy the gold the PMMC has licensed a network of 750 gold buyers across the country. The aim of this government company is to bring a fair price to local miners and thus cut off the gold smugglers who pay lower rates to local miners and then slip the gold out of the country, avoiding taxes. When the PMMC was set up in 1989 it was thought that 80,000 ounces of gold were being handed over to smugglers each year, and the government was losing millions in taxes. With the government acting as a guaranteed buyer, miners got a better price and smugglers were pushed out of the market, but there was a fatal flaw in the plan.

To make sure it gets all the gold mined, the government buys gold brought to a PMMC office, like the one I visited with its great stacks of cash, *with no questions asked*. The government wants its cut on all gold, no matter how it is mined, whether it is legal, illegal, or simply stolen. Having a "no questions asked" policy means the government can help the small miners get a good price, and also act as a "fence" for any ill-gotten gold, no matter the origin. This means that illegal miners who use slaves and decimate the environment always have a ready buyer for their gold. The smuggling problem is solved, and two other problems are made worse. The contradiction in the government's position is clear, and turns especially ugly (and lucrative) if the licensed gold buyer is the same spiderlike person who bankrolls and controls the illegal and slave-based mines. Like mercury, corruption bonds with gold.

Of course, the main volume of gold isn't coming from the small-scale miners; it comes from the large-scale production of international companies that have contracts with the government, and who don't take their gold to little local PMMC buyers. Billions of dollars are in play and the companies both work hard to protect their land from poaching and expect the government to use force to safeguard their mines and equipment. For the big companies the illegal mines are a nuisance. The companies complain they have to put up with accidents caused by illegal miners and bear the cost of replacing the equipment they sabotage or steal. In 2008, Johan Botha, the managing director of Gold Fields Ghana, warned that a big new mine was ready to open. "But we're not going to do it as long as illegals are on the site, as they will follow us down there." According to the mining companies, illegal miners threaten and disrupt normal operations: "Illegal miners intimidate, or in some cases, physically assault mine employees to get access to mine shafts," explained Christian Luhembwe, a vice president of AngloGold Ashanti.

It is true that illegal miners steal from the big companies and from their concession sites. Old mines are reopened on the sly, or new paths are cut into areas where freshly dug ore can be stolen. And there are other deadly types of pilfering: illegal miners hide nearby and then sprint into open mines when blasting dislodges large amounts of ore. The trick, one illegal miner told me, is to get as close to the explosive charge as possible without being blown up, then to run into the blast site while you are still concealed by the dust cloud and grab as much of the ore as you can carry before running away. These desperate men are playing Russian roulette with dynamite. The closer they get to the blast the less likely they will be caught, but the more likely they will be killed or injured in the explosion.

I visited one illegal mine that had once been legal in the nineteenth and twentieth centuries. After being closed by the big companies, but still on their property, the mine had filled with water. Now someone had slipped in, installed portable gasoline-powered pumps to drain the mine level by level and brought in gangs of workers. The miners told me that there were great pools of water underground and that in the darkness of the mine it was easy to fall into one and drown. Given the haphazard pumping, sometimes the chiselers would break through between two old shafts, bringing a flash flood from an undrained section. The workers were terrified of being trapped and killed by a wall of water suddenly filling the mine shaft. Meanwhile, they showed me one old entrance tunnel that had been crudely sealed off with iron bars. Though it might be needed as an escape route, ore thieves had used this entrance at night so the illegal "owner" had sealed it off. For gold, thieves steal from thieves. Anyone who digs the "money stone," the quartzite ore, whether they are big legal companies or small illegal operators, knows there is always someone waiting for a chance to grab it away.

While the mines are deadly dangerous, illegal miners and especially those trapped in slavery tend to worry even more about the police. At mine after mine, I was told about raids by police and gold company security guards who beat up and arrested people, and destroyed or took anything of value. Pumps, electrical generators, shelters, beds, cooking pots, food, and tools—armed men, police, or private security would gather everything up and haul it away or destroy it on the spot. The miners would try to escape and hide in the forest, but many, especially those down in the shaft when the raid came, couldn't get out in time and were beaten with clubs, or jailed, or both.

Miners told me they feared the security guards and the police for different reasons. The security guards, they said, were more brutal, and injuries and destruction were much greater when they raided a mine. A story I was told several times—but never able to confirm—involved mining company security guards using a bulldozer to seal off a mine shaft, trapping and killing the miners inside. A report by the Ghana Commission on Human Rights in late 2008 claimed that in one instance mine security personnel set fire to car tires and placed them at tunnel entrances, suffocating those inside, and that attack dogs were routinely used in raids.

The police, on the other hand, are less brutal but cause a different long-lasting suffering. When police raid a mine, there are the same beatings, confiscation, and destruction, but any miners that can be caught are arrested. Even those held in slavery will be arrested and charged with illegal mining. Unable to afford a lawyer, they are quickly prosecuted and sentenced, and will spend the next two to three years in prison. Several miners who had been enslaved and arrested told me that the prisons, rife with violence and disease, were worse than the mines. The slaveholders, of course, are never apprehended, and the mines are up and working again within a week or so.

The truth is that no one in power really wants these mines to be closed. Yes, the mining companies would love to be rid of the irritation of ore thieves, but they wouldn't want to see all small-scale miners gone. Despite what they say, big mining companies often follow the illegal miners, letting them do the work of finding new productive shafts on their land holdings, then drive them off and take over. The government wants the gold, as do the local authorities and businesses that thrive on the cash skimmed from illegal operations. Blind eyes are turned at every opportunity; as long as the flow of gold is not interrupted the current state of affairs serves everyone—except the slaves and the natural world, but who speaks for them?

■ ■ ■

A government labor inspector *ought* to be speaking out for slaves, but he is getting a clear message from his superiors: "Don't rock the boat." The labor inspector I met in one town had been around gold country a long time, spending more than twenty years on the job, and he knew a lot about the mines. Even so, in front of a foreigner he tried to dismiss the idea of slavery, but try as he might, he couldn't quite pull it off. He started by explaining to me: "This is not forced labor, but if they go to the illegal mines to work they borrow money and then get threatened when it is time to repay it. When the workers realize they are not being paid, they're told to just hang on awhile and keep working, then they are still not paid. If they try to leave, the gang leaders drag them back, keep them working, and don't let them off the premises. If they do run away they lose everything, and children are working in this debt labor as well." That's a pretty clear description of debt bondage slavery, but officials like the labor inspector are told not to use the word "slavery." It's not just the government trying a cover-up. In African countries that suffered in the transatlantic slave trade, the word is loaded and touchy. "Slavery" is the great crime that Europeans did to them, not something that they would allow their citizens to suffer today. In addition, in Ghana in particular, there is a strong taboo against calling anyone a slave, or even suggesting someone is a descendant of a slave. Everyone in Ghana knows that slavery was both an indigenous activity as well as something exploited by the Europeans. They also know who of their neighbors and fellow citizens is actually descended from slaves. It is easy to tell that about a person, their last names testify to it. But to speak of it is completely taboo.

In spite of his nervousness about calling it slavery, the labor inspector told me he had seen plenty of court cases that forced indebted workers back to their "creditors," but he'd never seen or heard of a case charging a creditor with debt bondage or enslavement. This labor inspector was honest and knew what he *should* be doing about slavery, but his own superiors blocked him. "I tell mine operators to pay the workers," he explained, "and make it clear that it is illegal to hold workers against their will, but the police won't back me up. Anyway, most of the time I can't get to these mines. They are far out in the rural areas and I'm not allowed to use a government car for that." Even with the greatest will in the world, a single honest labor inspector who's not allowed a vehicle or police support is not going to make much headway against a large-scale and lucrative criminal enterprise.

Real change will have to come from the national government. Small-scale illegal mines could be made legal and inspected, and mining sites could be opened up to those needing work, but that would take a change in law and adjustments to existing contracts with the big companies. If such a law were passed, the enforcement effort would be vast, and since the gold is already flowing so nicely, why bother? Richard Quayson of Ghana's Commission on Human Rights put it this way: "Gold is at the heart of Ghana's economy, it is a very delicate sector to touch."

. . .

If only your wedding ring was as pure as your love . . .

It seems that everyone with power in the gold supply chain—governments, mining companies, local authorities, both large and small illegal operators, and slaveholders—all have an interest in business as usual. It is only the hungry displaced farmer, the young economic migrant, and the enslaved miner who are desperate for change. They are not completely alone; there are small local groups operating on a shoestring that are fighting for the oppressed and trying to protect the environment, often in the face of official opposition. But there is someone missing from this picture: the consumer.

The gold supply chain reaches much farther than the border of Ghana; it reaches through international markets and right into the shops and homes of North America, Europe, and other rich countries. There is a power for change in the supply chain, but it is power that is unrealized and disorganized—the power of everyone who buys gold.

Gold means hard cash for governments, investors, and criminals, but for most of us it has a special and emotionally delicate authority. Gold may be able to conduct electricity, but its greatest power is symbolic. We create that power when a decoration conducts our emotions, when we invest gold with meaning. For millions of people the purity of love, the eternity of commitment are symbolized in a little gold ring.

It is hard to know if the great symbolism we invest in our little gold rings is the key to taking slavery out of the mines and protecting the natural world, or the biggest obstacle to those goals. When your gold ring carries the profound emotional investment of symbolizing your love and your marriage, then it should be important to know that no slavery, no dangerous child labor, no mercury poisoning of rivers and streams taints that ring. Yet, for many people, those facts are just too ugly to think about.

Of course, some people want gold as a badge of wealth not love. They use gold as a blatant demonstration of economic superiority, and they don't really care where it comes from. Ropes of bling, chunky gold watches, solid gold MP3 players, and gold-plated car wheels are all just a way of saying, "This is *all* about me, and since I have things of obvious value, then I must be important and valued as well." It's a sad and pathetically hollow self-worth that depends on shiny jewelry, but it's so common it seems unavoidable, a kind of permanent flaw in human beings. Can people learn to see gold in a new way? All of human history seems to shout "No!" Human existence is littered with lives damaged and destroyed by the lust for gold. But history also shows us that change might be possible. Remember that for most of human history *slaves* were an important way of showing off your wealth. Their labor, their sexual use, even their ritualized murder could dramatically boost a person's status. A person's power and importance were directly measured by how many slaves he or she controlled. Today, it would be hard to find any sane person using slaves to boost their social standing; the very idea is repugnant, not to mention illegal. If that change was possible, can't we make a smaller and easier adjustment in our relationship with gold?

After all, we don't have to give up gold; we just have to give up the slavery and environmental destruction that make gold so ugly even in its beauty. We can do that by watching how gold is being mined, and refusing to buy gold that hurts people or the environment. Naturally, some people will want to avoid inspection and sneak slave gold into the economy, but the fact that criminals exist does not mean we give up and let them have their way. Tracing gold is a challenge, but it is easier to monitor than most commodities. Gold is stuck in place, it can't be replanted like a hidden crop of opium pop-pies. And since many large gold mines are already inspected, the cleanup can concentrate on the small and illegal mines where the greatest problems occur.

The cleanup will start when we decide what environmental and human rights standards we will require of the gold we own and wear. A lot will go into that decision, but everyone agrees on the fundamentals—no slavery, no child labor, no environmental de-struction. Then everyone along the chain, but especially the con-sumers, will need to agree on who is going to inspect the mines and certify that the gold is clean. Once these core decisions are made then it is a matter of searching out the mines, getting them in-spected, working with the operators to clean up their operations (or shutting down the criminals), and certifying the output. Naturally, there are plenty of things that can go wrong along the way, but once laws are passed that require "clean" gold, the market will push to expand the certified supply. Some patience will be required; envi-ronmental cleanups, converting illegal mines into legal concessions, freeing enslaved miners and helping them to start new lives, and letting gold that is already mined pass through the system in a way that doesn't hurt the economies of poor countries will all take some time, but the result will be gold that we can feel good about.

So who's going to pay for all this? That's easy, the answer is *every-one*: mine operators, big and little companies, governments, whole-salers, retailers, and us, the consumers. The volume of profit is so great along the product chain that tiny amounts can be deducted without disrupting the flow or driving anyone out of business. Note that engaged couples in the United States spend an average of $2,000 for their wedding rings, and there are more than 2 million engagements and weddings each year. If we add $5 to keep slavery and environmental ruin out of our wedding rings then there's $10 million a year to pay for certification. And wedding rings are only a small part of gold sales. In the United States alone jewelry sales hit $79 billion in 2013, and the United States still lags far behind India and China in gold consumption. A fraction of a percentage point added to prices along the chain would be invisible to both producers and consumers but enormously helpful to freeing slaves and preserving rain forests.

For a country like Ghana, achieving clean gold would be good for its economy in three ways: it would mean access to the premium market that is led by ethical consumers, it would achieve better control over its most lucrative export, and it would better protect both its most vulnerable citizens and its natural resources. In most cases this would simply mean enforcing laws already on the books. One such law says that the government can ask mining companies to surrender land to small-scale miners, thus making their sites legal. Since most illegal mines operate where the mining companies are not working, the result does not have to be a loss for the companies. In fact, agreements could have the companies providing environmental education and technical assistance in exchange for part of the extracted gold. For other small-scale miners, and particularly the miners escaping slavery, existing government programs designed to support alternative livelihoods would be appropriate—as long as the new jobs or skills were chosen with plenty of input from local communities. Add access to legal micro-credit at reasonable rates to such programs, and poor and enslaved miners would be on the way to new lives.

Tied to the help needed by miners will be the basic protections all citizens deserve. Once again, no new programs are needed, just the expansion of existing work and law. Two key areas will need to be beefed up: law enforcement and labor inspection. It is important to remember that this is not unique to Ghana; when it comes to some types of agricultural labor inspection the Ghanaian government is far ahead of the United States. In both countries, however, police lack the training to see slavery, and top officials are not committed to making their countries slave-free. But with Ghana's well-educated workforce, training labor inspectors and police to identify, confront, apprehend, and prosecute slaveholders should not be a problem, as long as the political will and resources are there.

That commitment can be based on both the idea that slavery is wrong and the fact that eradicating slavery is an investment in a better economy. Free workers produce more and spend more, they take their children out of the workforce and put them in school, and they are much more likely to pay taxes. And because Ghana has a vibrant anti-slavery movement already working in cocoa, fishing, domestic servitude, and other types of bondage, we may know as much about how to help people achieve sustainable freedom there as we do anywhere.

The odds that slavery in gold will end in Ghana are very good, if the dice roll right and companies, consumers, and the government step up and do the right thing. But if we stand next to Ibrahim, trapped in slavery and now aged twenty-three, freedom seems impossible and the future hopeless. My last night of research in Ghana I sat up late with Ibrahim and he bravely opened his life and his heart to me. I say "bravely" for two reasons—it was dangerous to talk to me, but also because many slaves feel terrible shame. Like rape victims, they often come to blame themselves for the abuse they suffer. On top of that shame the slaveholders regularly berate them, blaming the debts and enslavement squarely on the slave's laziness, weakness, stupidity, dishonesty, and inferiority. It is brainwashing, and to escape, the slave disappears into a blank place in his mind, avoiding thought, avoiding the truth of slavery. To look squarely at yourself in slavery is to look down a well of hopelessness. It can be excruciatingly painful to speak honestly about a stolen life, but Ibrahim, sometimes shaking as he spoke, faced his devils and told me his story.

"I've worked in several mines, and lived through many raids by police and security guards," Ibrahim told me. "When a raid starts, there is usually a warning shot from a lookout, and then everyone runs for their lives. We know that anyone caught will be beaten badly. You just have to sleep in the forest that night, and then sneak back to the mine the next day. It is always the same, everything is destroyed, and anything you didn't carry into the forest is gone. But the gang leader is there with the guards, and you have to go back to work, cleaning up, getting the mine ready to start producing again.

"Once, when I was seventeen, the police surrounded the mine and I was grabbed as I ran into the forest. They beat me up and arrested me for illegal mining. After a night in jail I was taken before a judge. I couldn't understand what was happening; it was all going so quickly. Then I heard the sentence—two years in prison, and that was that. I was taken to the town of Kumasi and locked up. The prison was packed, really crowded, and it was dangerous. Bad things happened there. We got one meal a day. Inside I realized many prisoners were just teenagers like me, and I thought about how the gang leaders and the moneylenders were never arrested, never paid fines." When Ibrahim was released he did the only thing he knew, he went back to the mine and rejoined his uncle, taking the debt back onto his shoulders.

It was clearly hard for Ibrahim to speak of life in prison and in the mines. I suspect there are things, especially what he might have suffered in prison, that he can't bring himself to talk about. Trying to get an idea of the damage he's suffered, I gently asked Ibrahim questions aimed at revealing the extent of his trauma. Did he ever have flashbacks? Memories of bad things that just filled him up? "Oh yes," he said, "like last Tuesday, it was a kind of slow, kind of a quiet day, and for a moment I began to doze off. When I did, all the scenes came into my head, they were so real, and I was frightened. This is common for me. Sometimes, also, I wake in the night in a panic, so afraid, shaking and sweating." These, and every other psychological indicator of post-traumatic stress disorder that I mentioned, Ibrahim recognized in himself—the constant nervous edge of hypervigilance, the inability to concentrate, an emotional deadness, and a deep unshakable sadness. "About two and a half years ago," he told me, "a raid destroyed everything I had, and I just felt it was the end, that I had lost all control over my life. What little I had was gone, but the debt remained. I know there is no future for me in the mines, no security, no chance for medical care, someday I will just get sick and die."

Unless change comes to gold, the odds are that Ibrahim's prediction will come true. He already has the nagging cough that comes with silicosis, and has had pneumonia a couple of times. Malaria spirochetes swim in his blood and when he is weak the chills and fevers begin. There is no mosquito netting where he sleeps on a piece of cardboard on the ground, and certainly no chance of anti-malaria medicine, so he spreads and receives fresh malaria infections all the time. Another rock fall could leave him disabled, and the lack of food and rest means he stumbles through work, dazed and clumsy, an accident waiting to happen.

"This work is dangerous," Ibrahim explained, "but the men with money, the men who make the profits, force us to work just as we do. If the debt disappeared I would walk away and leave here forever. I would learn a new skill and do some other kind of work." I asked what he would feel about a legal mining lease; what if Ibrahim and the crew he works with could mine legally. "Yes, that would help. When you are illegal all your work can be stolen in a raid, all your possessions and all the ore you have dug. Between the interest on the debt and the raids that take everything, you can never get free."

If there is anything that softens the bitterness of his situation, it is Ibrahim's belief that God is watching. "God plans everyone's life," he told me, "and knows what is good for them. God knows his creature is suffering and in trouble, and one day God will bless him." I asked Ibrahim if he was ever angry with God. "No," he said, "it is wrong to think bad things about God, and anyway, many who are closer to God went through worse hardships and came through it. If God will not provide for you, he will not let you see the next day, so when you wake up strong and able to work, then God is providing." Ibrahim told me he goes to the mosque whenever he can and prays for a better life, but that no one at the mosque ever talks about slavery. "The Imam," said Ibrahim, "just cautions us to be careful, especially when there are raids."

As we came to the end of our conversation Ibrahim confessed to me what he felt was his worst failure. A few years earlier his younger brother had come down from the north, looking for work. His brother believed what so many young migrants believe, that gold mining would make him rich. Ibrahim tried for weeks to convince his brother of the truth, to help him find other work away from the mines. It was no use, and rather than let his brother become indebted Ibrahim added to his own debt to buy tools for his brother so he could operate independently. The experience left him frustrated and committed to never letting anyone else start work in the mines. "I will never again allow any relation or family member to be involved in this work," he said.

It was hard for Ibrahim to talk, hard to confront the facts of his life. At the same time he was anxious to make it clear that he was telling the truth. "I assure you my story is true, and I know others whose situation is even worse," he told me. Talking about his experiences left him with strongly mixed feelings. "I feel good that you are listening to me, for the first time someone is letting me talk about my pain," he said to me. "I am happy that I have been listened to and understood. But it also makes me feel very sad that all this is happening to me, and I do not have a clue about how to get out of it. I know from what we have talked about that I am a slave."

Then Ibrahim, tears running down his cheeks, said that he wanted to ask something of me. "I want to be remembered," he said. "When my story is written and your book is ready, will you send me a copy? I want to show it to others, to show them that I am not completely useless. I just want to show that something good can come out of my life."

8

AS WITH TREES, SO WITH MEN

AM I SCARED? I AM. I AM A HUMAN BEING, I GET SCARED.
—JOSÉ CLÁUDIO RIBEIRO DA SILVA

When Brazil decided to build a new capital city in 1956, it seems they let a group of twelve-year-old boys design it. Playing off a couple of narrow lakes, the streets of Brasília sweep in cow horn curves, with a central bulbous avenue making up the cow's face. And what a face! Like the cover of a science fiction novel, great swaths of empty space draw the eye to buildings that look like spaceships, or cereal bowls, or barbecued ribs standing in a circle, or duck eggs, or a pair of eyelids on a stick. Everything is pointy or bulbous and stark white, connected by long smooth spiraling walkways, the sort that robots love to whiz along beeping and flashing. It seems odd that the locals are not wearing collarless stretch unitards, a futuristic V-shape across their chests.

An adolescent's sense of organization shines through as well. Instead of old-fashioned ideas like "marketplaces" or "neighborhoods," the designers grouped buildings together by function. Hotels are found in the hotel sector, apartments in the apartment sector, restaurants in the restaurant sector, and so on. Luckily, they spread the toilets all around instead of concentrating them in a special excretion zone. It must have been fun in the 1960s zooming down the broad empty avenues in your tail-finned car, zipping from the government sector to the entertainment sector for a night out. Of course, that was before the population exploded and everyone got a car. Now everyone just sits in the traffic jam that locks down the city every day, trying to get across town to pick up their dry cleaning, or some Chinese takeout, since no one really lives in any of the function zones. There's little in the way of public transportation, since the handful of public buses are caught in the same jam as everyone else. How this city escaped without a monorail is beyond me, but it is not too late. It could at least connect the various government buildings replacing the now required taxi rides that sneak through underground parking lots, risk U-turns across six-lane roads, and descend into confusion when it's time to find a building's entrance—where does the door normally go on a duck egg?

The people who live in Brasília have learned that if you think too hard about their city and its vast idiosyncrasies it can make you glum and a little feverish, so they just don't. It is a detached approach I strive to copy as I wander from the hotel district through a collection of Buck Rogers Bauhaus to a celebration meeting in a big modernist building somewhere. (Sorry, that's the best I can do. I was never clear about where I was or what building I was in as I traveled around the city, though one building looked so much like a flying saucer I thought I was about to be abducted by aliens.)

. . .

My job in the capital was to help celebrate the seventh anniversary of something uniquely Brazilian—a national plan for the eradication of slavery. Everywhere else I went in researching this book the same themes were repeated—corruption, violence, and grinding and seemingly unstoppable environmental destruction. In Africa and Asia ecocide and slavery were running hand in hand over the lives of people and the natural world. Brazil is different.

Different, but it's still a country suffering severe environmental threat and ongoing ecocide. In many ways, Brazil is ground zero in the fight to end global warming. Here is the world's largest forest, the great Amazon basin, recognized as a crucial center of biodiversity, as well as being the "lungs of the planet." This is also a country with a long history of slavery. During the transatlantic trade of the eighteenth and nineteenth centuries Brazil received a huge number of slaves from Africa. Ten times more slaves were sent to Brazil than to North America. From the beginning of colonization until the 1880s, about ten million people were transported from Africa and enslaved in Brazil. Yet because the death rate on sugar plantations was so high, the slave population of the country, around two million, was never more than half that in the United States. It also took much longer to bring legal slavery to an end. When full emancipation finally came in May 1888, Brazil was the last country in the Western Hemisphere to abolish legal slavery. As happened in so many other countries, making slavery illegal did not make it disappear. It simply continued under different names. By the mid-twentieth century slavery underpinned a number of Brazil's key export industries, but it was also bringing unwanted attention, and the government moved to blind outside observers to the realities of slavery in the country.

Denouncing slavery at the United Nations, condemning it in the European press, assuring the US government of their earnest efforts, the Brazilian government dodged its responsibilities at home until 2002. With the country under a military dictatorship from 1964 until 1985, this was not surprising. But even after the return to democracy, Brazil's Ministry of Labor and Employment unit called the Executive Group for the Suppression of Forced Labor had only four small and poorly equipped squads. Clearly, if the whole neighborhood is full of cockroaches, four small cans of insecticide won't go very far. Four squads in a country the size of Brazil, with tens of thousands in slavery, simply weren't enough.

A small example is telling: in the late 1990s I met with a government labor inspector in his strangely stripped-down office in a small town in western Brazil. He knew where the slaves were and he was ready to take official action—but when local bosses realized that he was serious about doing his job his telephone was taken away, the furniture removed from his office, and his official car was "recalled." The charcoal camps using enslaved workers were many miles away and deep in the forests, and on the occasions when he did manage to hitch a ride into the countryside, someone always seemed to tip off the slaveholders and the workers would go missing. The government had no real intention of dealing with slavery; the influence of rich landowners who benefited from forced labor was too strong, and the slaves themselves were seen as irrelevant and disposable. In this context of official indifference, slavery popped up like a deadly mushroom wherever profits could be made from human sweat. In agriculture, land clearances, mining, charcoal production, prostitution, and small factories, men, women, and children lost their free will and sometimes their lives to the slaveholders.

This all began to change in October 2002 when Luis Inácio Lula da Silva, known as "Lula," was elected president. Lula had a background in organized labor that predisposed him to take real action against slavery. He was also a person who understood poverty, having grown up in an impoverished family that his father abandoned when Lula was just two weeks old. Lula left school after the fourth grade to earn money to help his destitute family. At fourteen he went to work in a copper smelter, lost a finger in a factory accident at nineteen, and then worked his way up in trade union politics. President Lula made it clear that he believed that Brazil's history of slavery was still hampering its development. In October 2006 he stated, "This [slavery] system channeled wealth to a powerful elite and dug a social abyss that still marks the life of the nation."

Four months after entering office in 2003, Lula set up a National Commission for the Eradication of Slave Labor as a permanent part of the government and tasked it with rewriting and extending a National Plan for the Eradication of Slavery that had been shelved by the previous administration. Perhaps for the first time in the history of abolition, a government proceeded in the right way, making sure that everything was in place *before* taking action instead of rushing unprepared into liberation with often disastrous results The commission brought together the relevant government agencies, the police and national law enforcement, as well as the anti-slavery and human rights organizations that had been doing most of the work up to that time. It was the right team to attack the problem.

The national plan included some excellent ideas. The law against slavery would be tightened and the penalties increased. One of the strongest new proposals was also very radical: the expropriation, without compensation, of land belonging to slaveholders. If approved, expropriation would provide a significant sanction. It was also suggested that expropriated land could be distributed to freed slaves and poor landless farmers, which would help prevent re-enslavement—a serious problem in Brazil. According to the Brazilian Department for Labor Inspections, up to 40 percent of people freed from slave labor had been re-enslaved and freed more than once. Lula understood that rural Brazil was caught in a cycle of poverty, economic crisis, and enslavement; providing access to land and a better chance at employment would prevent workers from falling back into slavery.

■ ■ ■

By 2014 the plan to confiscate the land of slaveholders was still intensely controversial and hadn't been enacted, even though it passed the Chamber of Deputies in May 2012. On one hand it seems perfectly reasonable. Many countries, including the United States, allow for the confiscation of property from criminals. America's earliest laws against the slave trade, enacted long before the Civil War, ordered the seizure of slave ships and other property. But in Brazil a great deal hinges on land, who claims it, who controls it, and what you can do with it. Over time, the historical slavery system and the vast fortunes made by the owners of slave-driven coffee and sugar plantations established an elite class of landowners, often referred to as the "landed oligarchy." The descendants of these landowners still exert a powerful control over the country. This group is one of the key players in the drama of slavery and environmental destruction in Brazil.

To shed light on slaveholders, the national plan also established a "dirty list" of people or companies that use slave labor. The list is published in newspapers and on a special website. Anyone put on the list is excluded from receiving any sort of government funds, grants, or credits. Since much of the process of opening and developing new land relies on government permissions, tax credits, or other support, slave-using companies and individuals are driven out of land development. This is important because in Brazil "land development" is often a euphemism for destructive deforestation—by driving slaveholders out of land development, the government is also sparing the land from the kind of reckless destruction slave drivers often engage in.

Most important in the short run was the expansion of the Special Mobile Inspection Groups, the anti-slavery squads that had been starved of funds and equipment by the previous administration. These teams were increased in number, given good four-wheel-drive trucks, and, crucially, linked to new "mobile courts." The mobile courts included a judge who traveled with the anti-slavery squad and was empowered to impose immediate fines, freeze bank accounts, and seize assets, making it much easier to force farm owners to pay workers "back wages" within hours of their rescue. With this money in their pockets, freed slaves had the means to find their way back to their families.

The National Plan for the Eradication of Slavery achieved immediate and dramatic results. In 2003 the number of slaves freed more than doubled, to 4,879, and people began to think that the government might actually hit its target of eradicating slavery by 2006. Sadly, the number of newly liberated slaves fell in 2004 to 2,745 as slaveholders began to hide their slaves better. Slaveholders also began to fight back against the government's campaign, and in late 2003 violence and intimidation increased dramatically against anti-slavery workers, especially in the rural states of Pará and To-cantins. Anti-slavery activists in Tocantins were forced to flee in the face of repeated death threats. State officials were also targeted. In October 2003 both a labor judge and a prosecutor had to leave town after repeated death threats; three months later the judge's deputy was killed. On January 28, 2004, three officials from the labor min-istry and their driver were murdered while investigating reports of slavery on farms in the state of Minas Gerais.

It is a simple and tragic truth that when anti-slavery work is suc-cessful it provokes a violent response from slaveholders. As the number of liberations increased, more liberators were martyred. In February 2005 an American nun, Dorothy Stang, who had been working for many years in the frontier state of Pará, was gunned down as she walked to a community meeting. "Dot" Stang was from Dayton, Ohio, and had been living and working with rural peasants, helping them to make a living on their small plots through sustain-able forestry. Her murder was assassination pure and simple: a hired gunman stopped her on the road, shot her in the stomach and then, after she had fallen forward onto the ground, shot her in the back and then four more times in the head. The triggerman was appre-hended and convicted eleven months later. After more investiga-tions, others were arrested and tried, including Regivaldo Galvão, a ranch owner who had ordered and paid for the killing. During Galvão's trial a witness against him was murdered just before he could give evidence; Galvão was still convicted and sentenced to thirty years. Hardly a year goes by without the murder of one or more anti-slavery or environmental workers in Brazil. After I left Brasília and headed up into the Amazon in May 2011, a husband and wife team of environmentalists, well known for protecting the forest and resisting slavery, was stopped on a rural road not far from where I was staying, and shot dead. They had been receiving death threats since 2008 because of their work to save the (already legally pro-tected) rain forest in the state of Pará, and prevent illegal charcoal production and land clearing for cattle ranches. As with Dorothy Stang's murder, this was clearly assassination. Nothing was stolen from them and the police reported that the husband's ear had been cut off after death, most likely as proof that the hit had been made. Less than a week later, another campaigner, Adelino Ramos, was murdered in the far west of the Amazon near the Bolivian border. He had reported those who were illegally cutting the forest to the authorities. When those who profit from ecocide and slavery feel threatened, they hit back, and in Brazil the battle lines are clearly drawn across a landscape of corruption, greed, and poverty.

The remarkable thing about the slavery eradication plan is the brutal honesty that shines through its bland official language. At the meeting in Brasília, the government workers and the anti-slavery activists were clear about the underlying causes of slavery and ecocide and willing to name them. Behind every murder, every ruined forest, every enslaved crew of men, they said, are the drivers of corruption, greed, and poverty. Slaves around the world understand this, but most governments are loath to admit it.

In Brazil there is enormous tension around the role of corruption, greed, and poverty in the national narrative. The parallel and contrast with the United States demonstrates the situation. While the United States opened its vast frontier to individual small farmers, giving out family homesteads and building small communities, Brazil extended their frontier with a system of great landlords and dependent peasants, feudal practices they had inherited from Portugal.

Immensely powerful, and relatively unchallenged in the nineteenth century, this landed oligarchy used the military dictatorship from 1964 to 1985 to reestablish and solidify their position. Rural trade unions were shut down, and vast plantations were mechanized, driving peasant sharecroppers, tenant farmers, and small farmers off the land and into the cities. The military government paid for this land grab and mechanization with subsidized credit, tax breaks, and price supports for the big landowners. Added to this was an even greater handout scheme for the rich—free or very cheap land. In the decade of the 1970s, about 79 million acres were handed over to the oligarchy, an area the size of Germany. Some individuals who were government favorites received land grants as large as 15 million acres. This "land to the rich" program ended along with the dictatorship, but it left 60 percent of the country's agricultural land in the hands of 2 percent of landowners. Meanwhile, 70 percent of families living in rural areas of Brazil had no land at all.

The results of this inequality are clear to see in the simplest measures of wealth and poverty in Brazil. Economists often measure inequality by comparing the richest one fifth of a country's population with the poorest one fifth. In the high-income countries of North America or Western Europe the highest fifth of the earning population normally receives about six times more of the national income than the lowest earning fifth of the population. Put another way, families in the bottom 20 percent, on average, earn one dollar for every six dollars earned by families in the top 20 percent. For comparison, while North America has a 6:1 ratio, most of Africa has a 10:1 ratio (reflecting even greater poverty and less widely distributed wealth), and Latin America has a 12:1 ratio (wealthier rich people than Africa and plenty of very poor people). And even though it is easy to think of countries that are much poorer, the ratio for Brazil is 30:1. This is the greatest inequality in the world.

Inequality at this level is dangerous, as the World Bank explains: "High inequality threatens a country's political stability because more people are dissatisfied with their economic status, which makes it harder to reach political consensus among population groups with higher and lower incomes." So when I say there is tension around the issues of impunity, greed, and poverty, I don't mean they are just having a lively debate in the blogosphere. People die because of slavery all over the world, but in Brazil they also die in battles over the *issues* that underpin slavery.

In spite of a National Plan for the Eradication of Slavery, at the moment these battles add up to an ongoing war with no clear winner. What is clear are the stakes: a victory for the slaveholders in this war means a catastrophic loss for the planet, since it would likely mean the end of the great Amazonian forest.

In Brazil the conflict around slavery and environmental destruction is a repetitive but ever-changing drama. Big landowners find they have more restrictions on what they can do with their land, and the truly immense areas of state-controlled land, which include a large part of the Amazon basin, come under more and more protections. At the same time there is a powerful group in the national parliament representing the landowners and big businessmen, ready to block any proposed human rights or environmental protections that they think might get in the way of development and profits. If this drama is starting to sound familiar it's because this is a common plot in novels and films about the American Wild West. While both sides have supporters in the national congress, on the ground it's big ranchers versus sod-busting families all over again, but on a vastly larger scale. To understand how this drama is played out, hold in your mind a picture of Dodge City, Kansas, or Tombstone, Arizona, in the Old West.

. . .

Few of us have lived on, or even visited, a real frontier, the zone between the uninhabited natural world and the "civilized" world. Growing up in a small town on the banks of the Arkansas River in Oklahoma, I could sense only the faintest echo of what had once been the wild Great Plains around me. With the land cut into perfect one-mile squares, and the sprinkled houses of the countryside coalescing into towns at regular intervals, it required hiking out to a rare piece of raw prairie to find a spot where a plow had never sliced the sod. Sometimes, when night would draw in the horizon and the high yip and call of a coyote rang in the distance, I could imagine what once had been—the land that Walt Whitman described in his travel notebook ". . . a sky of limpid pearl over all—and so evening on the great plains. A calm, pensive, boundless landscape—the perpendicular rocks of the north Arkansas hued in twilight—a thick line of violet on the southwestern horizon—the palpable coolness and slight aroma . . . (profounder than anything at sea), athwart these endless wilds." The always moving line of the frontier had rolled over what would be my hometown a couple of generations before, and just on the edge of living memory was the prairie of the late nineteenth century when ". . . a herd of four million [buffalo] had been spotted near the Arkansas River . . . The main body was fifty miles deep and twenty-five miles wide." But as S. C. Gwynne explains, ". . . the slaughter had already begun. It would soon become the greatest mass destruction of warm-blooded animals in human history. In Kansas alone the bones of thirty-one million buffalo were sold for fertilizer between 1868 and 1881." By my boyhood, all that was long gone, yet there was something, no more than an image glimpsed in peripheral vision, that still whispered of wildness.

I'm reminiscing about my roots in Ponca City to remind us that everywhere was once a frontier. And while the previous wild state of Manhattan Island seems frankly unimaginable, in other places nature is just now being pushed back and could still recover from the crushing weight of humans if given a chance. Most of us like the idea of wilderness and share a feeling deep in our guts that wild places need to be saved. Most of us have even been to some sort of semi-wild place, a protected nature reserve, along the seashore, or canoeing up a river, and have felt touched by that experience. The north of Brazil, however, is the real deal, one of the last truly wild places.

●　■　●

The city of Açailândia is in the northern state of Maranhão. The frontier passed over this place some years ago, and the great açai trees are gone, their wild berries left only in the city's name. Gilberto is a handsome young man who has taken time out of his Sunday to talk to me. He's brought his wife with him, and the two are clearly crazy about each other, and make a handsome couple. As Gilberto tells me his story, his wife alternates beaming with pride and frowning and worrying when he describes what he has been through. Gilberto was a slave. His job was destroying the forest.

"My family, like most families, had no land," Gilberto explained. "Sometimes we would try to 'earn the land.' That meant finding a piece of public land, or unused land, and planting a crop on it. Once we got some land cleared and the crop started, and then a big farmer came and said the land was his. We had no way of knowing if this was true. He said we could stay and he would pay us for harvesting 'his' crop. Then someone came from the Ministry of Labor and stopped us farming there altogether. They said the conditions were too bad, and it was true we had no water, no toilets, and not really any shelter. We mostly just slept in the field, some people had pieces of plastic sheet to sleep under. We were hungry all the time, and the ants were biting us. We tried planting some vegetables, but got pushed off before we could harvest them. When the corn we had planted was ready, we went back to harvest it. We worked through the field pulling the ears of corn and then stripping away the outer leaves. The big farmer paid us about 5 reais [$2] for every 130 pounds of shucked corn. This was all of us working, even the small children worked.

"After this I went off with my cousin looking for work further north, up near the forest. This is where the *gato* [cat, slang for a dishonest recruiter] caught me. The *gato* is like an actor, he comes along and is very nice, he understands how much you need a job, and he says he can help. He'll recruit several young men at a time in town, but when you get to the countryside, up on the edge of the forest, the *gato* becomes a villain.

"When he recruited me, he said I would be paid 12 reais [about $7] for every 'line' of trees I cut. A 'line' was about 50 square meters, and was about all you could cut if you worked hard from four A.M. until sundown. This is the raw forest, and the vegetation is very thick, some of the trees are enormous, but there are others of every size, along with thornbushes, vines, snakes, and lots and lots of in-sects. To do the work we had to buy equipment from the *gato*, boots, knives, hooks, machetes, and axes, and they were really expensive.

"When we started to work there, we realized this was a bad situ-ation. For breakfast the *gato* only gave us a little coffee and some manioc flour, at lunchtime there would be a small amount of rice, maybe some beans if we were lucky. Working this hard we were really hungry, and after a couple of days we just said, 'Forget it! We want to leave.' But the *gato* said, 'No! You owe me money, a big debt for the tools and the food and the cost of bringing you out here.' And then he showed us his gun. So we thought, 'Okay, we'll work out this debt and go,' but the debt just kept getting bigger and big-ger. And the situation just got worse, our only shelter was a little bit of plastic over sticks, rats were running over us in our sleep, our only water was from a dirty pond, and our only toilet was the forest.

"One of the worst things was what the *gato* was doing to two young guys who were thirteen or fourteen. At night he would come to the shelter and take one of them away at gunpoint. Off in the middle of the forest, he'd put his gun to the boy's head, and rape him, forcing him to do things. Sometimes he'd hit him with his pis-tol as well. It was terrible, we wanted to help them, but we were afraid that he'd shoot us. These boys were in bad shape.

"After five months I had just had enough, and I told my cousin I was going to run for it. He was frightened and told me that I would be killed. By this time the *gato* had two other men watching over us with guns. But I was determined and willing to take the risk. So, on a Sunday afternoon I walked about five miles through the jungle and found a road. It is hard to believe, but I actually met a guy I knew on the road. When he heard what had happened he gave me 30 reais and I was able to get a bus into Açailândia. There were men hanging around the bus station, so I asked some of them where I should go to report what had happened. 'Don't bother going to the police,' they said, 'they won't do anything. You've got to go to the Center for Defense of Life and Human Rights.' At the center I met Brígida, a specialist who seemed to know all about what had happened to me, she said it was happening to a lot of young men. She took down all the details and where the men were being held and started a report to the Special Mobile Inspection Group so they could raid the site and rescue them. She told me it would be several days, possibly even weeks, before there could be a raid.

"When she told me this I started to worry about my cousin. He was pretty sick when I left and I didn't want him to die there. So, I went back to help him. The *gato* was angry, but also very surprised to see me come back. I told him I had gone off to see a girl, and he just sent me back to work. I think it was the water, but now everyone was getting really sick, and my cousin was getting worse. He was so sick the *gato* didn't care when I asked to take him out to the road, so I got him off and he made it home. I stayed around waiting for the mobile squad to show up. I wanted to see what would happen, and be there to tell the truth. Finally, one day, the mobile squad arrived at about noon. The *gato* ran out with his gun, but realized the soldiers were a lot stronger, so he had to surrender. The workers started shouting, they were very happy, and were rushing to meet the mobile squad. The farmer who owned the land had to pay us 'back wages' immediately, and most of the workers left for their homes.

"We told the police that the *gato* had raped those two teenagers, but he wasn't arrested, I don't know why. Somebody said that they couldn't physically prove he'd raped them, but I feel like those boys were victims and their word should have counted. The rest of us had seen the *gato* take the boys away, and then we had been with the boys when he brought them back. I don't understand why the *gato* wasn't punished for that.

"Most of the men returned to the south, but when I got to Açailândia, I looked for work. I also met my wife; she was working in a restaurant. We hit it off right away, and got married not long after the raid. She still works in that restaurant and I'm working in a big kitchen. Everything is different now, I've got a whole new life."

Gilberto's story has a happy ending—for him. We don't know if his cousin recovered, or whether the *gato* was ever brought to justice. We don't know what scars the other workers carried away with them, and we don't know how those two teenagers have fared after suffering sexual assault. It's likely that the forest Gilberto was cutting belonged to the government; virtually all of the uncut northern forests are under government control or held by Indian tribes—so the "farmer" he thought he was working for was almost certainly a local businessman trying his luck with an illegal land grab. The odds that this man came to justice are also remote.

All this points to flaws in Brazil's plans to eradicate slavery and preserve the Amazon forest. Note that the actors that stopped this particular crime were a local human rights group and national anti-slavery police, not local or state police or prosecutors. This pattern is repeated all over Brazil and especially in areas with the most severely threatened environments. Big landowners still control local governments, and often, local law enforcement as well. That means this is a war of words as well as bullets. While the national government talks about preservation, local bosses talk about the jobs and economic growth that will come when the forests are cut. It's hard for a local, poorly paid, policeman to buck the influence of local bigwigs. For the local human rights group the job of expanding local minds to a global viewpoint that includes the idea of justice is an uphill slog and starts with the young.

After my talk with Gilberto I followed the sound of drums to a warehouse of a building where teens were practicing a play they have written about slavery, part of a program run by the Center for Defense of Life and Human Rights. With more song and dance than dialogue it followed nineteenth-century slaves from Africa to Brazil, and then telescoped into the present to talk about slavery today. The teens had interviewed freed slaves to write their script. Even though this was just a practice session, it was a dazzling performance—pounding rhythms, dance that is part jazz and part capoeira, and a sharp plot of loss and triumph. The show is to be taken out to rural villages as a form of outreach, enlightenment, and community building—as well as empowering the kids who take part. Very proud parents look on, and little brothers and sisters yearned for a chance to join in, mimicking the teens' every movement. These are the ideas and the words that will win over the local people, but will they win in time?

.   .   .

The next day I'm in a small plane headed north to the forest. This is the best way to see the great sweep of the frontier, and watch the deforestation reverse itself, like a film running backward. Around Açailândia the forests are long gone, and the cutover land is rough grass and lost soil. From this altitude the white Brahma cattle on the light-green grasslands look like lice crawling through a short green crew cut. The effect of different herbicides, insecticides, or toxic wastes is stark in the cutover land, a patchwork of rust, chartreuse, mottled bottle green, etched with the pink and red threads of dirt tracks. Some of the low mountaintops have been scalped of their forest, leaving the sides uncut. It is hard to know why anyone would do this except for a quick timber grab since there are no crops or cattle to be seen, and no dirt roads wind their way to the mountaintop. As we fly north, the light green of the grasses and the yellow-red streaks of erosion are squeezed out by the deep green of the forest. Trees seem to spread from low mountaintops, normally the last areas to be cut, and creep down the slopes into the valleys. What would it take to preserve these steep mountain slopes? This is land where the forest can thrive, but once the trees are cut, it quickly erodes into a dead zone. We make a quick stop on a precarious mountain airstrip in Carajas. Coming in low, at a thousand feet, the forest looks like a rich display of broccoli, the canopy trees pushing their stalks above the undergrowth and spreading into dark bulbous heads of foliage in the afternoon light. It's a forest world waiting to be steamed and served with pasta.

Another stopover and we reach the booming little frontier town of São Felix do Xingu, landing on a tiny airstrip that's used so rarely that tall weeds are growing up through the concrete. The town's name comes from its position on the banks of the Xingu River, one of the larger tributaries of the Amazon. The Xingu is a contested river. In its basin the first "Indian Park" reserve was set aside by the Brazilian government in the late 1950s. At that time, anywhere west of the Xingu was far in the wilderness, but now the frontier has caught up and passed over the river. Some of the protected lands and remaining sections of forest along the Xingu are threatened by a plan to build the world's third-largest hydroelectric dam at a place called Belo Monte. Controversy has surrounded that plan since it was leaked to the press in 1987, but in 2014 the struggle ended and construction began. In any case, illegal deforestation keeps spreading along and across the river. In September 2011 astronauts on the International Space Station took photographs showing fires raging in the forests along the Xingu, part of illegal slash-and-burn clearance, fires so large they were easily visible from space.

For most travelers São Felix is the end of the line. If you want to fly farther into the forest, you have to hire a plane, and landing it is restricted to a few places where a dirt road has been flattened and smoothed. (To land, the pilot has to swoop a few times to announce his intention and get the horse carts, motorcycles, old trucks, and sleeping dogs to move out of the way.) São Felix is also the end of what passes for a paved road; from here west the roads are mostly rough tracks and need four-wheel drive. Larger trucks hauling goods in or timber out crawl along at a walking pace, and stop altogether when it rains and the road becomes river, mud pool, bog, or a sudden new ravine.

I've come here to meet Father Danilo, who will be my guide across the Xingu. Danilo is a Catholic priest in his sixties, who has been working in this region for decades. He's part of the Comissão Pastoral da Terra, usually just known as the "CPT," the social justice wing of the church that works against slavery and for environmental protection. The direct translation of Comissão Pastoral da Terra into English is "Pastoral Land Commission," but in Brazilian Portuguese the meaning is more like "the group that cares for the people and the land." Out here on the frontier, the CPT sets up farmer cooperatives, provides education, handles all sorts of human rights cases, and negotiates with politicians and businesses, anything that helps bring peace and justice to the region. Danilo is Italian, partly educated in the United States, and in his long time serving in São Felix has seen great changes around the Xingu and the forest. He is a gentle, firm, and jovial man, greeting everyone with a calm and trusting dignity. For the days to come he will be my traveling companion, wrestling the wheel of a tall four-wheel-drive, extended-cab pickup truck.

Leaving São Felix, we cross the mile-wide Xingu on a ferry that's like nothing I've ever seen, a rough and rusted iron barge with a motorboat permanently attached to its side by a hinged steel pole that allows the boat to push it in any direction except straight ahead. On the far side of the river, the road seems wonderfully smooth, but Danilo explains that this will last only till we reach the entrance to a ranch owned by the mayor. Sure enough, soon we are in a tangle of ruts and ravines and stream crossings, crawling along in low gear.

Along the road walk tired and dusty men. These are the *sem terra*, the landless. Because of Brazil's completely lopsided economy and extreme income inequality, and in spite of its success in the world markets, there are thousands and thousands of these men trying anything anywhere to find work. Think of the droves of wandering workers in America during the Great Depression of the 1930s, men willing to do anything for a meal. What is so out of kilter is that there is no depression here, these destitute men are living in a rich and booming economy but have fallen off the bottom rung of a ladder that keeps rising above them. The grapes of wrath flourish here, along with weeds of desperation. Poorly educated, skilled only in hard labor, these men, women, and children make easy prey for slaveholders. Yet, they are also men and women that know they live in a free country. It may be unfair country, but in this vast frontier where anything can happen, people still hold to a sense of their rights. For some of them, this seed of dignity is a death sentence.

■ ■ ■

Three men are walking into the rain forest. There is no clear path, but they follow a track where the undergrowth has recently been pushed back or beaten down. Over them tower the great canopy trees. They look like three friends out for a day's hiking, until you notice the automatic pistol strapped to one man's leg. In a shaded darkened glade, they slow down and carefully approach a pile of new earth and a rectangular hole in ground. Gently leaning over it, they see a scrap of cloth, and looking more closely, a human jawbone smeared with red clay. A fast-growing undergrowth tree shoots straight up from the corner of the grave.

Carefully, the man with the gun opens his small backpack, puts on surgical gloves, and takes out a few hand tools. Reaching down into the pit, he brushes lightly with his fingertips and soon the rest of the skull, turned on its side, is exposed. Stretched along from it, but doubled up, are the long bones of the skeleton, the humeri and radii of the arms, the femurs and tibiae of the legs, white and bulbous at the joints of elbow and knee. As he brushes more soil away, the teeth emerge. It is clear this was not an old man, the teeth are white and strong and even. The man with the gun is wearing a white shirt with the words "Perícia Criminal" printed in large letters across his back and above his breast pocket. He's a crime scene investigator; this is *CSI—Amazon*. But this is nothing like TV, there are no fast cars, no glamorous or craggy cops, just bugs and dirt and a rotting shirt and muddy bones in a hole in the forest on a hot and steamy day.

When more of the bones are exposed, the investigator climbs out and starts taking pictures with a small digital camera. Then he turns the camera to a nearby dirt pile. This is where the men who dug into this shallow grave tossed the first things they found. A single flip-flop rests next to a rib bone, a dirty plastic bag weaves around and under both. Leaves and sticks are jumbled together with hand and arm bones. There's an orange colored T-shirt, now ripped and filthy, emerging from the loose earth near the bones. Something was written on it once, but only "sion" is visible now.

A man with a mattock begins to scrape a clear space next to the grave and the crime scene investigator spreads some newspaper on the ground. Gently, reverently, the bones and clothes and fragments of the young man are lifted out of the grave and placed on the newspaper. As they emerge from the dirt, the investigator slowly assembles the loose skeleton. There are puzzled pauses as a small splinter of bone, or a piece of cloth, is carefully examined to discover exactly where it fits. The skull comes out last, clay jammed into the eye sockets and mouth. Fleshed out with clay, the skull seems more like a person. Tenderly, as the earth is removed, the bare facts of the skull emerge. Brushed clean, two neat holes are easy to see. The bullet entered above and behind the left ear, ripped through the young man's brain, and left through his forehead just above his nose.

In 2008 this young man and his friend had been offered work clearing land for a new cattle ranch. They worked hard for more than a month in terrible conditions, and then, fed up, they went to the landowner to demand their wages. The landowner promised he would send payment to them at the camp where they were working in the forest. Instead, he sent a gang to kill them. It took three years for the story to leak out and for the police to find their graves deep in the woods. The killers are long gone. Unable to tie the landowner directly to the murders, the police did what they could and jailed him for forty days, charged with the crime of cutting and clearing in a nature reserve.

■ ■ ■

These young men were victims of a new and insidious variant of slavery. The cost of acquiring a slave in rural Brazil is practically zero. Desperate for work, a potential slave only needs to be offered a job, chivied along with some food, and transported into the forest. For the slaveholder there's no purchase price, no up-front payment, just the expense of finding them, feeding them, moving them, and providing the axes, saws, and shovels needed for the work. The cost of getting a slave is so low that the length of enslavement has short-ened, in many cases, to around a month. At first glance that doesn't seem to make sense—once you have a slave, why get rid of him after just a month? But for the criminals tearing out the forest, short-term slavery is a great way to maximize profits while minimizing risks.

It works like this. Arriving in the forest with the promise of con-tinued employment and good pay, the workers will do their best to do a good job. Told that they owe money for the tools they've been given and the food they've eaten, they work that much harder, honor bound to pay their debt and keen to move into profit. Isolated in the forest, it's hard to see it any other way, so the workers knuckle down and look forward to when the wages will start to flow. If they do realize they've walked into slavery and try to escape, they'll be run down with horses and dogs and dragged back. Beatings will follow, and some may be murdered like the two young men in the forest grave. In time, after a month or so of hard labor, the poor food, poor sanitation, violence, and accidents take their toll and the workers begin to collapse from illness and exhaustion. Now the workers are treated as disposable, like plastic drink bottles or Styrofoam cups, and can be taken out to a road and dumped.

If the enslaved workers make it to the police, little will be done. The slaveholders are careful to conceal their identities and the loca-tions of their farms—giving false names and transporting the work-ers into the forest at night. Hauled away and used up, then dropped in an unfamiliar area, the exhausted slaves usually have no idea where they are or where they have been enslaved. All they want to do is get back to their families.

The criminal slaveholder has stolen a solid month of intensive work, and if he is ever found and questioned he simply claims the workers ran away without paying their debts and should be arrested for that. Meanwhile, in the nearest town his thugs are recruiting their next crew of unknowing slaves. Ambiguity feeds this short-term slavery: Was it really slavery if it lasted only a month? Was it the boss's fault they got sick or injured? Aren't these crazy accusations just the word of a lazy worker against that of a respected landowner? Even the slave is left unsure about what has happened: Was that slavery or just a terrible misunderstanding and bad luck? Certainly the experience is something the workers want to put behind them, something they try to forget about as they look for decent work.

This is "just-in-time" slavery, and it works like a charm for the slaveholders wanting to make a quick buck wrecking the protected forest. It's also a reaction to increased law enforcement (in this case "increased" means *some* as opposed to *none*). And it's also a risk reduction strategy. The workers are easier to conceal and less likely to report the crime if they get free or after they are dumped. Short-term slaves may not even realize what has happened to them until later, assuming instead it was just poor conditions and the bad luck of being ripped off for their wages. For the slaveholder, a shorter period means they can play on the worker's sense of hope and obligation to maximize productivity. In the twenty-first century, the *gatos*, the slave recruiters, have opened a temp agency.

Not long after the bodies of the two young men were found, thirteen more were exhumed on another farm nearby. I was just beginning my trip into the forest and I was shaken. In this gorgeous and vibrant countryside there was murder, bodies in shallow graves, and killers and slaveholders walking free. The job of CPT, and the job of the organization I helped to start, was to protect these workers, to find a way to end slavery and rebuild lives. But how could we do that in the face of hard-to-detect short-term slavery and even quicker death? Isolated from any law, facing armed men, even facing martyrdom like Dorothy Stang, would we ever be able to do more than care for a few survivors as the natural world and more human lives were destroyed and consumed?

.   .   .

If you've ever seen a Hollywood Western, you've got a sense of what I found on the other side of the Xingu River. All the stock characters are here: the tough but kind woman who owns the local saloon, the sodbuster family trying to make a go on land that is slowly killing them, the big cattle baron running roughshod over anyone who gets in his way, the lawman who is outnumbered and outgunned, and the good-hearted priest who won't give up. I found all these characters and more in a little hamlet called Primavera.

Father Danilo and I reached Primavera after a long slow slog along a road that sometimes flowed with mud, and other times disappeared into rifts and holes. We were lucky we had a truck. Just fifteen years ago this land was untouched, and when a mining company pushed through this rough track, rogue mahogany cutters were right on their heels. Mahogany is beautiful wood for furniture, increasingly rare, and very valuable. There is no legal cutting in the protected forests, and certainly not on Indian reserves, but mahogany cutters are criminals and are not interested in the law. Not surprisingly, as they penetrate into the virgin forest they use slaves to do the dirty work. These slaveholders are slash-and-burn specialists—first the mahogany and then any other valuable trees are cut and dragged to the road.

If the thieves are lucky they'll find a pernambuco tree. This highly threatened species, because of its special characteristics, has been used for the last four hundred years for a single product—to make the bows needed to play violins and cellos. Every great violinist and cellist you've ever heard was using a bow made of pernambuco, but today bow makers are scrambling to get more trees planted and Brazil may soon enact a total ban on pernambuco exports. Attempts to cultivate this slow-growing tree are difficult because they thrive only in mature rain forests, and falter in commercial, monoculture settings. With growing awareness symphony musicians are suddenly very interested in saving the rain forest and have organized to protect the pernambuco trees.

Once they've logged any tree of value, the slaveholders normally set fire to the remaining forest and then trick a poor farmer into paying for the right to occupy the illegally ruined land. These poor landless farmers have arrived on foot, hoping to build a new life. Single men come first, hiking in with tools to further clear the forest and cultivate crops. Finding or paying for a plot to claim, they'll scour the land for any valuable tree the criminals have missed. Cutting these, they'll receive only a fraction of the tree's value, but it is money they need to get started. When weather conditions are right, the rest of the forest will be torched again, leaving scorched earth and an annihilated ecosystem that is easier to clear away with hand tools. All over the trans-Xingu are patches where the blackened three-story-high trunks of dead Brazil nut trees tower over ash, rubble, grass, and weeds.

The burning of Brazil nut trees, even by land-hungry homesteaders, is a good example of all that is wrong in Amazonia. Strangely, these enormous trees belong to the same plant family as blueberries and cranberries. Growing as tall as a fifteen-story building with trunks more than twenty feet around, they are known to live for 500 to 800 years. Taller than all other trees, they dominate the forest canopy. Yet, because the bumblebees that pollinate them and the rodents that spread their seeds can't survive land clearance, they're only found in wild pristine forests. Brazil nuts are valuable as a food source and especially for export, which is why killing any Brazil nut tree is illegal in the countries of Brazil, Bolivia, and Peru. In spite of this law, illegal deforestation is wiping out the Brazil nut trees. Brazil harvested 104,000 tons of nuts in 1970, 40,000 tons in 1980, and 8,000 tons in 2000. For every Brazil nut tree that is lost, so goes a herd of little agouti—an increasingly rare jungle dweller that looks like an overgrown cross between a guinea pig and a jackrabbit. The agoutis are one of the very few species that have evolved teeth strong enough to penetrate the Brazil nut seedpod and feed on Brazil nuts. They eat the nuts, but they also dig holes and store them in the ground for later. Some of these buried seeds germinate and grow, thus spreading the range of the trees. It is a classic example of the balanced harmony of the forest. The king of the forest is exquisitely dependent on a high-flying, solitary, ground-burrowing bee for pollination and a dirt-digging rodent for survival. Break these subtle links that have evolved over millennia, and the ecosystem comes crashing down.

The painful irony is that for most of the settlers the Brazil nut tree they destroy is actually worth more to their families than the cattle they try to raise on the ravaged and denuded land. This is because most of the poor families that occupy land in the forest are laboring under a delusion. Life on a homestead is arduous, grinding, and dangerous. Occupying around two hundred acres, they burn the forest or hack it away one machete-swing at a time. They dream that they will become like the well-off ranchers who sit at the pinnacle of rural society. But this is a poisoned dream. The rich ranchers control thousands and thousands of acres, and their cattle, even though environmentally damaging and economically inefficient, exist in such numbers that even low profit margins can grow into large fortunes. Imitating the big landowners, settlers destroy their forest plots and risk everything to buy cattle for the two hundred acres they've cleared. But the fact is that their herd will be too small to make money, but still large enough that the herd's grazing leaves the land useless for other crops. At the same time, an untouched forest yielding Brazil nuts and other products can easily generate as much or more income as what can be made from cattle. If the naturally occurring forest products are complemented with a few cocoa and açai berry trees, the yield can be double or triple what a family might earn from cattle. But the cultural imperative is very strong, and the uneducated rural poor will tell you: "Cattle make a man rich." So, the forest dies and all but the cattle barons are impoverished.

. . .

As a frontier opens, while the slaveholders are ripping up the land and then fleecing the settlers, the only law in the newly opened land is the law of the gun. At the edge of the frontier, murders for land theft are commonplace. Vulnerable single farmers just disappear in the night, their land sold again within a few days. Or, as one landless farmer explained to me, "After we started the farm, a man came to me one day and said, 'Well, you can either sell me this land now at this price, or I will just buy it from your widow.'" The man sold up and moved on.

This rolling wave of frontier chaos and lawlessness is not a thing of the past. Today, the day you are reading this, and every day, the front line of assault just keeps pushing into the great forest with murder and slavery. There are only two ways that this violence will end. Either it will end when the forest is gone, or it will end when the forest is truly protected. We have to hope it will end when the line of assault comes to a halt, and the rule of law, instead of chaos, embraces the edge of the forest.

Like all frontier towns, little Primavera has grown up just behind the line. It's completely true to type—dusty, scrappy, and desperately boring, until something happens. There's a single dirt street lined with low wooden buildings: a bar, a stable, a couple of churches, a mechanic's shop, a school, a few houses, and a small general store. Dogs sleep in the street and people move at a slow easy lope. Some of the shelters are made of raw tree trunks with a palm-leaf roof. Under a shade tree is a pickup truck on blocks, its rusty engine hanging by a chain. It's easy to imagine *pistoleros* squaring off in front of the saloon, and sometimes they do.

The waiter in the combination bar, café, shop, and dance hall told me that he'd been living on the town's single street for two years, and that the police had visited the town just once, about a year before. "But last week," he told me, "there were some workers from out of town doing a building job for the Pentecostal mission. Their job had finished and they were hanging around and drinking in the bar. They got drunk and got into an argument with a local man who was also drunk. The local man threatened them with a pistol, but these young workers just took his gun away from him and shot him with it. There were plenty of witnesses, and someone called the police, but they never came. Late the next day his widow took the body away to bury."

In spite of this story, I enjoyed Primavera. The telephone lines and the cellphone towers are a long way away, which makes this a quiet reflective place where people still talk to each other, telling stories and sharing laughs. The only electricity comes from small gas-powered generators; only a few people have them, and they run them only part of the time. The café-bar runs their generator at night to power the lights strung up over the open patio where people drink beer and play foosball. The generator also runs the scratchy sound system and the TV behind the bar that shows videos of ancient kung fu movies. Bruce Lee is big in Primavera.

But before midnight, people roll home and the generator is shut off and slowly the world reappears as it once was. With no artificial lights for hundreds of miles the darkness is pure and the stars make a dazzling comeback. Slowly, as the eyes adjust to the night they've actually evolved to see, the light of the stars covers everything in silvery whiteness and clarity. Overhead the Milky Way becomes a luminous river, and I remember the words of John Muir: "We travel the Milky Way together, trees and men." Without electricity, without generators, without the humming and chugging and buzzing of a normal town, the silence unfolds into a symphony of nature. Seeing it clearly in the starlight I can also hear the wings of the big owl that swoops over my head. The bats are quieter and darker, their presence more of a flickering absence in the silver light. Weaving around and through it all are insects, calling, chirping, sawing, and flitting, flashing, and flying in all directions. Big and little, animals and reptiles rustle unseen through the grass and bushes. Tree frogs pipe in a chorus that starts and stops in perfect unison, according to their own private logic. A dog barks, a cow lows, a snore echoes out the open window of a nearby shanty. It is the all-sound, gentle but everywhere, the sound of life unchecked.

. . .

About the time I was being absorbed into the glistening night, an assassin was afoot not far away. He was a paid killer and his target was an older couple that just wouldn't get out of the way. Later the police weren't able to say if the pair died on Monday night, or early in the morning of Tuesday, May 24, 2011, but the motive and the method of their murder were clear.

José Cláudio Ribeiro da Silva (often known by his nickname, Zé Cláudio) and his wife, Maria do Espírito Santo, weren't well-off or well educated. As one of their close friends told me, "They were peasants." They came from poverty and stayed poor, but they were smart and they had big dreams. The core of their dream was the idea of living in harmony with the forest, especially the gigantic Brazil nut trees. Those trees meant something special to them, and were the symbol and focus of their lives and work.

When they first got together Cláudio and Maria grew rice, beans, and corn in their garden, like all Brazilian peasants, and took care of their young son. But somehow, at some point, they began to see the forest in a new way, as a source of life and livelihood, not as an obstacle. Soon they were reaching out, finding people to teach them about forest ecology and how to live in a sustainable way. Their curiosity and intelligence pushed them out into the wider world, and then they'd come home and tell others what they had learned. When they were getting started, Cláudio had only a fourth grade education. Maria had done a little better, but as time passed they became more and more self-educated on environmental issues and more confident in their knowledge. Their friend told me, "No one could tell they were peasants, they just seemed really smart." By the time they were murdered, aged fifty-two and fifty-one, Cláudio still hadn't gone beyond the fourth grade, but Maria had just completed a teaching certificate, gaining the skills she felt she needed to spread the word to others.

Their friend told me that Cláudio and Maria made a great team. Cláudio was fervent and a little serious, Maria upbeat and funny, so they balanced each other. "They could hold their own in a discussion with experts," their friend said, "they could argue their corner easily because they really knew what they were talking about." They had a way of making things real. When they moved into the forest in 1996, Cláudio and Maria started a small farm, but this was something new, a productive and profitable farm that didn't require clearing the forest. They moved onto land that was owned by the government, near to other new farms, some legal, some illegal, and some where the legality was unclear. A few of these farms had already cleared forest and put in cattle, others were trying to do things in a new way. About three hundred families lived in the area.

Using the knowledge and skills they had carefully assembled, they grew vegetables and kept some livestock, but they concentrated on harvesting the many natural fruits, nuts, and products of the wild forest. The centerpiece of their farm was an immense Brazil nut tree that they nicknamed "The Majesty." It took eight people to circle the trunk with their arms, and its nuts were an important cash crop. Cláudio and Maria welcomed all visitors, letting people stay in their home, and introducing hundreds to sustainable forestry. After a while the state government approved what they were doing and supported their claim to use the land and forest. So far, so good; but loggers also had their eyes on this virgin forest.

Cláudio and Maria had set up an eco-friendly demonstration farm, but it was in the equivalent of a war zone. The families living in the area had come years before from northeastern Brazil looking to make a better life, but by the end of the 1990s three factors converged to put great pressure on this rural community. The first was the age-old fallacy that small farmers could grow rich from raising cattle. After some parts of the forest had been clear-cut and small cattle operations began, these new small-time ranchers learned they

had made a disastrous mistake. Their cattle were too few in number
to support their families, and the land was now useless for most agriculture. After investing everything, they were left with ruined land
and poor prospects. The second pressure came from the logging
companies that had been working their way toward this part of the
forest for years. In spite of the fact that this was government land,
the companies knew they could easily log it illegally, even if some of
them were caught and fined in the process. Just when many local
families were trying to change their lives and circumstances by
switching to sustainable forestry, the logging companies arrived in-
tending to trick them or drive them off and cut their trees. It was a
recipe for conflict.

Then, around 2005, the third pressure began to build—an increasing demand for charcoal driven by rapidly expanding iron
smelters in Marabá, the nearest large town. Brazil is a country with
a lot of iron ore, but almost no coal. Without coal, charcoal made
from wood provides the fuel needed to refine iron ore into what is
called "pig iron," portable blocks of iron that are then sold around
the world. Production really took off after 2007 when the government enacted a Program of Acceleration of Growth for a number of
industries. This program provided a number of incentives aimed at
increasing exports. By 2010, the mining sector was earning $157
billion in profits and generated $51 billion in foreign earnings for
Brazil, about a quarter of all exports from the country. A large part
of the exported pig iron goes to the United States, where it is used
to make plumbing fixtures like bathtubs, sinks, and toilets, as well as
car parts, bridges, washing machines, microwaves, and any of the
other thousands of iron- and steel-based products American consumers buy and use.

The big companies that own the smelters and export the pig iron
don't make their own charcoal, they buy it from small producers
who arrive in Marabá with open-backed trucks stacked high with
loose bags of new charcoal. Charcoal producers have a long, ugly
history in Brazil. They rapidly construct low clay furnaces and then

transform forest preserves into wasteland. It's environmental hit-and-run, quick and dirty, and their modus operandi is slavery. Cláudio and Maria were standing in the way of both the timber companies and the charcoal burners.

"Cláudio and Maria were the elected leaders of the local settlement," their friend told me, "and they did everything they could to stop this encroachment. So a lot of people wanted them dead." In 2008 the couple reached out to the local government and to the Pastoral Land Commission (the CPT) and told these agencies they were getting death threats. A CPT lawyer helped them make official reports and complaints to government agencies, and they got some response. The Brazilian Institute of Environmental and Renewable Natural Resources (IBAMA) is the Brazilian equivalent of the US Environmental Protection Agency—but with more teeth. After reports from Cláudio and Maria, IBAMA went in and closed several logging and charcoal camps, but these actions weren't enough to warn off other companies and charcoal makers. Soon the logging trucks were back on the road that ran through the settlement where Cláudio, Maria, and their neighbors lived. Frustration was growing on both sides, and in 2009 Cláudio took action, standing in the middle of the road with an old shotgun, stopping trucks and warning them that if they tried to pass and cut trees illegally he would shoot their trucks. Soon the couple were taking pictures of all the trucks that carried illegally cut timber and sending them out to anyone who would listen. The threats escalated and many of the people in their community were scared off, backing away from Cláudio and Maria. As their neighbors abandoned them, their friends in the CPT stuck with them. Meanwhile, their stand against illegal logging brought widespread media attention and suddenly Cláudio and Maria were known all over Brazil and in other parts of the world.

With all the media attention, Cláudio was asked to speak at the TEDx conference in Manaus in 2010. His speech there was calm but powerful as he explained the situation he and Maria were facing:

In 1997 . . . we had a vegetation cover of 85 percent, made up of native
forest, which was mostly made up of nut and cupuaçu trees. Today,
with the arrival of the loggers, and pig iron producers in Marabá, today
there is only 20 percent of this forest cover left, already fragmented in
many places. It's a disaster for those like me that live in and from the
forest. I have been extracting nuts since I was seven. I live off the forest,
I protect it in every way that I can. That's why I could get a bullet in my
head at any moment. Because I don't just stand around, I denounce
loggers, I denounce the charcoal burners, and that's why they think I
shouldn't exist. The same thing that was done to Sister Dorothy
[Stang], they want to do to me. I may be talking to you here today, and
in a month you may hear the news that I have disappeared.

I ask myself: Am I scared? I am. I am a human being, I get scared.
But it doesn't make me shut my mouth! As long as I am able to walk, I
will be denouncing those who hurt the forest. The trees in the Amazon
are my sisters. I am a son of the forest. I live off them, I depend on
them, I am part of them. When I see one of these trees on top of a
truck going to the sawmill, it gives me such pain. It's as if I were watching a funeral procession, taking the dearest person I've got.

Why? It's life. It's life to me. It's life to all of you who live in cities!
Because the forest is purifying the air, it is giving us a return. And the
crimes of a group of people, who can think only of profit, of themselves, and not of future generations or anything else—they are doing
whatever they want in our town. It's a shame because nobody takes any
brave steps to solve this problem. This is the obstacle.

The forest needs to be preserved because everything it contains
generates money, profits! And the forest is there, providing for me.
Whenever I want, I just go there and get it. Now, some people think it
can only provide resources if it is cut down, if it is burned to make
charcoal. This makes me sad.

Now I am going to ask something of all of you. When you buy
something that was made from timber that came from the forest, check
the origin. That is the only way we can start slowing things down.
Something we can't do from there. If you start to say no to timber of
suspicious origin, the market will begin to weaken. They will either
abide by the law, or they will close down. However, as long as people
keep buying illegal timber, or purchase illegal forest products, this will
continue. And those who lose are those who live in the forest, and you,

because you won't have the forest later, it will be gone one day. And if it's gone, how are people going to survive? How are we going to survive? . . . Is deforestation viable? No! The forest is viable when it is standing! You don't have to water or fertilize the forest. All you have to do is go there and gather what it produces.

There, on my little piece of land, I produce nut oil, cupuaçu butter and pulp, I make crafts with liana vines and timber, using the timber that nature brings down, the timber that nature puts on the ground for me. I go there and use it, and in place of the one that fell I plant another. So that when I am gone, things will continue, other people will come, and they will want the same thing I have today. The forest is twice as sustainable when it is standing because when you cut it down, you have only one chance, whereas when you leave it there, you will always have it. You will have it today, tomorrow, when you're gone, other people stay there and they will enjoy the forest the same way you did and they will live well.

In predicting his own death Cláudio was pretty accurate. Not one month, but six months later, he and Maria were traveling down the road near their house on a motorcycle, as they crossed a river bridge gunmen opened fire. Given that both pistol bullet casings and shotgun shells, fifteen altogether, were found on the scene, it is likely there were two killers. Before they ran, one of the assassins severed one of Cláudio's ears as a trophy.

Two days after the murder I sat with their old friend and leafed through photos of Cláudio and Maria. Here is Maria in a sheltered area growing medicinal plants, talking to a group of visitors about mixing horticulture and forestry. In another shot she's leading them single-file across a field on a tour of the forest. Here is Cláudio with his teenage son, standing proudly beside the small oven they've just built from bricks and cement. There are images of gorgeous jungle flowers, handfuls of nuts and fruit, monkeys in trees, and spectacular orange, red, blue, and green parrots. In front of "The Majesty," the gigantic Brazil nut tree, Cláudio and Maria, along with a cute young couple, are grinning, posing, and mugging for the camera.

But there are also photos that tell a darker story: Cláudio stand-ing by the stump of a newly felled canopy tree, images of burnt-over land and timber trucks carrying enormous logs barreling down dirt roads, charcoal camps operating at full tilt, and land that's been de-nuded and scraped clear of life. Sometimes Cláudio stands in the shot, grim-faced and worried. And then there are images taken at home: Cláudio slumped back in a chair, his face slack with fatigue.

On the same day that Cláudio and Maria were killed, the Brazil-ian congress was debating a proposed law that would loosen protec-tions on the country's forests. If passed, the bill would scale back provisions of the national forest code designed to guard the Amazon against loggers, farmers, and other commercial interests. The new law would open more land to deforestation and grant a blanket am-nesty to those guilty of illegal logging. During the debate, José Sar-ney Filho, a congressman and former environment minister who opposes the changes to the code, received word of the murders. Standing to speak in the congress chamber, he spoke about their deaths. *The New York Times* explains what happened next:

> He was greeted by boos from the audience, including fellow deputies. "I couldn't believe it," said Mr. Adário, the Greenpeace director, who witnessed the speech. "They were booing the news of a murder. It was terrible, but it happened."

Over the next few days, two more environmental activists were gunned down. Eremilton Pereira dos Santos was shot not far from where Cláudio and Maria were murdered. Then, in the Amazonian state of Rondônia, Adelino Ramos, a farmer and labor leader, was killed while selling vegetables. About a week later environmental and anti-slavery activists submitted to the government a list of 207 people who had received death threats, including 42 who had al-ready been killed. A few months later the Pastoral Land Commis-sion released their annual report of the "walking dead"—naming 918 people who had been killed in the Amazon since 1985. No one knows how many just disappeared into unmarked graves in the forest.

. . .

As the death toll unfolded around me I felt hammered by despair. In America we talk a good line about saving the Amazon, but no one came to stand with Cláudio and Maria, and I was just as conspicuous in my absence. We all believe deeply in ending slavery, but where were the abolitionists ready to dig in and fight? I seemed to be trapped in a place where every choice was wrong. If we keep trying to save the rain forest and stop slavery, people are going to die. If we don't try to stop the slavery and the destruction of the forest, people are still going to die, and our natural world will die with them. The forces that crushed a sweet couple like Cláudio and Maria keep growing. And when people in power are so callous that they shout down and jeer the murder of anyone who opposes them, what hope is there? How can we stand when unbridled greed is joined to unchecked and rampant violence? And it was happening here in Brazil, a fast-developing nation that had attempted a genuine, good-faith effort at eradicating slavery.

As I was leaving her, Cláudio and Maria's friend said to me, "They were the only ones standing in the road, so what happens now? Today, right after the murder, all sorts of police are all over the place, but we know that will end soon. The people of the settlement are very afraid; many of them are distraught. Cláudio and Maria were their friends—they all shared a dream. Lots of their neighbors are thinking about leaving. If someone doesn't go and take over the job, then everyone forgets. Cláudio and Maria made this a national issue, but now where are all the people that shouted agreement?"

The next day I was talking to an IBAMA agent. A pistol strapped to his leg, he'd been involved in arresting illegal loggers and busting slaveholders in their charcoal camps, but he's frustrated too: "No labor inspectors are going out," he says, "they wait for one of the groups like CPT or the police to denounce a logger or a charcoal camp. Then they have to go. That's why we don't see light at the end of the tunnel—if we say something, they do something, if we don't say something, they do nothing. But to have something to report we have to be able to get out in the field and investigate, and we don't get the tools we need to do the job. We need vehicles, radios, GPS, and more people, the problem is much, much bigger than our little crew. We end up relying on groups like CPT to find the crimes. Then we're often told to wait on other government agencies for permission to raid a charcoal camp where we know there are slaves. And we wait and wait as they go to the top of their agency for authorization. So people are dying and nobody shows up to enforce the law—is it any wonder that people just assume that the police don't care?"

I'm left feeling more depressed. The forces assaulting the forest and enslaving people are driving forward; they have friends at the top and guns in their hands. They have trucks and radios and money. Not only are these slaveholders and illegal loggers dangerous criminals, they outnumber all who would stand against them. In the lawlessness of the frontier they are supreme. They won't stay around long, they are constantly moving with the edge of the frontier, and when they go they leave death, destruction, and slavery in their wake.

Father Danilo stands against them, but he is unarmed and for all his feisty energy he's an old man thinking about retiring to his native Italy to be near his family for the first time in decades. Xavier Plassat, anti-slavery specialist with the CPT, stands against them, but with no budget and few tools. Cláudio and Maria's friend stands against them and knows the price she may have to pay. An American nun stood against them and paid that price. Am I willing to pay that price? Are any of us? Or are we just all talk?

9

WE'VE ALL GOT A PART OF THE ANSWER

Behind me is the little town, before me the trees. This is the line of turmoil, the frontier, the edge of it all. On one side the bare and dusty detritus that comes with people, forest clearing, and settlement. On the other side the complexity and richness, the boundless balance and energy of the world's—*our*—greatest forest. If the truth is that our forest's days are numbered, then I will climb this little mountain, I will cross this stream into the raw world of our planet's deepest truth—and walk inside that truth, if only for a little while.

It's bittersweet, all this beauty, all this life. Just approaching the edge of the forest, life multiplies. The number of birds increases rapidly, great black and white eagles, buzzards, tiny gray doves, and multicolored finches. They flash through the bushes and the flowers, morning glories, purple foxgloves, wisteria, and happy sprays of yellow blossoms that hang like curtains from the trees. Here on the forest boundary clouds of big yellow and small cream-white butterflies spin through the air, then crowd together wherever there is a little water or animal dung into a pulsating carpet of fifty, sixty, a hundred or more.

Crossing the boundary, I'm in the rain forest and life really explodes. In the tangle of vines, bushes, trees, scrub, giant ferns, and mushrooms of all sizes, every step is a twisting limbo dance. As I climb a steep hill I grab a small tree trunk for support and a river of ants flows over my hand. My steps dislodge a small ball that rolls near my foot. It's about the size of a grapefruit, a perfect globe of dried leaves and dead grass. I touch it with the tip of my boot and it rolls again, and breaks in half against a stone. Inside is a spherical chamber littered with eggshells and bird droppings. Another stride and I nearly step on another brown ball, but this one is furry and it unfolds and scurries into the bush.

One tree has smooth, light green bark punctuated with rings of needle-sharp spikes. Stumbling on the slope I reach up and grab before I look, and the thorns slip into my palm. Mushrooms grow everywhere in white, orange, brown, and black. Overhead, squawking shrilly, fly mated pairs of parrots, some black, some green, some a light blue with bright flashes of yellow under their wings. One red parrot has the soaring wingspan of an osprey, broad, streamlined, delicate.

. . .

As I turn into the slight opening of a glade at the base of a hill, I glimpse what I first think is a bird. Its rich blue wings are larger than my spread hands, but it flies in fits and starts, and I realize this is the biggest butterfly I have ever seen. I try to hush my clumsy feet and move toward it, hoping to trace it as it moves through the undergrowth. It's hide-and-seek, I see it, then it is gone. I catch another look, and keep following, slipping between the trees as the lowering sun begins to send shafts of light into the glade. Suddenly I am blinded by a bolt of hot blue light and duck down by reflex. Disoriented, I shake my head and look ahead to see the butterfly cross between two trees. As it does so, another beam of sunlight touches it, and its wings, like mirrors, throw the full force of the tropical sun back at me, and a blinding ray of blue shoots out and penetrates the thousand greens and browns of the forest. Dazzled and a little hypnotized, I can't believe the power of this butterfly, and stumble after it, seeing it flash once more before it disappears completely into the ferns.

Puzzled, dazed, I stop and feel deflated. The flashes of light had distracted me from my sorrow and confusion. Now I'm just tired and sweaty and bug-bitten. But looking down at the saturated green of a branch I see a tiny echo of blue, almost like mist, hovering above the leaves. I shake my head, and lean in until I see this is another butterfly, but one as timid and discreet as the other was showy. It is small, with wings shaped more like a dragonfly's, but perfectly clear, exactly transparent, only the edges glisten with a trace of cornflower blue. It is all but invisible, but as it moves the light green leaf behind it seems to have a faint ghost of rippling blue, just a whisper, a half-formed thought, a question.

From big to small, from blinding to pale, in my mind it all spins together. The delicate white butterflies feeding on dung, the blue bolt of light, the rolling ball of an empty nest, the rich and delicate balance of this complex forest, and an answer comes to my feeling of hopelessness. A thorn pierces my hand, a flash blinds me, and something vociferous and relentless burrows into the flesh of my belly underneath my shirt—and I see *that* is our job—to bring the light, to protect people *and* forests, to dig in and in, and not give up.

If we love our world, then we have to be those thorns and protect it. If we hate slavery, then we have to be that light and expose it. If slavery and ecocide are growing together like tumors, then we just have to dig in and root them out—knowing and accepting that doing so, like anything that really matters, may take generations and may exact a high price. I don't know how to do it, but Cláudio and Maria learned one way to do it, even though it killed them. We've all got a little of the answer, and now is the time to bring those pieces together.

■   ■   ■

I come down from the mountain and straight into the home of a frontier family. Not too far outside of Primavera, this family is digging in, building up a life that keeps the forest alive and, at the same time, lets them live with hope for their children. This gentle family is the slaveholder's nightmare; they live on the land with a light step, coexisting with and protecting the forest. Their farm is typical of many others. It's not the eco-teaching farm of Cláudio and Maria, but one that is applying some of those lessons and learning more.

Mom and Dad, with two teenage sons, live together in a three-room house they've built with their own hands. Two rooms are for sleeping and the third is for storage and sitting and whatever is needed. Cooking happens on a sheltered back porch in a great clay oven (also handmade) fired with wood. Pot-sized holes in the oven cradle the pans above the fire. Most meals are eaten on benches around the porch where the cooling breezes can play as well. I sit down to a late dinner with them while ducks waddle around my feet, hoping for a handout.

Because of the land-use laws in Brazil, this family doesn't own the land, but they have been given the right to farm it. They have about two hundred acres, the usual allotment for a homestead. The land is virtually free, but the government has this requirement—if the land has been cut over illegally, then the homesteader has to return half of it to forest, planting trees and letting the wilderness return. If the land is still uncut, then the farmer can't cut trees on half the land, but can manage it as a forest resource in the way that Cláudio and Maria worked with their forest. This requirement pays off for everyone if done correctly. The families make more money and have more security than they would if they cleared the land for cattle, and the government protects the forest. Still, it's a delicate balance; it's a long way up a dirt track and a lot of things can happen in the woods.

This family is keeping to the rules. The wild forest I climbed through is part of their land, and they leave it untouched except to harvest Brazil nuts and other forest products. They call the ridge and hill beyond the stream Monte Cristo, and their farm by the same name. On the flat land by the stream and near the road, where they've built their house, is the amazing mix of plants and animals that sustains them. Chickens run underfoot, there's a sow with her piglets, and a few cattle that they raise mainly for milk. The cows produce three gallons of fresh milk every day, and the tall teenage sons look like they've had plenty of it to drink. Mom makes some of the milk into fresh farm cheese that they eat and sell. Around the house they've planted lime and lemon trees, papaya and passion fruit, peppers and vegetables, and a field of pineapple. Soon they'll be putting in some cocoa trees too. All their water comes from a well they've dug by hand and lift with a bucket. It's a frontier life, but they're happy and their sons are thriving. Poor, but well fed, they can afford to help others, and when Danilo comes to get me they put a piglet in a sack for him to take to another family that they've heard has been sick. I've always heard of "a pig in a poke," but it's my first time to carry one around.

They're just one family, but they stand for thousands. Around the world, family farms are disappearing, vast land holdings are put into monoculture, often using genetically modified crops as agribusinesses standardizes production. Brazil is the only country on the globe moving in the other direction, where the number of family farms is increasing, up 350,000 between 1996 and 2006 to a total of 4.5 million. These small family farms are a powerhouse, producing 70 percent of the food consumed in Brazil on just 30 percent of the active agricultural land. In a fair market, without huge subsidies to big agribusinesses (that kill off family farms in America and Europe), they are simply more efficient. This is one of the reasons why Brazil is overtaking other countries in the world economy—local food production means greater price stability and a stronger balance of payments. Local farmers supply food that is fresher and without the fuel costs of long-distance transport. "Buy local, eat local" may sound like a foodie mantra, but in Brazil it is backed up by government policy that is good for the economy, good for local communities, good for protecting the forests, and good for the farm families. And extensive research shows that slavery in Brazil happens in illegal land grabs on the frontier or on the big farms of agribusiness, not on small family farms.

. . .

Once upon a time Brazil was the center of the chocolate universe. Cocoa trees are native to the Amazon and Orinoco river basins and the last wild cocoa trees still grow there. Cocoa was one of the first domesticated plants in the Western Hemisphere and spread from the Amazon north to Central America. In Mexico, four-thousand-year-old ceramic pots have been found to contain traces of cocoa drinks. The Maya thought cocoa was a gift from the gods, and even its Latin scientific name, *Theobroma cocoa*, translates as "food of the gods."

When cocoa reached Europe in 1528 its popularity grew very slowly, the bitterness of raw cocoa making it an acquired taste. But from the eighteenth century with the development of milk chocolate and sweet drinking chocolate, demand for cocoa began to soar. After that, and especially after eating chocolate bars became a working-class pleasure in the nineteenth century, Brazilian cocoa exports rose rapidly in competition with the new cocoa farms planted by Europeans in West Africa and the Philippines.

In the Brazilian state of Bahia, on the Atlantic coast, cocoa became a major crop, but shortsighted landowners sowed the seeds for an ecological disaster. Cocoa trees are understory trees, the type of bushes and trees that grow in rain forests under the canopy of tall trees. At their tallest cocoa trees are unlikely to grow higher than twenty-five feet, and their productive life is short, around forty years. Hoping to cash in on a boom market, farmers in Bahia cleared land of both the canopy trees and the understory vegetation and then planted cocoa trees packed closely together, increasing the virulence of any plant disease that might strike them. As growers wrung out a few years of production, but didn't care for the trees by weeding, trimming, and fertilizing, output fell nearly 40 percent as the trees aged. By the late 1970s Brazil's cocoa trees were weak and vulnerable and unable to resist when an airborne fungal infection swept through the country. Called "witch's broom" for the way it left stunted clusters of little branches on the dead trees, by 2001 the fungus had wiped out the world's third largest producer of cocoa, cutting production more than 75 percent. And while the immediate effects of the fungal infestation were severe, the knock-on effects were disastrous. In 2008 Joanne Silberner of National Public Radio reported on what happened next in Bahia:

> Before the fungus hit, the region had more than a million acres of lush rain forest. The soil was moist and absorbent and soaked up moisture during the rainy season. During the dry season, the absorbed water slowly drained into the Cachoeira River. But with the death of the cocoa trees, people cut down the forest to make money from timber and pastureland. The exposed soil was tamped down by animals' hooves and burned by the sun. In the watershed . . . the ground is now hard and dry.
>
> The shift from forest to pasture greatly altered the area's water flow, says Neylor Calasans, who works at the Universidade Estadual de Santa Cruz in the city of Itabuna, on the Cachoeira River. "As long as we change it for pasture, the water is not able to enter the soil," he says. "It just touches the soil and runs off." Calasans has been monitoring water flow, temperature and precipitation in the watershed. His charts reveal that instead of being absorbed by the spongy soil, the water rushes straight off the hard-packed dirt and into the river, sometimes leaving no water in the ground to feed the river during the dry season. "This is causing several problems," he says. "In Itabuna, they are having problems of water supply for the city, especially during this period of the months when we receive less precipitation, from May to August." There have been days in the city of Itabuna when the river simply does not flow.

The fungus pushed farmers into a rush to grab land and raise cattle; the result was the same as in all other parts of the Amazon, lush forests became desiccated pasture. But it doesn't have to be this way.

Back along the Xingu River, not too far from the pioneer family on Monte Cristo farm, is a general store and warehouse belonging to a group called CAPPRU (in English, the acronym stands for the

Alternative Cooperative of Small Rural and Urban Producers). Here I meet a man named Jose Barros. Jose used to be a landless peasant, but now he grows cocoa. "Cocoa has changed my life," he told me. "I only have a fourth grade education, and most of my life I've been knocking around, trying to earn enough to feed my family. I worked for different farmers, I even went down in the mines." About seven years ago Jose managed to make a claim on a hundred acres of land and, like the family at Monte Cristo, began to grow some vegetables, corn, and manioc to feed his family. To obtain permission from the government to use the land he had to promise to leave 60 percent of the original forest intact, and he worried if he could make a living on the remainder. Then he met someone from CAPPRU and learned about cocoa. A government program, trying to rebuild production in the aftermath of witch's broom, was giving away seedlings; and Jose asked for some and planted them in about six acres of forest. With guidance from CAPPRU he planted the trees spread out as understory, leaving the big canopy trees to shade them and keep the moist soil protected from the sun. He nurtured them carefully, re-planting if any died, and in four years his trees began to make cocoa pods.

"That's when our lives started to change," he told me, "that first year I sold about 1,000 kilograms of cocoa beans. For the first time in our lives we were able to buy more than just the food and clothes we needed. We bought a cow for milk, and a motorcycle, we improved our house, and ate much better food. We got decent clothes and good shoes. Our children were growing then and leaving home, and we were able to help them get started." With a look of wonder and pride on his face, Jose told me how he and his wife had recently done something they had never dreamed possible: "We took a trip," he marveled, "we went to a city on the coast, just to visit!" Their horizons were expanding, and Jose understands it was due to sustainable farming. Now he has nearly 5,000 cocoa trees on 15 acres, and about 1,200 of the trees produce around 3,000 kilos of cocoa beans; the remaining trees are still too young but will start making cocoa pods in the next two or three years. "When I started I used a little herbicide," he says, "but now I manage without. I watch my trees carefully, and sometimes witch's broom will appear, but I cut it away immediately and burn those branches. I trim the trees, dig around their roots, and fertilize with manure. And one of the best things is that the canopy trees make money too, there's Brazil nuts, it's great!"

Jose's story shows another way forward. His family enjoys a decent life while 60 percent of the land he "farms" is a protected virgin forest. Remarkably, staff at the cooperative told me Jose could hardly hold a candle to another farmer, their best producer, who had significantly diversified his plantings, growing herbs and other specialty crops, and as well as coaxing large amounts of cocoa beans from each tree. As I asked questions of the farmers and the co-op staff I realized that this wasn't just cocoa, this was organic, eco-friendly, fairly traded cocoa that would make the chocolate we want, chocolate untainted by slavery, child labor, or environmental damage. The only problem was that the co-op, a small rural producer of just 1,000 tons a year, hasn't been certified as organic or fair trade so their special cocoa just flows unrecognized into the millions of tons in the global market. Fortunately, that's a problem that can be fixed. Meanwhile, in 2011, the co-op began a program to help its 800 farm families plant one million more cocoa trees.

. . .

Leaving the deep forest, Father Danilo and I traveled back along a rough road toward the town of Taboca. The frontier passed here thirty years ago as first gold prospectors, then loggers, and finally mining companies walked into the forest from a landing on the Xingu River. Where the town of Taboca now stands geologists found the mineral cassiterite that is used to make tin and solder, one of the same minerals that brings such misery, crime, destruction, and slavery to the Eastern Congo. In the 1980s and 1990s Taboca was a boomtown, as the personal computer took over the world and the demand for cassiterite soared. When the price collapsed, the big mining company pulled out, but Taboca still thrives as a gateway to the frontier and supplies the small-scale miners who have moved in.

Like other questions about land in Brazil, it is not clear who has the right to mine around Taboca, but after witnessing the horrors of cassiterite mining in the Congo I knew I had to visit these mines as well. What I found was eerily familiar yet completely different. At a mine near Taboca I found the same great ragged hole in the earth with a diverted stream being used to wash and process the ore. On the surface it looked like the open-pit gold mines in Ghana and the cassiterite and coltan mines in Congo. But up close, the picture was very different. Down in the pit where I would see slaves in the Congo, a big Hyundai excavator was doing the heavy work of digging the ore. Workers still scrambled around turning jets of water on the ore, or hauling it up to rough contraptions that would shake and sift it, but they didn't move with exhaustion and fear. Yes, they were caked with mud, but then, within minutes, so was I, after I sank up to my knees in the sucking yellow mud and then thrust my arms into the goo to recover my shoe.

A man came out to meet me and I asked if he was the boss. He answered my question with his own question: "Good morning, are you the federal police?" After I assured him we weren't police, and not even Brazilian, he began to talk about the mine and the work. "The land here," he explained, "still belongs to the big mining company, but they were thrown out by IBAMA [the federal environmental police] for ecological destruction. So now, we're here in a sort of semi-legal way, IBAMA knows we're here and since we're being careful with the environment they don't interfere. The town government can't recognize us officially, but are glad for the jobs and business. It's all a sort of informal arrangement.

"Back when the big mining company was here," he went on, "mines like this were wild and dangerous, bars and prostitutes would set up around the mines and drug dealers would be everywhere. But we don't allow any of that, this is a safe place, clean, and the food is good." Everything I saw backed this up, and the workers freely chimed in—one man, who seemed to be mainly concerned with playing a game of checkers in the large shelter where they slept and ate, explained, "We have two four-man crews working here, but today one of the crews, my crew, isn't working because the motor of one of the ore-washing machines burned out and we're waiting for a replacement. But the mine works like this: each man gets 4 percent of the proceeds when we sell the cassiterite. We normally produce about 300 kilograms of semi-refined cassiterite a day and sell it for 18.5 reais [about $11] per kilo. So, 32 percent of what we make goes to the workers, the 'owner' gets 10 percent, and most of the rest of the money pays all the other expenses, like the rental of the excavator, all the food we eat, a salary for the cook, tools, fuel, you name it."

This arrangement seemed to be working well. In the shelter next to the mine I found a field kitchen and a full-time cook preparing vegetables, chicken, and rice for lunch. Clean clothes were hanging from ridgepoles and hammocks covered with mosquito nets were rolled up for the day. There were rubber boots lined against the wall, laundry drying on a line, neat stacks of scrubbed pots and pans, an arrangement of clean glasses next to a water cooler, and chickens pecking around the little hut where the cook, a woman, lived separate from the men.

In the shelter I struck up a conversation with another man who seemed to be in his early twenties, and after a few minutes his wife joined our conversation. "Before I came here," he told me, "I was like some kind of machine at other mines. My wife and I left the little piece of land we had in [the Brazilian state of] Rondônia, we were just peasants there. Here I can make good money. On my land I could earn around 5 reais [$3] a day; on a good day in this mine I can make 200 reais [$300]. Sometimes other companies come from Taboca and try to recruit me, but I like it here. It's kind of fun; you make your own time." As we talked and joked I saw something I had never seen before, something that verified in a clear and simple way what this man was saying—his young wife, so recently a "peasant" was wearing braces on her teeth—exactly the sort of thing only decent and reliable wages makes possible.

As I had in other countries, I asked the men if they knew how the mineral they were mining was going to be used. And, like so many other miners around the world, they had no idea. Several of them had heard the Portuguese word for "solder," one of the main uses for cassiterite, but even then they weren't sure what it was. The idea that the gooey black sludge they mined ended up in their cellphones was a revelation and a couple of them took out their phones and just stared at them. The term "conflict minerals" just left them confused, but they did know that sometimes in Brazil people were enslaved in mines, and especially on farms and charcoal camps.

The man that might have been the boss chimed in, "To mine here we had to promise IBAMA we would fill in the pit, reshape the land, and replant it when we are done. That's okay, we're setting aside money for that, and who would want to leave a big ugly pit like this next to the river? Our biggest problem is with the bureaucracies! All these different agencies, they all have different rules and agendas, yet none of them seem to have the power to really assign us this land or to regulate what goes on here. IBAMA protects the environment, but they can't assign a mining lease. It's frustrating."

It may be frustrating, but like the farmer cooperative growing cocoa, this little outfit is showing how economic development from the grass roots can provide jobs, protect human rights, *and* preserve the environment. A big global economy probably needs big companies, but scale means distance, and the greater the distance the harder it is to see the source of what we buy and use. The successful operation at the cassiterite mine in Taboca would work in the gold mines of Ghana and the coltan mines of Congo as well, if they had protection from criminal gangs and some training in how to run their mines. Building local communities and enterprises has proven to be the best way to get people out of slavery and keep them free—it can also be a way to protect the natural world.

On the edge of the Taboca mine is what appears to be an ancient, gigantic cannon. Overgrown with weeds, the great rusty barrel is pointed toward the road, as if guarding the riverbank. This monster, along with the iron floor and smashed machinery scattered around it, are the remains of the mine as it was run by the big mining company—all destroyed and abandoned when they were thrown out for environmental violations. This rusty wreck is also a strange echo of the huge abandoned mining equipment in Ghana that was also surrounded by small-scale mining. It's another indictment of big-ness. While the company could afford to run these big and relatively efficient machines, they couldn't afford to stick around when the price of cassiterite fell, or to honor their commitments to protect the environment around the mine. Operating at a smaller, appropriate scale the current crew makes a good living when the global price for cassiterite is low, and a great living when it is high. The same can be said for the small farmers in the CAPPRU cooperative. While the price of cocoa on the global market swings up and down, with a mixed range of crops, and proportionally lower overheads, the farmers are secure.

Jose's healthy cocoa trees, the informal cooperative running the eco-friendly cassiterite mine, and the pioneer family in the little house in the forest of Monte Cristo, these are just single instances in a much larger, often confused, and very dynamic frontier. But what is important is that in each example people have moved from vulnerability to stability, from desperate poverty to, if not comfort, then a healthy and decent level of security that allows children to thrive and lives to be more than just grinding work. These examples show that alternatives to smash-and-grab ecological destruction are possible, and equally demonstrate that this isn't about charity. This is actually a more viable economic model for frontier development since it preserves and extends the potential profits and benefits the great forest can provide. Go beyond the shortsighted clear-cutting of forest and the delusional investment in cattle ranching, look just a little further into the future and you see the medicines, the rich biodiversity, the renewable and sustainable products. You see the future that Cláudio and Maria saw on the horizon. It's a pattern of development that makes the most of the Brazilian trend of expanding numbers of family farms. It's smaller-scale, decentralized, more organic and responsive growth, and it doesn't fall into the same traps that ruined the Brazilian cocoa crop, or plague the biofuel industry today.

·   ·   ·

Solutions like these can seem very simple, but let's not kid ourselves: getting the balance right between agriculture, environmental protection, economic sustainability, workers' rights, and consumer demand can be tricky. Sometimes the road to hell is paved with the good intentions of governments, businesses, and consumers.

In Brazil under President Lula "agroenergy" became a flagship project. Watching the rest of the world spiral into deeper and deeper insecurity about oil during the period of the Iraq war, President Lula and his government saw a tremendous opportunity. Traveling the globe Lula talked up the idea of biofuels, signed cooperation agreements with a number of nations, including the United States, argued for biodiesel at the United Nations, and used his presidential power to support a new "green" export market for Brazilian agriculture. With leadership from the top there was explosive growth, and a burgeoning desire to make Brazil "the Saudi Arabia of biofuel." In 2008 Brazil overtook the United States as the world's leading producer of soybeans, the primary ingredient in biodiesel, and by 2010 Brazil had more than 45 million acres, almost half of all the country's cultivated land, in soy production.

But there are other drivers that have nothing to do with the price of gasoline. Another reason for the explosive demand for soybeans since 2005 is the dramatic increase in meat consumption in the developing world. Shifting farmland from plants to animals has pushed small farmers onto less and less viable land, often up the slopes of hills and mountains as the valleys are converted to large-scale monoculture such as soybeans or cattle ranching. In the Amazon we already know the cost, both economically and environmentally, when a diverse ecosystem is denuded and then used for cattle, but this shift in land use seems to be relentless. As countries like India and China grow their middle class, meat-eating increases rapidly, and given that these two countries together have more than two billion inhabitants we're talking about a lot of beef, pork, and chicken on the table.

The important point here is that the increase in meat production also increases the amount of grains being raised, which means more and more protected forests are under threat. It takes around fifteen pounds of grain or soybeans to produce a pound of meat. The United States actually uses 95 percent of its soybean crop (the second largest in the world) as animal food, mostly for pigs. Leaving aside the fact that the soybeans could have fed hungry people much more efficiently, there's another problem: high-input annual crops like soybeans and corn release about 1,000 pounds of CO_2 per acre per year which comes to 144 billion tons of annual carbon emissions in the United States from these two crops alone.

That's a lot of numbers about crops and cattle, but what it adds up to is that the demand for grain and meat was already pushing ecosystems into crisis when oil went over $100 a barrel. The added demand for biofuels unleashed a new gold rush, a scrambling grab for land and labor. In places like Brazil much of this grab was driven by outside investment, speculators reasoning that this was like buying Saudi oil wells when they were still cheap. The result has been disastrous for poor people. Though grain production increased, the price of food made from grain also increased as corn and soy were diverted to making fuel. A classic case study of this phenomenon happened in Mexico in 2007 as the United States launched programs to blend more gasoline with ethanol. As the price of corn skyrocketed, the cost of corn tortillas in Mexico, a staple of the local diet, increased 400 percent. With soy and rice prices doubling and corn prices quadrupling, many poor countries were suddenly unable to pay for the imported food needed to feed their people. When this started happening across the world, the first outcry came from a surprising source.

Just as Presidents Lula and Bush were signing an agreement to boost ethanol biofuel, both the United Nations and the International Monetary Fund issued stern warnings. The IMF spoke of serious implications for the world's poor, but United Nations experts went much further. Converting food stocks to fuel is "a crime against humanity," stated the UN's Special Rapporteur on Food, Jean Ziegler. He added that "What has to be stopped is . . . the growing catastrophe of the massacre [by] hunger in the world." He noted that it takes 510 pounds of corn to make 13 gallons of ethanol, which is enough corn to feed a child for a year in Zambia or Mexico. Admitting the positive outcomes of using biofuels, such as a cleaner environment and less dependence on fossil fuels, Ziegler still called for a five-year moratorium on biofuel production in order to develop techniques "to make biofuel and biodiesel from agricultural waste," rather than edible wheat, corn, sugarcane, and other food crops. No one listened and more land was rushed into biofuel production.

By 2012, 40 percent of US corn went into ethanol, and more and more land was being devoted to corn for the ethanol market. It is unclear exactly how much this diversion of the corn crop increased overall food costs in the 2005 to 2012 period, but the average of the different independent estimates is around 25 percent. For Mexico, a country that imports one third of its corn, this has meant extra expenditures of between $250 million and $500 million each year, much more than the Mexican government has been able to invest in supporting their own small-scale corn farmers. All of that has meant greater food insecurity: the cost of the basic food basket in Mexico increased 50 percent, and meat and dairy prices were pushed up by higher animal feed costs. By 2011, the government there estimated over half the population was having periods of food shortage, and five million children were regularly malnourished.

There was already slavery in deforestation for charcoal production or the sale of high-grade timber like mahogany, but biofuels pushed and pulled workers into bondage in soybeans and other crops in new ways. The CPT and the government noted an increase in slavery parallel to the increase in biofuel farming. Desperate, landless families became even more desperate as the price of food increased. Their hunger pushed them into taking risks with recruiters promising good pay and a good job at the edge of the forest. Meanwhile, big farm owners who had previously had little use for slave labor on their highly mechanized farms, now needed "root collectors," slang for the short-term workers needed to clear forest land, exactly the type of work for which Gilberto was enslaved in the last chapter. The possibility of employment exercised a powerful pull on workers from the poorest regions of the country, some of whom ended up in slavery.

By 2011 deforestation for soybeans matched that for cattle ranching, creating a double threat to the Amazon. As the first scientific studies came in, it became clear that soy, like cattle, had a serious and detrimental impact on the land, through loss of moisture and the compaction of dry soil. Communities and ecosystems in soy-growing areas began to suffer the same problems linked to cattle lands. Not surprisingly, a good deal of this degradation occurred in official Environmental Preservation Areas.

Back along the Xingu River, nature reserves and protected Indian land are experiencing both increased water pollution and disturbed water flows. At the headwaters of the Xingu, just outside the protected areas, and encroaching into the river's buffer zone, soybean plantations channel herbicides, pesticides, fertilizers, and silt into the river. The knock-on effects are diminished fish stocks and game animals, concerns about the safety of drinking water, and flash floods that occur when rain falls on the plantations and runs off all at once instead of soaking into the soil and vegetation of the forest. It's a situation with a dark echo in American history.

On May 31, 1889, the greatest disaster in US history up to that time occurred when more than two thousand people died as a wall of water, set in motion by a dam failure, swept away a series of small towns and the city of Johnstown, Pennsylvania. While the immediate cause was the collapse of the dam, a larger cause was ongoing deforestation that channeled more and more water at high velocity into the lake behind the dam. David McCullough, in his bestseller about the flood, explained that: "Forests not only retain enormous amounts of water in the soil (about 800 tons per acre), but in mountainous country especially, they hold the soil itself, and in winter they hold snow. Where the forests are destroyed, spring thaws and summer thunderstorms would send torrents racing down the mountainsides; and each year the torrents grew worse as the water itself tore away at the soil and what little ground cover there was left."

At the headwaters of the Xingu River there is no question of snow or a spring thaw, but that part of Brazil gets twice as much rain every year as Johnstown, Pennsylvania, with proportionately disastrous results. Paradoxically, the lush wet climate of the upper Amazon is especially rich because it evolved with a cycle of slow seasonal floods. Many tropical rivers have seasonal flooding, but few are so impressive as the *igapo* (swamp forest) and the *varzea* (flooded forest) of the Amazon basin. When the floods come, large areas of rain forest are inundated to depths of forty feet for long periods, the water so high that the tops of some rain forest trees are accessible from boats. The flooding is so widespread that the central portion of the South American continent sinks several inches because of the extra weight and then rises again as the waters recede, the largest rise and fall of the earth's crust ever detected. The upriver ecology is fine-tuned to the rhythm of the floods—fish have evolved to eat fruit and seeds in high water and to breathe air directly from the atmosphere as low water leaves them stranded in shallow pools. Some of the plants on the forest floor spend as much as six months each year under water, and seem to have evolved a way to continue photosynthesis while submerged. The extremity of these conditions has generated amazing biodiversity, but all that is under threat from the deforestation linked to biofuels.

. . .

The other key biofuel crop in Brazil is sugar, a principal source for ethanol. Sugar and slavery have a very long and very ugly history in Brazil and other parts of the Western Hemisphere. In the eighteenth and nineteenth centuries mortality on sugar plantations in the Caribbean and Brazil was notoriously high, requiring constant importation of new slaves from Africa to make up for the losses. The historian Stuart Schwartz has written extensively on sugar slavery in Brazil and describes a process that "closely resembled the modern industrial assembly line . . . The labor was exhausting . . . The nighttime scenes of boiling cauldrons, the whirring mill and the sweating bodies caused more than one observer to evoke the image of hell." Hell it must have been for the slaves who were regularly punished and "burned or scorched with hot wax, branded on face or chest, tortured with hot irons, had their ears or noses lopped off, or suffered sexually related barbarities . . ."

Extensive torture and death no longer haunt Brazilian sugar fields, but some 300,000 people are seasonal cane cutters, migrant workers who are especially vulnerable to abuse. Leonardo Sakamoto, who heads up Reporter Brasil, explained, "Brazil has a great climate, great land and technology, but a lot of the competitive edge for biofuels is due to worker exploitation—from slave work to underpayment." In 2008, mobile anti-slavery squads liberated around three thousand sugarcane workers. They reported harsh and dangerous working conditions—not surprising, given that harvesting sugarcane with a machete is thought to be one of the worst jobs a person can do.

Once again Brazil shows us both sides of the equation, what can go wrong and what can go right. On one hand is worker abuse and some enslavement, on the other is the National Commitment to Improve Labor Conditions in the Sugarcane Activity, signed in 2009 by 331 companies representing 80 percent of sugar producers. In spite of the fact that slavery was found soon after on the plantations of one of the signatories, the industry-wide agreement has helped achieve a year-on-year decrease in labor violations. And supporting this change is the ineluctable progress of mechanization. In the past both sugar and cotton were thought to be crops that "required" slave labor given the backbreaking and onerous nature of their cultivation. Antebellum American planters argued that without slavery the vast wealth that poured into the United States from cotton exports would dry up and plunge the country into depression and chaos. Now both are much more efficiently cultivated and harvested by machines. In Brazil, it tends to be only the smaller and more remote farms that still use individual cutters to harvest sugarcane, and these are the farms where most slavery cases occur. Speaking with Brazilian anti-slavery workers in 2012, they reported very few slavery cases in sugar, but pointed to the fact that mechanization also means bigger and bigger plantations that have a larger environmental impact. With increasing international demand for biofuels, sugar fields are also pressing hard against the Amazon forest, threatening biodiversity and the protected forests. Even a rumor linked to the biofuel boom can set off widespread environmental destruction. In the state of Bahia in 2009 a South Korean group announced their intention to build an alcohol/ethanol processing plant in a nature area called Caatinga. The news caused a scramble for land. Forests were cut and small farmers pushed from their land, false land titles were issued by corrupt politicians, frivolous but devastating lawsuits were brought against poor farmers who wouldn't sell out, and other, more ominous, threats and intimidation were used to scare people away. The result was that long before the processing plant was built, and without any reference to state and national regulations for land preservation and use, a large clear-cut area of forest appeared at the headwaters of a tributary to the Amazon.

. . .

We all want to reduce greenhouse gases, we all want to protect endangered species and keep people out of slavery, but at what cost?

Calculating the real cost of biofuels is complex and, for most of us, pretty confusing. Mixing ethanol into gasoline really does cut some of the worst emissions and that's a good thing. But ethanol doesn't make sense if the price for fractionally reducing emissions from cars in America is the loss of rain forest in the Amazon. Deforestation damages the greatest power on earth to remove and store away atmospheric carbon. Any threat to the "lungs of the planet" has to be balanced against the good done by ethanol-enriched gasoline. Probably the greatest wisdom on this question was expressed by the voice most ignored, that of UN expert Jean Ziegler with his call for the five-year moratorium on biofuel production from food while continuing to improve our ability to make biofuel from other non-food sources.

The US Environmental Protection Agency counts these costs by using "life-cycle analysis." This measures all the ways that something like biofuel can generate CO_2 in the long process of getting from the farm to your gas tank—adding up the carbon generated by deforestation, planting and harvesting, processing, transporting, and its ultimate use by the consumer. Critics say that the EPA's criteria aren't good enough, and don't account for all impacts, especially when it comes to the loss of ecosystems before farming even begins. At the same time, in 2012 the EPA ordered that biodiesel made from palm oil, a rapidly expanding crop that is decimating the rain forests of Indonesia, has an environmental cost too high to be acceptable as a fuel in the United States.

In this calculus of conservation Brazil is walking a very fine and very dangerous line. It is a path that looks very familiar to anyone who knows the history of the United States. The level of political and economic corruption in Brazil, and how that corruption generates and supports slavery and environmental destruction, mirrors the American experience in the late nineteenth and early twentieth centuries. In the United States today it is hard to imagine that at the beginning of the twentieth century the country's remaining forests were in danger of being handed over to timber companies and clear-cut. At that time the Adirondacks, what is now Glacier Park, and hundreds of thousands of square miles of government forestland were pretty much up for grabs. Most politicians were for sale, so it's no surprise that they were happy to sell off government forests for low prices and high bribes. The fact that America still has extensive forests today is due to a crusading young president who was willing to risk his political future in the name of conservation.

Theodore Roosevelt was elected vice president of the United States in November 1900. His calls for health and safety regulations, control of large corporations, and environmental conservation meant that many politicians and business leaders were pleased to see him sidelined into this symbolic but low-power job. But six months after the inauguration, with the assassination of William McKinley, Roosevelt became president. One of his first acts was to call on Congress to exercise greater control over businesses and to press for the preservation and conservation of America's forests and wild places. After his landslide election to the presidency in 1904, controversy erupted over what to do with the nation's forests. Working closely with the head of the Forest Service, Roosevelt began setting aside some 150 million acres of federally owned forests for America's future. Congressmen, especially from the western states, wanted to sell those forests, so to block further conservation they added a provision to the 1907 Agriculture Bill taking away the president's power to protect forests. Not wishing to veto an important and needed bill, Roosevelt and Gifford Pinchot of the Forest Service worked feverishly to choose land for protection. Just minutes before Roosevelt signed the Agriculture Bill and lost the power to do so, he signed orders designating more than 16 million acres of western land as national forests. These became known as the "midnight forests" marking the late hour they were set aside. It was audacious, but it was also the right time to act. By 1900, half of the original forest cover in the United States had been eliminated, and logging peaked in 1906 at 46 billion board feet.

That quick and controversial action by a president who was not afraid to stand up to special interests meant that America preserved a portion of its great forests. Today, even though Brazil has set aside areas of forest, it is caught in a fight between those who would cut and "develop" land, and those who would conserve and preserve. It is a fight seemingly without end, and made worse by the fact that the rule of law is stretched thin along the frontier. It is important to understand that some preservation measures have worked, that *legal* timber cutting and lumber production in Brazil has fallen rapidly over the past ten years. Legal timber companies have shed thousands of jobs and some have gone out of business. According to research by the government's Amazon Institute, log consumption fell from 24.5 to 14.2 million cubic meters. Their 2010 report noted that this decrease was due to more rigorous monitoring of felling and processing of trees by legitimate timber companies. The system works if people play by the rules, but rules mean nothing to criminals.

Demand for wood continues and criminals rush into the vacuum created by the reduction in legal logging. The decline in legitimate timber cutting has been more than made up by illegal sources. As I discovered in all the countries I visited for this book, environmental regulations have slowed legal logging and protected some forests, but into that space have stepped criminals ready to exploit not just private land, but the nature reserves, protected ecosystems, national parks, and the land belonging to indigenous peoples. In the Brazilian state of Para "ghost" timber companies have multiplied, felling trees and grabbing logs from prohibited and protected areas. Workers for ghost companies may claim the right to cut trees, have a logo on their truck, and produce what appear to be logging permits, but the company is usually fictitious, not legally registered as a business, and certainly doesn't have a permit to fell trees. In a 2011 report, the investigative group Social Observatory explained how this works.

In the state of Para, businessmen who want to sell charcoal to companies smelting pig iron for export will bribe officials in the state environmental department. The corrupt officials issue an authorization for the removal of "wood scraps" from legal agricultural land in the area near the smelters, or will reauthorize expired permits, some over ten years old, to "finish" work on land previously approved for logging. These permits are then used as legal cover for illegal cutting in preservation areas nowhere near the location given in the permit. The key to a successful timber raid is speed. Waving the permit if anyone asks, the chainsaws roar and the trees fall like dominoes. If anyone goes to the city to check up on the permit papers, or goes to the police questioning the legality of the logging, by the time they are back on the scene the cutters and the trees have disappeared. And once the trees have rolled away on the back of trucks bound for a hidden charcoal camp or sawmill, that's it, that section of forest is basically gone for good. Within a couple of weeks the downed trees are processed, reduced to charcoal for the smelters, or cut as timber ready for export.

When the Social Observatory investigators traced the license plate numbers for the double-trailer trucks delivering charcoal to the smelters, they found most of the license plates were actually for motorcycles, stolen cars, vehicles that didn't exist, and only rarely an actual truck. False license plates meant that trucks couldn't be traced to owners, businesses, or logging sites. Tipped off by the investigation, some honest environmental police began to dig into the story. But when the officers began to uncover wrongdoing, the governor of state, Ana Julia Carepa, wrote to the national head of the environmental police asking him to suspend the officers who had exposed the links between crooked businessmen and the state government. Using an argument often repeated by those pushing deforestation, the governor condemned the police for being "against the development of the region" and charged that "the activities of the [police] office . . . contributes to nothing happening." The honest officer in charge wasn't suspended, but he was transferred to another city, which had the same effect, and the illegal deforestation and charcoal sales continued.

• • •

I grew up on the American Great Plains. Never a forest, it was still, once, a complex and vibrant ecosystem. The prairie grass grew up to six feet tall, and millions upon millions of elk, deer, and buffalo roamed and fed and enriched the land. People lived there as well, living the transhumance life, following herds and creating cultures just as beautiful and rich, and sometimes as foolish and misguided, as most others. When the settlers came and "developed" the plains, the well-balanced ecosystem was smashed. The native plants were plowed under, and the buffalo and other fauna slaughtered in one of the most rapid near extinctions in world history. The Native Americans living on the plains suffered plagues of new diseases and then, in spite of protective treaties, were massacred by armed groups. I grew up with children from a tribe that, in the span of a single generation, the time of our grandfathers, had seen the majority of their population dead of disease or violence. In that time of dying, memory was lost, every family reeled from trauma, and more than decimated, the tribe was forced from their homeland and driven hundreds of miles to inhospitable reservation land. Marginalized and treated with vicious racism, many of the remaining members descended into alcoholism and despair.

Many tribal groups of the Great Plains, their culture and livelihood shattered, and crushed by the US military, reached for religious and mystical answers. A special ceremony called the Ghost Dance spread rapidly among the tribes after 1890. Many hoped that this five-day-long ritual of purification and unification would renew the earth and wash away the evil the whites had brought. Experiencing extinction, they called out for divine help. It was not to be; and federal attempts to suppress the Ghost Dance led to the infamous massacre at Wounded Knee that left 153 dead, mostly women and children.

We all know this sad story, but it is what followed these events that is important as we try to understand the links between slavery, deforestation, and the economic pressures of development. On the Great Plains, with the arrival of the white settlers, however well meaning their efforts, the land degraded faster and further. Wheat was planted and produced enormous harvests, for a while. When the radically variable climate of the high plains caught up with the plowed fields and lonely homesteads, the result was drought, soil degradation, and the dust bowl. More than 100 million acres of land were severely damaged. The native deep-rooted grass species that held moisture and bound the soil together in drought had been swept away, and now the exposed earth itself, dried to dust, was blown away. Dust storms left more than 500,000 people homeless immediately, and within five years 2.5 million people had fled this environmental catastrophe, leaving abandoned farms and towns scattered across the plains. Today people continue to drain out of the high plains, and there are an estimated 6,000 ghost towns in Kansas alone.

We look back to the destruction of the Great Plains ecosystem and shake our heads, blaming the ignorance of our ancestors and their rapacious disregard for nature and indigenous peoples. We can say that they didn't understand what they were doing, believing that "development," civilization, and their own betterment went hand in hand. That they didn't understand that mature and highly evolved grassland was a treasure. They didn't grasp that forcing its "development" meant ruin, and in the case of the Great Plains actually released more CO_2 into the air than cars or coal-fired power plants.

But today we *do* understand. We know that trying to turn a grasslands ecosystem into plowed fields is just as stupid and destructive as turning a forest into grassland for grazing cattle. We might as well make umbrellas out of toilet paper, or shoes out of concrete. We understand that it takes hundreds of thousands of years of evolution to assemble an ecosystem that works, one where plants and animals and insects and climate and weather and soil and water are fitted together into something that flourishes and produces, that is stable and maximizes the conversion of sunlight (our main energy source) into everything that makes life possible. There is a human contradiction to these facts, but it is venal and ugly. It is the argument used by some individuals that their immediate desire for riches is more important than anything else, and one of the favorite rationalizations for this greed is the worn-out lie of "development."

If this sounds a little cosmic, if it sounds like a mystical call for tree hugging, it's not. This is not the call of the Ghost Dance, an anguished last song when all was already lost. This is the living testimony of people like Cláudio and Maria, whose words and actions demonstrated the possibilities of a sustainable partnership with the forest. It is, however, a dangerous message, and it is no coincidence that Cláudio and Maria, like the Ghost-Dancing Sioux, were murdered when they stood in the path of greed.

. . .

For many people, in Brazil and around the world, it seems outrageous that the grinding destruction of the Amazon continues, that the Brazilian government doesn't better safeguard this essential and rich resource. But in addition to the criminality of slaveholders illegally destroying the forests, Brazil suffers from another terrible threat to the environment—politics. Theirs is a very polarized political system. The extreme distance between rich and poor also divides the country politically, and on one side is a powerful coalition of landowners and businesspeople that see the Amazon as their own to exploit in order to build their fortunes. As I write this, a bill is working its way through the Brazilian political system that would open the Amazon to more cutting and reduce protections to already reserved forests. President Dilma Rousseff is sitting on the bill, as millions of emails and messages flow in from around the world calling for a veto.

Certainly from the perspective of the United States there should be no sense of superiority to Dilma's dilemma, for America also has extreme division and rancor in its political system, as well as facing

very serious threats to its remaining forests and wild places. If anything, the American political debates over the environment are
more confusing than those in Brazil. In the United States, ending
environmental protections and allowing the destruction of preserved wilderness are somehow justified as being "conservative."
Strange linguistic acrobatics allow conservation to be condemned as
"liberal," and the liberal waste of our shared natural heritage is pre-
sented as "conservative." And to further muddy the waters, some
politicians build platforms linking together socially conservative positions important to religious groups, like opposition to civil marriage rights for gay people, to environmentally destructive positions
like oil drilling in protected forests. The result, in the minds of some
citizens, is that Christianity is somehow brought into the argument
on the side of environmental destruction. Actually, there is wide
variation in the environmental views of American citizens, including
Christians, and a growing faith-based movement for environmental
protection. The key problem is that the environment has become
one more political football, its importance measured only in its use-
fulness in winning the next partisan scrap. In both America and Brazil, the question of managing the environment needs to be removed
from these immediate political arguments and framed with a view to
the long term. Environmental policies may have dramatic short-
term effects, like producing more oil or increasing the cost of food,
but what is more important is that their outcomes are long-term and
irreversible. The politicians are too often like children fighting over
a toy, but their shortsightedness is putting at risk the viability of the
world we leave to our children and grandchildren.

It's possible to get this right, and Brazil has a lot going for it. The
cocoa cooperatives and the mine that produces cassiterite without
slavery or environmental destruction, demonstrate alternatives that
are not just viable but preferable in many ways. The Brazilian "dirty
list" of slave-using, ecocidal companies works. The environmental
police are too few in number, but those in the field are as effective as
they are allowed to be and often more so. In Brazil there are also

smart and active groups and a free press ready to name names and expose wrongdoing. And, perhaps most important, there are people who are ready to put their lives on the line for what is right.

On the other hand, the rule of law is fragile or nonexistent on the frontier, and fails to protect those who risk their lives for right. The government is the guardian of the protected lands, but will not hire enough guards, like the environment police, to keep them safe. In the little frontier towns there's no marshal, no tin star–wearing law-man to keep things honest. Worse, the Brazilian judiciary can't de-cide who has jurisdiction over crimes like slavery and ecocide, so they bounce from court to court and criminals walk free. Then when the government itself, whether in the United States or Brazil, gets caught up in the biofuel fad, there's no clear voice from below explaining why the whole idea needs more thought.

So, the situation is normal—all messed up, confounded by poli-tics and greed, but still not without hope. There is the countervail-ing power of people who want to end slavery and protect the environment, and smart folks who are trying to fit all of these seem-ingly ill-matched pieces together. One of the most promising strate-gies is to bring together the Amazonian forests and the global market in carbon credits. The value of the global market in carbon credits in 2012 was something like $150 billion, with the price of a metric ton of CO_2 expected to stay around $35 till 2020. This is a market that is growing, in part because of laws like the one that came into effect in California in 2012 that placed mandatory caps on carbon emissions for big companies. If companies aren't able to re-duce emissions to their legal limit, they can buy carbon credits from groups that are actively reducing CO_2 in the air. This is what is often referred to as a policy of "cap and trade."

Two dots that don't yet seem to be connected in the Brazilian puzzle are the challenges of getting people out of slavery and carbon reduction, and how they might, if they are connected, generate a win-win situation. We understand how slaves are being forced to create environmental destruction and huge amounts of CO_2. We also understand that a key obstacle to their liberation is finding the money to pay anti-slavery workers and help freed slaves to support themselves once freed. What no one seems to see is that while slaves can be forced to cut down trees, *ex-slaves* can be immediately employed to plant trees. Brazil's official minimum wage in 2010 was $288 per month—less than $10 per day—but to generate a $35 one-metric-ton carbon credit requires planting six to ten trees, which might be a day's work if you took a lot of breaks. Could cap and trade fund the end of slavery while reducing atmospheric CO_2? It's time we find out. When we better understand the interrelationship of environmental issues and human rights we're likely to see in many ways that working to solve one can help to solve the other.

■ ■ ■

When I came out of the woods, bug bit and blinded, I knew it was going to take all of us to crack these interlocked problems, to build the unified field theory that shows us the way forward. Brazil has part of that answer, and in smaller ways so does the Congo, Bangladesh, Ghana, and everywhere else that the two ugly ogres of ecocide and slavery team up. I certainly don't have all the answers, and may have some things just flat wrong. But I do know that a key part of what's needed is people—people to bring the light and expose the truth, people willing to protect what we love in nature and humanity, and people who are mature enough to make a commitment and dig in until slavery and ecocide are rare and diminishing. The really important things take time, sometimes they require whole cultures to change their thinking, but we know that can happen. In spite of all the obstacles, human rights and civil rights keep spreading, and in some places the rate of change in the last few decades has been astounding. Yes, it is daunting to have to measure our work in decades, but the prize is worth it. We just have to start now while the prize is still possible.

10

YOU CAN'T UN-KNOW WHAT YOU KNOW

In the summer of 1942 a young couple traveled home to visit their families in poor and rural southern Oklahoma. A few years before, aged twenty-two and nineteen, not long after their marriage, they made the almost unimaginable leap from the Dust Bowl to Washington, DC. A government job notice found on a post office wall had catapulted them into the great human-powered information-sorting machine of the Federal Bureau of Investigation. These two young people were just the way J. Edgar Hoover liked his recruits: resilient, loyal, uncomplicated, and grateful for the chance they were being offered. They had never known anything but hard work, and they may have been ignorant Okies, but they were smart as whips and their rise was smooth. The young husband performed so well in the fingerprint division he was given the chance to become an agent, a real G-Man. Well regarded, he helped his young wife apply for a job searching and sorting crime files. Before long they had a car and dressed like city folk. To their families, still living perilously close to the hunger and poverty they'd experienced in the just waning Great Depression, they were proof that life could get better.

Their families had gathered to see the couple, to hear about this

miraculous rise and the shining city so far away. When night came
the small farmhouse was packed, all the beds were full and the floors
were covered with people sleeping on pallets of old quilts. It was
also hot, the mercury had topped 100 degrees that day and the still
and humid heat barely eased when the sun went down. The best one
could hope for was a breeze, a breath of moving air, so the young
couple took their bedding and spread it on the grass away from the
house. Lying on the ground together, looking up at stars in a hazy
sky, excited to be home, too hot to sleep, they murmured and kid-
ded, talking about all the changes they saw around them.

After the last light had gone off in the house, when only the thrum
of the cicadas filled the air, edging toward sleep, the young husband
began to speak in a lower and slower voice. "Sweetheart, I want to
tell you something, but you have to promise that you'll never discuss
it with anyone, ever." She quietly agreed, understanding that when
America had gone to war seven months before, security meant se-
crecy. He continued, "There's a bunch of scientists that have been
got together to make a new kind of bomb. If it works it will be more
powerful than anything, not just bigger than a blockbuster bomb,
bigger than hundreds of blockbusters." He paused to collect his
thoughts. "They're using some kind of atomic power like in those
science fiction stories I've told you about. If they can get it to work
they'll be able to destroy a whole city with a single bomb, it's a power
like nothing ever before." There was no triumph in his voice just a
sober dark accounting. Her mind was stretching, trying to imagine
such destruction, trying to imagine the people of a whole city dead
in an instant. It was no good; the image, the horror of it repulsed
her.

"And there's something else," he said, and she could hear him trying to keep something fearful out of his voice, to be the strong and
protective man she knew. "Before too long they think they'll be able
to test this new bomb. Some of the scientists think it won't work at
all, some think it might. But some scientists say that if it does work
the explosion could start a chain reaction that would burn up all the

oxygen, all the air, in the whole world. If that happens, well, that's the end of everything, this world will be over." She had put her hand on his chest, and felt a shudder, all the while trying to understand why anyone would take such a risk.

For a little while they were quiet, looking at the stars but seeing everything in new way. Their world, their solid ancient world, could be snuffed out. Their new promising and happy lives, everyone's lives, could go in an instant. They'd already been learning to accept the nearness of death. With friends and family members going to war, with casualties already mounting up in the newspapers, they knew death was prowling their generation. But this was not the risk of war, this was the Book of Revelation, the end-time, the fire that consumed everything. That knowledge filled their minds and they were changed forever.

Changed, but still resilient and loyal, still uncomplicated enough not to dwell on oblivion. Hard work and grit had got them this far; a world-destroying bomb shook them but that didn't change the jobs they had to do. After that night, their lives unfolded as lives do: children, struggle, losses, gains, but they never said a word to any-one about what they knew of this atomic bomb, not when it was unleashed against Japan three years later, not even when the Rus-sians tested their bomb. They kept this knowledge to themselves, but it touched the way they lived. It made their love for each other that much more precious, it moved them to value all life and want to help make a world where that horror could never occur. They didn't tell anyone their secret because they were honor-bound not to, but their actions testified to their permanently altered state.

This young couple, in time, became my parents. Parents who tried their best to make my childhood as free from care and worry as they could, parents who set an example of moral strength, stability, curiosity, hard work, and fun. I don't know if they ever told anyone else about the A-bomb, but just before her ninety-first birthday, as we were discussing a biography of Harry Truman we'd both read, my mother told me about that night under the stars. I was astounded.

I will never know how my father, a new entry-level FBI agent, could have known so much about the Manhattan Project, when even those in the research labs were being kept in the dark. But somehow he did know, and it is hard to imagine the weight of that knowledge on his and my mother's hearts and minds.

. . .

My parents, knowing what they did, kept going, and in their way made a difference in the world. The deep excitement my father felt investigating crime somehow passed to me, and even though it takes me places that are hard to experience, the drive is there: I can't not go, I can't not know. In the late 1990s that drive took me around the world to investigate the vast hidden crime of slavery. From 2007 that dogged curiosity took me around the world again. This time on the trail of a criminal combination, a secret assault not just on people, but also on our shared and precious natural world. And now we know some things that we didn't know before:

- *We know* that the hidden crimes of slavery and environmental destruction are not just inextricably linked but mutually reinforcing and reach around the planet.
- *We know* that slaves are used to destroy the environment, and that when an ecosystem is devastated the people who live within it are pushed closer to slavery.
- *We know* that this destruction and slavery feed the global market and that we eat and wear and use the spoils of this crime every day.
- *We know* that slavery, our old enemy, is also a major cause of global warming, our big new enemy.
- *We know* that environmental laws and treaties stopped much legal deforestation and that slave masters rushed in to fill the hole in the market.
- *We know* criminal slaveholders go straight for the sweet spots—the national forests, the wildlife preserves, the UNESCO World

Heritage Sites, and the protected homes and territory of indigenous peoples.

- *We know* these slaveholders don't care about obeying environmental laws; to them the world is to be pillaged and slaves are the
tools they use to smash and grab.
- *We know* the profits generated when we buy things flow back
down the supply chain to fuel the assault on the natural world,
drive more people toward slavery, and then feed more goods into
the global supply chain.
- *We know* these crimes go round and round, a criminal perpetual
motion machine that devours people and nature like a cancer.
- *We know* that to save our planet we have to fight slavery, and that
to end slavery we have to protect our environment.

And we know that knowing these things changes the way we see the
world and how we act. From now on we can't plead ignorance, only
indifference. We're now part of the generation that came to know
better. It's a burden on us, just as the knowledge of the A-bomb was
a burden on my parents, but it's also an opportunity. A new way of
seeing the world doesn't come along very often, and when it does it
can be a jarring awakening, a responsibility as well as a privilege.
The new challenge of global warming and the age-old challenge of
slavery, both seemingly insuperable, now have a linked solution.
Knowing that makes us the people our children will fairly ask: *What
did you do when you learned the truth about slavery and environmental
destruction?*

Understanding the truth and feeling concerned about it are important, but if the arc of our moral universe is that narrow, then it's
hard to be optimistic about the future of our planet or our species.
Though, in fact, very little will be asked of us if we *do* act on our
concerns. There may be people, like Cláudio and Maria, who will be
asked to give up their lives to serve this truth, but for most of us the
greatest sacrifice will be some inconvenience. We'll have to think
about the origins of the things we buy and maybe pay a little more

for some items. We'll have to make small donations to support people, like Cláudio and Maria, who are doing the jobs the rest of us know must be done to solve this problem. We'll all have to decide if our goal is worth the inconvenience it brings to our lives. At least we can be assured that the decision to accept some inconvenience is immensely powerful. *We know* it can bring families out of slavery, stop deforestation and pollution, reduce greenhouse gases, protect endangered species, lessen corruption, suppress violence, unleash the creativity and productivity of free workers, improve public health, and help eliminate systems of cruelty and exploitation that have plagued us for centuries. What we don't know, however, may be just as important. How would making that decision change *us*?

What kind of world do we create when we choose not to live with slavery and ecocide? That choice doesn't have to be all consuming, but to be real it does have to be a consistent part of our lives. Small choices, made at the right moment, can bring very big changes. Rosa Parks chose to not give up her seat on the bus, Fannie Lou Hamer chose to register to vote, Aung San Suu Kyi chose not to give up and give in; we can choose to act on what we know. If we do that, and make those little actions part of our lives, then our children will learn from our examples to be the people we deeply hope they will be. Jonathan Safran Foer noted that "compassion is a muscle that gets stronger with use, and the regular exercise of choosing kindness over cruelty would change us."

As our compassion gets stronger it has to be guided by our sense of responsibility. We can't blame ourselves for the ecologically unbalanced and destructive things our parents and grandparents did while living in a kind of innocent ignorance. Much of what they did they did for the right reasons: caring for their families, making a better life, and enjoying the fruits of hard-earned progress. It's hard to say if they would have kept up the actions that led to global warming if they had known their children would find themselves in such a perilous situation. Maybe some of them would have chosen to join those who remain in denial in the twenty-first century, but I want to think not. I want to believe that they'd never want to land their children with the big ugly problems of global warming, slavery, species loss, and systematic and brutal exploitation of people and the natural world. And I want to believe that we don't want to dump these problems on our children.

We have to be honest; we don't have a silver bullet. If we could end slavery tomorrow it wouldn't stop all global warming, and if we could end environmental destruction that wouldn't bring all slavery to an end. If we could miraculously end both slavery and environmental destruction, that wouldn't solve all the world's problems, but it is remarkable how many of those problems intersect where slavery and ecocide meet. It seems improbable, even impossible, that we could actually effect change at the global level, but no one can seriously doubt the influence of American consumers on the rest of the world. Wendell Berry said that every time we make a decision about the food we eat, we are "farming by proxy." The same goes for our relationship with all the goods that come from the intersection of slavery and environmental destruction. We are mining by proxy every time we buy a cellphone or a piece of gold jewelry. When we choose to load up the barbecue with shrimp, we are fishing by proxy. When we buy furniture or cars or kitchen sinks, we are cutting down forests by proxy, burning them into charcoal by proxy, and smelting iron by proxy. What we eat, or choose to wear, the things we buy for our homes, or choose not to buy, all link us in one relationship after another to people in slavery, national economies, and protected forests.

To avoid or ignore the inconvenience of thinking through our actions is surely the easiest decision. Who wants to be bound by these pesky concerns? Can't we just feign the ignorance of our parents? Surely our little choices don't really change anything, right? Yes, each choice is small, like a tiny drop of water. But the act of choosing is repeated every day of our lives, and carries into the lives of our children and their children. These millions of little choices turn into a great river of economic pressure, a powerful river that can either erode or sustain people's lives and the natural world. We know what happens if we do nothing—it is happening every day in Brazil and Congo, Ghana and Bangladesh. It's easy to imagine a future if we do nothing, a future with few forests, more slavery, children dying in mines and fish camps, no gorillas, rising sea levels, no tigers, farmland dried out and exhausted, and people hungry. It doesn't have to be this way, and the best reason to think that there could be a better future is the fact that we know just how bad the future could be.

Rationally, slavery is just so obviously wrong in so many ways. Hacking away at the environment that sustains us, that is the *only* source of our sustenance, is both wrong and stupid. There's no credible defense for either, just a tangled mess of rationalizations and justifications that mask hurtful greed. Slavery and environmental destruction are irrational, but then so is, all too often, culture. When a whole culture is convinced they are right in their wrongheadedness, we've all got a problem. Our cultures have a lot to answer for when it comes to slavery and how we treat the natural world. When a culture decides that women are inferior to men and acts on that decision, life for women can get ugly. When a culture decides that people who look a certain way, or pray a certain way, are evil or subhuman or a threat, then it becomes a lot easier to use them or enslave them or just dispose of them. When a culture decides that its immediate well-being is more important than the livelihood of others, more important than a healthy and vibrant environment, then we're on a path to disaster.

Stopping our walk down that path is about much more than slavery and environmental destruction. We've had plenty of facts about slavery on one hand, and facts about global warming on the other, for a long time. Knowing the truth of their dangerous alliance gives us even more reason to act, but sometimes reason is not enough. This is beyond reason, it is about our core. This is about the earth we all spring from and will all return to. This is about being human, and though we are thinking and reasoning animals, being human is more than reason. Our truest essence is found where thought meets desire, where facts and dreams collide, where being human presses against the rest of the natural world. The choices we make at those intersections transcend our lives and reach far into the future. What seem to be small decisions and small actions actually determine our intrinsic human worth, what it means to be human, as well as the judgment we will receive from future generations.

Slavery will come to an end because of its wastefulness. It is bad economics and essentially unsustainable. The earth will ultimately shake off any threat that engages in wanton destruction. Ecocide is also bad economics and unsustainable. The question is whether we will be shaken off as part of that threat. The feelings we have about our freedoms are powerfully resonant, but so is our need to provide for our families and ourselves, our love of nature, our protectiveness of those we love and what we have. These resonances can be harmonic or dissonant, controversial or inspiring, threatening or comforting, but they will always be filled with meaning. Slavery matters and the environment matters and the dark and violent congress of slavery and environmental destruction matters even more.

The end of slavery is an aspiration we all share. The protection of our marvelously beautiful and life-sustaining natural world is something we all know is right. The possibility of reaching such ideals comes rarely, and when it does, it usually comes at the dangerous crossroads of opportunity and crisis. What we decide to do at this intersection is a test of how we respond to the most distant, the powerless, and the voiceless. No one is forcing us to choose one way or the other. We don't have to be consistent, but we have no choice but to engage. Either we act to make our ideals reality or we do nothing and attempt to un-know what we know.

■   ■   ■

Is there anything quite as adorable as little children dressed up for a school play? In an elementary school in the city of Araguaína in Brazil, the gym has been turned into a theater, and the folding chairs are filled with beaming parents. The room buzzes with lively chatter and giggles, and a skit about the importance of vaccinations is just coming to an end. As we watch a little girl dressed in a doctor's white coat, stethoscope dangling from her neck, her mouth covered in a surgical mask (just in case there is any doubt of her profession), is congratulating a little girl dressed as a student. The student holds a book and a folder, and it is clear from her serious but happy expression that she now fully owns the important knowledge of good hygiene and inoculation. The parents applaud and smile and the little doctor seems especially proud, she pirouettes before leading her patient from the stage.

Taking up a microphone a young teacher introduces the finale. This is a play about modern slavery, she says, how it traps people and how we can stop it. Two little boys walk nervously onto the stage. They have identical curving mustaches and tiny goatee beards painted on their faces and are wearing broad-brimmed hats so we know they are grown-ups who live in the countryside. "I am a big farmer," says one little boy into the microphone, "I need some workers!" "Okay," says the other boy, "I'm a *gato*, I can get you some workers from the city." And with a little nervous fumbling and nodding between them, and a little shove from the "farmer," the *gato* dashes offstage to the "city."

"There are people in the city who need jobs," narrates the teacher, "when the *gato* promises them good jobs, they come with him to the country." As she says this six "poor" children troop in, four girls and two boys with bandannas wrapped around their heads, floppy rubber hoes and shovels are self-consciously perched on their shoulders. Lined up on the stage, the *gato* shouts at them "Get to work!" and with a nervous giggle they flail about with their hoes and mattocks, "clearing land." The teacher explains that they are working all day long, then a little girl steps forward. "I'm tired, I need to rest," she pleads. "No!" orders the *gato*. "Get back to work!" and a nervous laugh echoes out from the audience. More flailing about and another girl steps up, "I'm hungry!" she says, "We need food!"

"No food for you," shouts the *gato*. "Get back to work!" But now, explains the teacher, one worker escapes to the city, and a little girl zips across the stage before the *gato* can grab her. In a moment, she is back, but this time with the police—their captain is a little boy in a suit jacket that looks like a six-year-old Barack Obama, the only boy without a painted goatee. With him are a girl and boy, "police officers," the little boy captain's chin is thrust out, he's glowing.

"Hands up!" says the captain, and everyone, even the enslaved workers, throws their hands in the air. "Who's the landowner here?" he asks with firm authority, and all the workers as well as the *gato* point to the farmer and shout, "It's him! It's him!" The other "officers" move quickly. One secures the farmer's hands behind his back, and the little girl officer arrests the *gato* with such enthusiasm that she bends him backward, gives him a bounce, and his hat falls off. The workers begin to laugh at the *gato*, then cheer when their new freedom is announced. At a signal, they shout out together, "*Escravo nem pensar!*" and the applause and laughter well up as they bow over and over to the audience. The whole play has lasted a little over two minutes.

A literal translation of "*escravo nem pensar!*" would mean something like, "slavery, don't even think about it!" but Brazilians tell me a better translation into English would be "Slavery, no way!" The play in Araguaína is no one-off performance, but part of a national *Slavery, No Way!* campaign. For these children the knowledge of slavery and environmental threat is simple and clear. They know already whose side they're on; we just have to catch up with them.

APPENDIX:

———

ORGANIZATIONS WORKING IN EASTERN CONGO

THE PANZI HOSPITAL

Renowned for its treatment of survivors of sexual violence and women suffering from severe gynecological conditions, the hospital has received a great deal of international attention and publicity. You can help support the Panzi Hospital at http://www.panzihospital .org/about/support-panzi-hospital.

FREE THE SLAVES

Free the Slaves helps those in slavery escape the brutality of bondage. It helps prevent others from becoming trapped by traffickers. It helps officials bring slave holders to justice. It helps survivors restore their dignity, rebuild their lives, and reclaim the future for themselves, their families, and their communities. Free the Slaves is building a world without slavery by demonstrating that ending slavery is possible. In the Congo, Free the Slaves works with local groups to support education and access to schooling, good governance, citizen advocacy and government accountability, law enforcement, workers' rights associations, increased transparency by companies that use Congo minerals, micro-credit, and the development of viable alternative livelihoods to mining—such as farming and animal husbandry. You can support this organization's work at https://www.freetheslaves.net/donate/.

LAKE TANGANYIKA FLOATING HEALTH CLINIC

The conflict-ridden, resource-rich Lake Tanganyika Basin has become vital to the well-being and interests of the planet, and this organization's work is now recognized as crucial to its stable growth and development. The Lake Tanganyika Floating Health Clinic (LTFHC) has been helping the communities living in the Lake Tanganyika Basin for more than five years. In this almost wholly neglected area it:

- Delivers vital healthcare
- Distributes necessary medical supplies
- Establishes important communications hubs
- Gathers essential medical data
- Builds strong relationships with the people and the governments of the region

You can support the LTFHC at: http://floatingclinic.org/support/.

ENOUGH

The Enough Project works to end genocide and crimes against humanity, focused on areas where some of the world's worst atrocities occur. This organization gets the facts on the ground, uses rigorous analysis to determine the most sustainable solutions, influences political leaders to adopt its proposals, and mobilizes the American public to demand change. The Enough Project has been a leader in getting slave-mined conflict minerals out of our electronics. Support them at https://ssl1.americanprogress.org/o/507/donate_page /support-enough.

THE AFRICAN GREAT LAKES INITIATIVE OF THE FRIENDS PEACE TEAMS

This organization strengthens, supports, and promotes peace activities at the grassroots level in the Great Lakes region of Africa (Burundi, Congo, Kenya, Rwanda, Tanzania, and Uganda). To this end, AGLI responds to requests from local religious and nongovernmental organizations that focus on conflict management, peace building, trauma healing, and reconciliation. AGLI sponsors Peace Teams composed of members from local partners and the international community. You can support their work at http://aglifpt .org/get/donate.htm.

ACKNOWLEDGMENTS

Many of the people who helped me explore slavery and ecocide are anti-slavery and environmental activists in countries where their work puts them at risk. The threat to these brave women and men comes both from the criminals who abuse slaves and the natural world, and, all too often, from local and national governments. I will not add to the danger they face by naming them here, but I thank them from the bottom of my heart. Great heroes of abolition and freedom walk among us unseen and unknown, they are the Frederick Douglass and Harriet Tubman and Sojourner Truth of today, and I long for the day when we can honor them as they deserve. Several other anti-slavery and environmental activists, whose lives are not threatened, who worked with me on the research for this book are mentioned in the text.

NOTES

CHAPTER 1

4 IN 2013 INDIA PRODUCED http://www.indianmirror.com/indian-industries /2013/granite-2013.html, accessed April 6, 2014.

5 "OBVIOUSLY IT MEANS THE GOVERNMENT HAS FAILED" Real Cost of India's Cheap Stone" BBC, http://news.bbc.co.uk/1/hi/world/south_asia/6233697 .stm, accessed April 7, 2014.

6 GERMAN FILMMAKERS RESEARCHING *Slave Labourers in Indian Stone Quarries* (2003), Director/Author: Henno Osberghaus, Frank Domhan. LavaFilm GMBH, Berlin.

9 BUT HOW CAN THE ESTIMATED For a full explanation of how the number of slaves in the world is calculated, see the Global Slavery Index at www .globalslaveryindex.org.

CHAPTER 2

22 AMBAYA ESTELLA'S THREE CHILDREN Basildon, Peta (Jan. 9, 2003). "Rebels 'eating pygmies' as mass slaughter continues in Congo despite peace agreement," *The Independent.*

23 NOW IMAGINE THAT WHEN THE GOVERNMENT Originally these armed groups were created for reasons that had nothing to do with the minerals. Some were linked to ethnic conflicts, like the Hutu FDLR (Democratic Forces for the Liberation of Rwanda) or the Tutsi CNDP (National Congress for the Defense of the People). Other forces, called Mai Mai groups, began as local self-defense teams to protect villages, but they now join in shifting alliances with the larger groups as well as doing their

own mining. The government force that should be clearing out these invaders and bringing order is the Congolese National Army (FADRC), but many army commanders and units have gone rogue and are now deeply involved in slavery and mining as well. To confuse matters a little more, the government tried to calm the situation by "absorbing" enemy militias into the national army, but allowing them to remain as intact units. This means that a brigade of the FARDC might actually be just an old Tutsi CNDP unit with new uniforms but little or no loyalty or obedience to the government. It is unclear whether the central government is too weak or too well bribed (or both) to impose order on its own troops.

24 THIS SYSTEM HAS AN EERIE PARALLEL An excellent introduction to post–Civil War peonage is Douglas A. Blackmon's Pulitzer Prize–winning *Slavery by Another Name: The Re-Enslavement of Black Americans from the Civil War to World War II*, New York: Anchor Books (Random House) 2008.

28 ENSLAVED MINERS OFTEN DISAPPEARED Op. cit., p. 397.

28 BLACKMON GIVES THE "CRIMES" Op. cit., p. 99.

30 BUT IT WAS NOT UNTIL FIVE DAYS Op. cit., p. 377.

34 "BECAUSE HE DID NOT THINK I WAS CAPABLE" Quoted in a report by the Harvard Humanitarian Initiative and Oxfam International (April 2010). "Now the World Is Without Me," An Investigation of Sexual Violence in Eastern Democratic Republic of Congo, p. 21.

35 PSYCHOLOGISTS DESCRIBE THE HOSTAGE See, for example, de Fabrique, Nathalie; Romano, Stephen J.; Vecchi, Gregory M.; van Hasselt, Vincent B. (July 2007). "Understanding Stockholm Syndrome," *FBI Law Enforcement Bulletin* (Law Enforcement Communication Unit) 76 (7): 10–15. ISSN 0014-5688.

35 ONE OF THE MOST REMARKABLE INVESTIGATIONS Kirsten Johnson, Jennifer Scott, Bigy Rughita, Michael Kisielewski, Jana Asher, Ricardo Ong, Lynn Lawry (Aug. 4, 2010). "Association of Sexual Violence and Human Rights Violations With Physical and Mental Health in Territories of the Eastern Democratic Republic of the Congo," *Journal of the American Medical Association*, 304, 5, 553–62.

38 THEY ALSO LIVE ON A SHOESTRING The international anti-slavery group Free the Slaves is based in Washington DC and works closely with two key organizations in Eastern Congo. You can read about their work there and how to support it at www.freetheslaves.net.

39 A ROCKET-PROPELLED GRENADE HAD KILLED http://news.national geographic.com/news/2007/08/070816-gorillas-congo_2.html.

40 "Hɪᴘᴘᴏs ɴᴏᴛ ᴏɴʟʏ ᴄᴏɴsᴜᴍᴇ ʟᴏᴛs ᴏғ ɢʀᴀss" Stefan Lovgren (Dec. 14, 2005). "Hippos—And Precious Dung—Vanishing From African Lake," *National Geographic News*, accessed at: http://news.nationalgeographic.com /news/2005/12/1214_051214_hippo_dung.html, March 17, 2011.

42 Oʀ, ᴀs ᴛʜᴇ ᴘʀɪᴍᴀᴛᴏʟᴏɢɪsᴛs ᴘᴜᴛ ɪᴛ Rogers, M. E., Voysey, B. C., McDonald, K. E., Parnell, R. J., Tutin, C. E. (1998). "Lowland Gorillas and Seed Dispersal: The Importance of Nest Sites," *American Journal of Primatology*, 45 (1): 45–68.

43 Nᴋᴜɴᴅᴀ ᴇsᴛᴀʙʟɪsʜᴇᴅ ʜɪs ᴏᴡɴ "ᴍᴏᴜɴᴛᴀɪɴ sᴛᴀᴛᴇ" Nkunda has also been linked by United Nations investigators to Tribert Rujugiro, an adviser to former president Paul Kagame and chairman of Tri-Star Holdings, an investment group involved in economic activities in Goma and rebel occupied territories. The UN Group of Experts reports that: "Mr. Rujugiro's United States–based legal representatives denied that he had purchased or invested in lands in 'Masisi district' [*sic*] while they were under CNDP control; held meetings with CNDP leaders, including 'General' Nkunda at his ranches in Kilolirwe in 2006; paid money to CNDP for 'protection' of cattle on his ranches; or appointed a CNDP commander to manage his ranches. The Group [of Experts] stands by its findings and provides further details in annex VI." Letter dated May 12, 2011, from the Group of Experts on the Democratic Republic of the Congo, addressed to the chair of the Security Council Committee established pursuant to resolution 1533 (2004). UN Document S/2011/345.

44 Sᴏᴍᴇ sᴏʟᴅɪᴇʀs ʜᴀᴠᴇ ɴᴏᴛ ʙᴇᴇɴ ᴘᴀɪᴅ ɪɴ ʏᴇᴀʀs James Owen (Jan. 19, 2007). "Mountain Gorillas Eaten by Congolese Rebels": *National Geographic News*, accessed at: http://news.nationalgeographic.com/news/2007 /01/070119-gorillas.html, June 25, 2011.

44 Tʜᴇ Cᴏɴɢᴏ ʜᴀs ᴀ ʟᴏɴɢ ʜɪsᴛᴏʀʏ "Congo's Curse." IRIN. Web. Oct. 5, 2010. http://www.irinnews.org/Report.aspx?ReportId=61006.

45 A ʏᴇᴀʀ ʟᴀᴛᴇʀ ʜᴇ ᴡᴀs ᴀʀʀᴇsᴛᴇᴅ ʙʏ ᴛʜᴇ Cᴏɴɢᴏʟᴇsᴇ op. cit.

CHAPTER 3

48 Tʜᴀᴛ ᴘʀᴇᴄɪsᴇ ᴍɪxᴛᴜʀᴇ ᴏғ ᴛɪɴ ᴀɴᴅ ʟᴇᴀᴅ The electronics companies that buy the solder are making things we'll end up buying, but they aren't likely to be companies we've heard of. All over Indonesia, Malaysia, Taiwan, China, the Philippines, and also in India, Europe, and North America, are small companies making and assembling components for electronics. Some

might be making a single type of transistor or capacitor, others might be assembling a logic board with hundreds or thousands of parts. They might be making disk drives or flash drives, headphones, microphones, or screens and displays. Some will be making parts for cars or kitchen appliances or hospital equipment. All of these will require solder. These parts and components will then be sold to the next step in the chain, the companies that actually assemble them together into the things we buy.

49 So MANY PEOPLE SLEEP PILED TOGETHER Scabies is also known as the "seven-year itch"; it's a skin infection caused by a tiny parasite which burrows into its host's skin causing an extreme allergic itching. Scabies is most often caused by direct prolonged skin-to-skin contact; a similar parasite causes mange in dogs and other animals. Think of scabies as mange for humans.

53 IT'S AT THIS STAGE IN THE SUPPLY CHAIN The term "ecocide" seems to have first been used in the late 1960s to describe the impact of war, and particularly the Viet Nam war, on the natural environment. The American spraying of large areas of Viet Nam with toxic chemicals resulted in desolation of the ecosystem as well as extensive human illness and death. In 2011 there is an ongoing campaign led by lawyer and environmentalist Polly Higgins to have ecocide recognized by the United Nations as an international crime against peace that can be tried at the International Criminal Court.

54 THEY AND THEIR COMPANIES KNOWINGLY PROFIT See: American Bar Association Antitrust Section (1982). "Jury Instructions in Criminal Antitrust Cases," p. 27. See also: US Justice Department (Jan. 1998). "Criminal Resource Manual 2472," a work of the US Federal Government, citing *United States v. Peoni*, 100 F.2d 401, 402 (2d Cir. 1938).

55 THREE COMPANIES DOMINATE Antonio Ruffini (2008). "Africa Remains Key to Future Tantalum Supply." *Engineering and Mining Journal*, pp. 68–72. See Cabot's policy here: http://www.cabot-corp.com/Tantalum /GN200809161037AM6983/. A spokesperson for H.C. Starck, Manfred Buetefisch, explained that, "While working through everything together with the UN panel, we found out that not every retailer had told us the truth concerning the material's origin—despite assuring otherwise. That's when we realized that—seeing the ongoing war in East Africa and the DRC—that they are not reliable partners for us, and that we cannot buy any material there anymore." Using microscopic X-ray technology, H.C. Starck is working with the German Federal Institute for Geosciences and Natural Resources to identify unique mineral "fingerprints" for minerals

from different mines. Quoted in *Deutsche Welle* (Aug. 13, 2010). "Coltan Mines to Be 'Fingerprinted,' German Scientists Say," accessed at: http://www.dw-world.de/dw/article/0,,5907446,00.html, June 29, 2011.

55 THE NUMBER IN THE UK If you'd like to try this yourself: Ningxia representative in the United States: Admat Inc. Tel: 610-783-5513 Fax: 610-783-0453; P.O. Box 1404, Southeastern, PA 19399, USA. ("Southeastern" isn't a region, it's a little place in the suburbs outside Philadelphia, a stone's throw from Valley Forge.) Ningxia representative in Europe: Elite Material Solutions Limited Tel: (country code) 1582-418423 Fax: (country code) 1582-418483; The Spires, 2 Adelaide Street, Luton, Bedfordshire, LU1 5DU United Kingdom.

55 UNDERNEATH THE BIG PLAYERS The following table shows the companies that bought minerals in Goma, DRC, over a three-month period in 2010; it was taken from an Internal Briefing Document, "Configuring Policy Approaches toward the Eastern DRC Mineral Sector," prepared for Free the Slaves by Resources Consulting Services in July 2010.

Buyers of Minerals from Goma, DRC, Jan-March, 2010, by Volume			
Quantity in Tonnes	Firm of destination	Country of Destination	Owner
949.49	Malaysia Smelting Corporation	Malaysia	The Straits Trading Company Limited
869.1	MSA Kigali	Rwanda	David Bensusan
800.08	Trademet SA	Belgium	Freddy Muyleart
265.77	BEB Investment	Canada	unknown
263.7	SDE Bruxelles, Belgium	Belgium	Elwyn Blattner Group International
177.15	Met Trade India	India	Gupta Group
163.8	Tengen Metals Ltd	Tortola/UK	unknown
44.46	Congo Russia Industry/OJSC	Russia	Rosspetsplav
33.9	Star 2000 Services Ltd	Hong Kong	unknown
22	Fogange Jiata Metals Co Ltd	China	Jiayuan Cobalt Holdings Co., Ltd, Macrolink Group & Hongkong Goldwei Group
20	MPA Gisenyi	Rwanda	Kivu Resources
10.1	Africa Primary Tungsten	Rwanda	Jean Paul Higiro
Source: Division de Mines, Goma			

55 SOME OF THESE ARE DOING When I called the ITRI offices, I was told that "ITRI" used to stand for something like "International Tin Research Institute" but that now it wasn't an acronym, the name was just "ITRI." They also couldn't explain why the letter "i" in iTSCi was lowercase. I'm guessing that since tin solder is used in iPhones and iPads, they were trying to be cool by association.

55 TIN SUPPLY CHAIN INITIATIVE From the ITRI website: "iTSCi (ITRI Tin Supply Chain Initiative) is a joint initiative that assists upstream companies (from mine to the smelter) to institute the actions, structures, and processes necessary to conform with the OECD Due Diligence Guidance

(DDG) at a very practical level, including small and medium size enter-prises, co-operatives and artisanal mine sites. It is designed for use by in-dustry, but with oversight and clear roles for government officials, in keeping with the recently published OECD Due Diligence Guidance for Responsible Supply Chains of Minerals from Conflict-Affected and High-Risk Areas. It also takes into account the recommendations of the UN Se-curity Council (UNSC) to expand due diligence to include criminal networks, as well as armed groups and to include violations of the asset freeze and travel ban on sanctioned individuals and entities. (UN 2010b: 88)," accessed at: https://www.itri.co.uk/index.php?option=com_zoo&task =item&item_id=2192&Itemid=189, May 8, 2014.

56 You'd think that everyone See: http://www.passivecomponent magazine.com/"itsci-is-in-very-real-danger-of-failing"-says-richard -burt-president-of-the-tantalum-niobium-international-study-center/, ac-cessed June 25, 2011.

57 In March 2011, a review Triodos Sustainable Bond Fund (March 2011). Triodos Bank, Newsletter, accessed at: http://www.triodos.com/downloads /distribution-partners/sustainable-bond-fund/newsletters/tsbfnews0311 .pdf, June 30, 2011.

58 One of the largest is Flextronics See: http://www.flextronics.com /partners/supplierinfo/WebPages/Supplier%20Sustainbility%20Report %202011/files/assets/downloads/page0020.pdf, accessed June 30, 2011.

58 One of the best known of these assembler companies From the Fox-conn Global Code of Conduct Policy (http://ser.foxconn.com/Group CocShow.do; accessed May 20, 2015): "Foxconn does not accept and does not use conflict minerals originating from the Democratic Republic of the Congo and its adjoining countries and regions. Foxconn requires suppliers to trace the origins of all products containing potential conflict minerals, including gold (Au), tantalum (Ta), tin (Sn), and tungsten (W), and provide relevant information sources to Foxconn. In addition, Foxconn's down-stream suppliers are required to fulfill their due diligence on free conflict minerals pursuant to the relevant laws requirements."

59 The combination of a lengthy supply chain Apple, *Supplier Responsi-bility 2010 Progress Report*, see page 23, accessed at: http://images.apple .com/supplierresponsibility/pdf/L418102A_SR_2010Report_FF.pdf, June 30, 2011.

60 Intel topped the list The global anti-slavery organization Walk Free mounted a campaign to push Nintendo to get its act together after the Enough Project stated the company's conflict mineral policy was a "mean-ingless piece of paper"—Walk Free "Enough Games Nintendo" campaign

at: http://www.walkfree.org/enough-games-nintendo/. Full report available at: http://www.raisehopeforcongo.org/content/conflict-minerals-company-rankings, accessed May 9, 2014.

61 WHY NOT WORK WITH THE ANTI-SLAVERY GROUPS In June 2011 I visited a cassiterite mine in the state of Para in Brazil (that's the same mineral being mined in the Bisie mine in Congo). I went over that mine inch by inch. I found workers that were happy with their jobs, eating good food prepared by a full-time cook, with freedom to come and go, and earning good money. The work was dirty and hard, but they had machines for the heavy lifting and digging. They had no idea what the minerals they were digging were used for, and also had no idea that they were producing "conflict-free" and "fair-trade" minerals. You can read more about this mine in Chapter 9.

61 "THE MORE YOU ENGAGE" "Peter Thiel Urges Investing in Human Rights in The Street": http://www.thestreet.com/story/11154811/1/peter-thiel-urges-investing-in-human-rights.html.

62 YOU CAN HAVE A LOOK Enough Project's report and rankings at: http://www.raisehopeforcongo.org/companyrankings.

63 PART OF THE MUCH LARGER DODD-FRANK BILL It takes a lot of people to get a law passed and Senators Sam Brownback (R-KS), Dick Durbin (D-IL), and Russ Feingold (D-WI), Representatives Howard Berman (D-CA) and Donald Payne (D-NJ), and Chairmen Chris Dodd (D-CT) and Barney Frank (D-MA), who ushered the bill through both houses of Congress deserve praise.

64 THE DODD-FRANK LAW HAS BEEN It's hard for people to resist gold. In June 2011 the UN Group of Experts on the Congo reported that: "Two high-profile investigations have drawn renewed attention to the role of regional and international networks involved in the illicit trade in natural resources from the Democratic Republic of the Congo. On 3 February 2011, a Gulf-stream jet [the favorite private jet of zillionaires] was impounded at Goma airport and its United States, Nigerian, and French passengers were detained during investigations into a gold purchasing deal. The detainees were transferred to Kinshasa and eventually released, after the State prosecutor of the Democratic Republic of the Congo, Flory Kabange, announced on 25 March 2011 that the individuals had paid a US $3 million fine and that the authorities had also seized 435 kg of gold [worth something like $21 million] and US $6 million in cash. In another case of interest, on 3 March 2011, at the request of President Kabila, a joint Kenya–Democratic Republic of the Congo investigation was launched into alleged large-scale gold smuggling [operation] through Kenya. On 11 May

2011, Kenyan police arrested three Congolese suspects in connection with this case."

64 THE SENIOR COUNSEL http://congress2014.cibjo.org/index.php?option =com_content&view=article&id=664:precious-metals-commission -debates-impact-of-dodd-frank-act-and-eu-proposals&catid=47&Itemid =290 accessed 20 April, 2015.

64 THE CONFEDERATION ALSO WROTE World Jewellery Confederation, Special Report, The CIBJO Precious Metals Commission (Feb. 2011). "Legislative Regulations for Heavy Metals in Children's Jewellery Spotlighted in 2011 Special Report of CIBJO Precious Metals Commission," accessed at: http://download.cibjo.org/PM2011REPORT.pdf, July 1, 2011.

65 THE DIRECTOR OF THE STATE-RUN LICENSING Nicholas Bariyo (May 18, 2011). "Congolese Military Withdraws from Tin Mine," *Wall Street Journal* (Online), accessed at: http://online.wsj.com/article/SB1000142405274 8703509104576330580910983012.html, July 4, 2011.

65 AT THE SAME TIME ALPHAMIN RESOURCES Here is the corporate announcement by Alphamin: http://www.alphaminresources.com/s/Qwik Report.asp?IsPopup=Y&printVersion=now&X1=449813,445677,445676 ,445675,394291, accessed July 4, 2011.

66 WHEN THAT IS COMPLETED See the April 2014 Activity Update at http:// www.infomine.com/index/pr/PB434969.PDF, accessed May 11, 2014.

66 JEFFREY MCNEELY, A RESPECTED SCIENTIST McNeely, Jeffrey A. (2003). "Biodiversity, War, and Tropical Forests," *Journal of Sustainable Forestry*, Vol. 16, No. 3/4, pp. 1–20.

CHAPTER 4

76 NINETY PERCENT OF THIS SHRIMP "US Shrimp Imports Fall 2.5 percent" *Seafood News Supply and Trade*, accessed at: http://www.seafoodsource.com /newsarticledetail.aspx?id=4294989242, July 23, 2010.

86 AS ONE LAWYER And who asked that I not give their name for fear of reprisals.

93 LIKE HURRICANES Cyclones and hurricanes are basically the same thing, those hitting North America turn counterclockwise, those forming below the equator turn clockwise.

94 THEY ADDED, "THIS IS A MEASURE Duke University (April 21, 2009). "Mangrove Forests Save Lives In Storms, Study of 1999 Super Cyclone Finds," *ScienceDaily*, accessed at: http://www.sciencedaily.com-/releases /2009/04/090414172924.htm, July 21, 2010.

94 AT THE CURRENT RATE OF FOREST LOSS American Institute of Biological Sciences (July 7, 2009). "Mangrove-Dependent Animals Globally Threatened," *ScienceDaily*, accessed at: http://www.sciencedaily.com-/releases /2009/07/090701082905.htm, July 21, 2010.

95 WHILE MOST SCIENTISTS AGREE See: www.350.org.

96 WHILE THERE IS A SMALLER AMOUNT OF BIOMASS The biomass in a mangrove forest scrubs about 50 percent more carbon from the air than does an equivalent amount of biomass in the Amazon terrestrial forest. For all details of this research on carbon sequestration in the Sundarbans, see: Ray, R., et al. (2011). "Carbon sequestration and annual increase of carbon stock in a mangrove forest," *Atmospheric Environment*, Elsevier, doi:10.1011 / j.atmosenv.2011.04.074.

96 SCIENTISTS AT BOTH THE US NATIONAL OCEANIC See: http://www.gfdl .noaa.gov/global-warming-and-hurricanes; and "Tropical Cyclones and Climate Change," an assessment by a World Meteorological Organization Expert Team on Climate Change Impacts on Tropical Cyclones, at http:// www.nature.com/ngeo/journal/v3/n3/abs/ngeo779.html.

96 THE COUNTRY OF BANGLADESH To give one example—Bangladesh is so flat that you get great cellphone coverage everywhere, and I mean everywhere. I could be miles and miles from any place that had electricity, much less a cellphone tower, and the reception on my old $20 handset was perfect. When the land doesn't so much as roll, where hills just don't exist, a tower that is 100 feet tall is basically always that high above you—at least until you move far enough away for the curvature of the earth to get in the way.

CHAPTER 5

99 IN THE LAST 800,000 YEARS Here is a chart of global temperature change over time, taken from Hansen, et al. "The Case for Young People and Nature: A Path to a Healthy, Natural, Prosperous Future." James Hansen, of the NASA Goddard Institute of Space Sciences, Columbia University Earth Institute, New York, is one of the leading scholars of climate change. This paper reprises his seminal work demonstrating the facts of global warming and has been disseminated widely on the Internet. I used a copy accessed July 14, 2011, from http://www.columbia.edu/~jeh1/mailings /2011/20110505_CaseForYoungPeople.pdf. That article included this figure showing the change in global temperature.

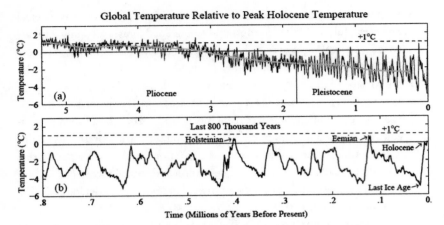

FIGURE 2. *Global temperature relative to peak Holocene temperature*
(Hansen and Sato, 2011).

100 BENJAMIN FRANKLIN FIRST LINKED See: Karen Harpp (Oct. 4, 2005).
"How Do Volcanoes Affect World Climate?" *Scientific American* (online),
accessed at: http://www.scientificamerican.com/article.cfm?id=how-do
-volcanoes-affect-w, on July 14, 2011.

100 IN CONTRAST, THE GREENHOUSE GASES Quoted in Jessica Marshall (June
27, 2011). "Humans Dwarf Volcanoes for CO_2 Emissions," *Discovery News*
(online), accessed at: http://news.discovery.com/earth/volcanoes-co2-people
-emissions-climate-110627.html, July 14, 2011.

102 SHIFTING OF CLIMATIC ZONES Hansen, et al. "The Case for Young People
and Nature: A Path to a Healthy, Natural, Prosperous Future." p. 2, accessed at: http://www.columbia.edu/~jeh1/mailings/2011/20110505_Case
ForYoungPeople.pdf, July 14, 2011.

102 COASTAL MANGROVES, LIKE THOSE OF THE SUNDARBANS Dittmar, Thor-
sten, et al. (2006). "Mangroves, A Major Source of Dissolved Organic Carbon to the Oceans," *Global Biogeochemical Cycles*, Vol. 20, GB1012, 7 PP.,
2006, doi: 10.1029 /2005GB002570.

103 THE FULL STORY ON THIS Daniel C. Donato, J. Boone Kauffman, Daniel
Murdiyarso, Sofyan Kurnianto, Melanie Stidham, and Markku Kanninen
(2011). "Mangroves Among the Most Carbon-Rich Forests in the Tropics," *Nature Geoscience*, DOI: 10.1038/ngeo1123.

106 THIS IS A SPECIAL KIND Kevin Bales (1999). *Disposable People: New Slavery
in the Global Economy*, Berkeley: University of California Press, pp. 121–22.

107 SPEND A LITTLE TIME ON GOOGLE MAPS If you'd like to see a Brazilian
charcoal camp in Moto Grosso do Sul, use Google Earth and its satellite
and aerial photographs. The GPS coordinates are 19°52'14.22" South

53°03'30.84" West. The beehive-shaped domes of the low ovens used to burn the forests into charcoal for use in the steel industry are lined up on each side of a dirt road. Smoke is rising from the ovens, and the ground is blackened near the road where charcoal has been spilled. To the east of the camp you can see where the forest has been clear cut to feed the ovens. Looking at satellite images you cannot tell if the workers in this camp are free or enslaved, but you do know exactly where it is.

108 THE SCALE OF THE OPERATION Douglas A. Blackmon (2008). *Slavery by Another Name: The Re-Enslavement of Black Americans from the Civil War to World War II*, New York: Anchor Books (Random House), pp. 344–45.

111 NO ONE KNOWS HOW MANY SLAVE-USING BRICK KILNS See, for example, Howard W. French, "Child Slave Labor Revelations Sweeping China," *New York Times*, June 15, 2007, accessed at: http://www.nytimes.com /2007/06/15/world/asia/15iht-china.4.6160781.html?pagewanted=all, Aug. 20, 2012.

112 THIS INCREASE IS ALARMING Yude Pan, et al. (July 15, 2011). "A Large and Persistent Carbon Sink in the World's Forests, 1990–2007." *Science*. Volume 333.

114 AS ONE ENVIRONMENTAL GROUP PUT IT See: http://www.greenpeace.org /raw/content/international/press/reports/carving-up-the-congo-exec.pdf, accessed July 19, 2011.

114 RECENT ESTIMATES SUGGEST THAT 88 PERCENT This piece by Greenpeace expands on these figures: http://www.greenpeace.org/usa/en/campaigns /forests/forests-worldwide/illegal-logging/, accessed July 19, 2011.

114 THE AMOUNT OF CO_2 SCIENTISTS SAY Intergovernmental Panel on Climate Change, "Summary for Policymakers," Climate Change 2007: The Physical Science Basis—Contribution of Working Group I to the Fourth Assessment Report of the Intergovernmental Panel on Climate Change, p. 3, http://www.ipcc-wg1.unibe.ch/publications/wg1-ar4/wg1-ar4.html. The exact amount of CO_2 emissions from deforestation has a large degree of uncertainty, with estimates ranging from 1.8 to 9.9 $GtCO_2$/year for the 1990s. It should be recognized that some sources report gigatons of carbon (C), rather than of CO_2; the conversion is 3.67 tons of CO_2 per ton of carbon.

114 TO 20 PERCENT CSIRO Australia (May 11, 2007). "Confirmed: Deforestation Plays Critical Climate Change Role." *ScienceDaily*, Web. Aug. 30, 2012.

114 TO 25 PERCENT Greenpeace, *Carving up the Congo* (2007).

114 TO "ALMOST 30 PERCENT" Al Gore (2006). *An Inconvenient Truth: The Planetary Emergency of Global Warming and What We Can Do About It*, Rodale Books, p. 227.

115 So, if 40 percent of deforestation is slave-based According to the US Energy Information Administration global CO_2 emissions from the consumption of energy in 2010 totaled 31.8 gigatons (million million metric tons). Twenty percent of that total, the amount estimated to be caused by deforestation, equals 6.36 gigatons, and 40 percent of that total, the amount estimated to be caused by deforestation using enslaved workers, equals 2.54 gigatons. According to the US Energy Information Administration China emitted 8.32 gigatons and the United States emitted 5.61 gigatons. Third after China and the United States, or fourth if we count slavery as a country, comes India at 1.69 gigatons. For comparison, the entire continent of Africa emits 1.14 gigatons. (For the country estimates see: http://www.eia .gov/cfapps/ipdbproject/iedindex3.cfm?tid=90&pid=44&aid=8&cid=regions &syid=2010&eyid=2010&unit=MMTCD, accessed Aug. 30, 2012.)

115 In 2009 two researchers Syed Nasir Ahmed Tahir and Muhammed Rafique (2009). "Emission of Greenhouse Gases (GHGs) from Burning of Biomass in Brick Kilns," *Environmental Forensics*, Volume 10, Issue 4, pp. 265–67.

115 As Elisabeth Rosenthal explained Elisabeth Rosenthal (April 15, 2009). "Third-World Soot is Target in Climate Fight," *New York Times*, p. A1.

115 About 52 percent of the carbon Kirk R. Smith, et al., "Greenhouse Gases from Small-Scale Combustion Devices in Developing Countries— Charcoal Making Kilns in Thailand." Research paper prepared for the US Environmental Protection Agency, Dec. 1999. This paper can be accessed online at the National Service Center for Environmental Publications (NSCEP) (http://www.epa.gov/nscep/index.html).

116 Plowing it into farmland For recent research on biochar, see: Dominic Woolf, James E. Amonette, F. Alayne Street-Perrott, Johannes Lehmann, Stephen Joseph. "Sustainable biochar to mitigate global climate change." *Nature Communications*, Aug. 10, 2010.

116 After all, we know that slavery For a complete plan for the eradication of slavery, see Kevin Bales (2007). *Ending Slavery: How We Free Today's Slaves*, University of California Press.

116 And it is worth remembering Great Britain produces (and consumes) about 200,000 tons of chicken feed per month. In 2011 chicken feed was selling there for about £265 per ton, that's £636 million per year or a little more than $1 billion. See the UK Department for Environment, Food & Rural Affairs, Animal Feed Statistics at: http://www.defra.gov.uk/statistics /foodfarm/food/animalfeed/, accessed July 19, 2011.

116 Eleven billion dollars is also the amount "Widespread failure of

forest governance—characterized by illegal logging, associated illegal trade, and corruption—undermines any nation's attempt to achieve sustainable economic growth, social balance, and environmental protection, according to the report Strengthening Forest Law Enforcement and Governance—Addressing a Systemic Constraint to Sustainable Development, released today by the World Bank during its Annual Meetings held in Singapore." World Bank: *Weak Forest Governance Costs US$15 Billion a Year*, World Bank News Release No. 2007/86/SDN.

117 ADD IN THE ATMOSPHERIC SCRUBBING A hectare of forest sequesters between 1 and 1.5 tons of carbon per year, every tree saved scrubs CO_2 from the air, we currently lose about 4.53 million hectares of forest per year according to the UN Food and Agriculture Organization (2010). *Global Forest Resources Assessment Main Report*, FAO Forestry Paper 163, Rome: UN FAO.

117 A KEY FACT HERE IS THAT CSIRO Australia (August 9, 2011). "Forests Absorb One Third of Fossil Fuel Emissions, Study Finds," *ScienceDaily*. Accessed at http://www.sciencedaily.com/releases/2011/08/110810093835 .htm, August 30, 2012.

117 IT INVOLVES ALL OF US DOING THINGS "The UN's Food and Agriculture Organisation has estimated that meat production accounts for nearly a fifth of global greenhouse gas emissions. These are generated during the production of animal feeds, for example, while ruminants, particularly cows, emit methane, which is 23 times more effective as a global warming agent than carbon dioxide. The agency has also warned that meat consumption is set to double by the middle of the century." Excerpted from Juliet Jowitt (Sept. 7, 2008). "UN Says Eat Less Meat to Curb Global Warming," *The Observer*. See also: Nathan Fiala (Feb. 4, 2009). "How Meat Contributes to Global Warming," *Scientific American* (online), accessed at: http://www.scientific american.com/article.cfm?id=the-greenhouse-hamburger, July 19, 2011.

119 SOME YEARS AGO A VERY BRAVE I'm not naming this man—he wants to be able to come and go from Bangladesh without threat. I will say that his images have been checked by experts and confirmed, as well as by someone who managed to infiltrate the island with him. I look forward to the day when abolitionist heroes like this man get the public honor they deserve, instead of having to watch their backs and protect themselves against reprisals from the corrupt accomplices of the slaveholders through anonymity.

120 "BODIES WASH UP ROUTINELY" Quotations from Ambassador deBaca, and those that follow from shrimper Paul Willis, were taken from a CNN feature entitled "Slave Labor Blamed for Falling Shrimp Prices" by Sean Callebs and Jason Morris, broadcast Dec. 3, 2009, accessed at: http://am.blogs

.cnn.com/2009/12/03/slave-labor-blamed-for-falling-shrimp-prices/, July 26, 2011.

CHAPTER 6

125 TODAY, OF COURSE, THE WORLD'S GOLD SUPPLY John Maynard Keynes (1924). *A Tract on Monetary Reform*, London: Macmillan, p. 172.

126 *TIME* MAGAZINE SAYS Marcus Webb, "Dubai: Ten Things to Do," #3 The Gold Souk, accessed at: http://content.time.com/time/travel/cityguide /article/0,31489,1849667_1849594_1849119,00.html, May 23, 2014.

127 THE FIRM IS KNOWN See: *From Child Miner to Jewelry Store*, The Enough Project, Oct. 2012, available at http://www.enoughproject.org/files /Conflict-Gold.pdf.

127 OR RATHER SOMEONE IS EARNING BREAD Abraham Lincoln, Second Inaugural Address, March 4, 1865. In this section of his inaugural address Lincoln is discussing the origins and impact of the ongoing Civil War. The highlighted sentence is a paraphrase of a Bible verse that would have been familiar to his audience: Genesis 3:19—"In the sweat of thy face shalt thou eat bread, till thou return unto the ground; for out of it wast thou taken: for dust thou *art*, and unto dust shalt thou return" (King James Version). The Inaugural Address reads in part: "One-eighth of the whole population were colored slaves, not distributed generally over the Union, but localized in the southern part of it. These slaves constituted a peculiar and powerful interest. All knew that this interest was somehow the cause of the war. To strengthen, perpetuate, and extend this interest was the object for which the insurgents would rend the Union even by war, while the Government claimed no right to do more than to restrict the territorial enlargement of it. Neither party expected for the war the magnitude or the duration which it has already attained. Neither anticipated that the *cause* of the conflict might cease with or even before the conflict itself should cease. Each looked for an easier triumph, and a result less fundamental and astounding. Both read the same Bible and pray to the same God, and each invokes His aid against the other. It may seem strange that any men should dare to ask a just God's assistance in wringing their bread from the sweat of other men's faces, but let us judge not, that we be not judged. The prayers of both could not be answered. That of neither has been answered fully."

132 AT FIRST THE EUROPEANS Hugh Thomas (1997). *The Slave Trade: The History of the Atlantic Slave Trade 1440–1870*, New York: Simon & Schuster, p. 226.

133 THE GOLD COAST, ACCORDING TO ONE EUROPEAN TRADER Ibid., p. 226.

142 HE DIED TEN DAYS LATER Associated Press (Apr. 1, 2008). "Colbert Man Dies from Mercury Poisoning," *Tulsa World*, accessed at: http://www .tulsaworld.com/news/article.aspx?articleID=20080401_12_80377, January 7, 2009.

148 SHE WAS PRETENDING TO BE A MOMMY I remember how proud I felt at the age of two when I filled the gas tank of my father's car using the garden water hose. Cars needed what came from hoses, I reasoned, and here I was helping out. Dad wasn't quite as pleased.

CHAPTER 7

157 ONE ECOLOGIST EXPLAINED Ehrenberg, Rachel (May 10, 2008). "Eight-Legged Bags of Poison," *Science News*, Vol. 173, No. 16, accessed at: http: //www.sciencenews.org/view/generic/id/31459/title/Eight-legged_bags _of_poison, Jan. 13, 2009.

157 SINCE THEN ILLEGAL MINING http://unpan1.un.org/intradoc/groups/public /documents/other/unpan022294.pdf.

157 THE BEST ESTIMATES ARE Ghana Forest Information and Data, accessed at: http://rainforests.mongabay.com/deforestation/2000/Ghana.htm, August 22, 2011.

157 IT HAS ALSO INCREASED "In Ghana, about 35 percent of the land surface experiences severe erosion and loss of productivity through deforestation and land degradation, amounting to a 4 percent loss of Gross Domestic Product (GDP). It has also been estimated that the original 8.2 million hectares of the closed forest in Ghana have been destroyed, leaving about 1.962 million hectares. Desertification in Ghana has come about as a result of population growth, deforestation, high incidence of bushfires and inappropriate land use practices, such as the slash and burn system of agriculture, which has caused the expansion of the savannah zone across the deciduous forest zone to the high rain forest ecozone." Accessed at: http://www.povertyenvironment.net/?q=ghana_in_the_fight_against _desertification_and_drought, Aug. 22, 2011.

157 *NATIONAL GEOGRAPHIC,* UNDER A HEADLINE READING "FOREST HOLO-CAUST" http://www.nationalgeographic.com/eye/deforestation/effect.html, accessed Aug. 22, 2011.

157 OR AS ROBERT D. MANN, A BRITISH TROPICAL AGRICULTURIST, HAS WARNED Quoted at: http://db.jhuccp.org/ics-wpd/exec/icswppro.dll?BU =http://db.jhuccp.org/ics-wpd/exec/icswppro.dll&QF0=DocNo&QI0=07

5326&TN=Popline&AC=QBE_QUERY&MR=30%25DL=1&&RL=1
&&RF=LongRecordDisplay&DF=LongRecordDisplay, accessed July 12,
2010.

159 GLOBAL SALES OF GHANAIAN GOLD "US economy recovery hurts Ghana's
gold sales—Dr Wampah"—See more at: http://www.ghanabusinessnews
.com/2013/07/25/us-economy-recovery-hurts-ghanas-gold-sales-dr
-wampah/#sthash.RIWXOD0g.dpuf, accessed Sept. 13, 2013.

159 IT IS BELIEVED THAT NEARLY ONE THIRD No one is certain since in 2006 a
new law—Act 703—retained companies' rights not to disclose how, where,
and when concessions are granted.

159 AND LEGAL PRODUCTION IS EXPECTED TO RISE World Gold Council, Market Intelligence, accessed at: http://www.marketintelligence.gold.org/news
/2008/12/11/story/10889/ghana_2007_gold_exports_total_173bn, Feb. 11,
2009.

159 GOLD EXPORTS BRING VAST SUMS Gold represents about 35 percent of
Ghana's total exports, about 4.2 million ounces in 2012.

161 ACCORDING TO THE MINING COMPANIES Helen Vesperini (June 17, 2008).
"Illegal Gold Mining on the Rise," *The Australian Business*, accessed at
http://www.theaustralian.news.com.au/story/0,25197,23878342-23850
,00.html, Feb. 22, 2009.

162 A REPORT BY THE GHANA COMMISSION ON HUMAN RIGHTS *The State of
Human Rights in Mining Communities in Ghana*, Commission on Human
Right and Administrative Justice of Ghana, 2008.

163 THE LABOR INSPECTOR He spoke with me on the promise of anonymity.

164 BUT TO SPEAK OF IT See, for example, Akyeampong, Emmanuel (2001).
"History, Memory, Slave-Trade and Slavery in Anlo (Ghana)," *Slavery and
Abolition*, 22 1–24. See also: Martin Klein (1989). "Studying the History of
Those Who Would Rather Forget: Oral History and the Experience of
Slavery," *History in Africa*, 16, 209–17. I am indebted to Dr. Laura Murphy
for helping me to understand this, and many other things about Ghana.

165 RICHARD QUAYSON OF GHANA'S COMMISSION ON HUMAN RIGHTS
"Ghana: Favouring Gold Over Miners," February 23, 2009, IRIN, the humanitarian news and analysis service of the UN Office for the Coordina-
tion of Humanitarian Affairs; accessed at: http://www.irinnews.org/Report
.aspx?ReportId=82624, Feb. 24, 2009.

167 NATURALLY, THERE ARE PLENTY OF THINGS I have greatly simplified ideas
about certification of gold. For a much more detailed and better explanation see *Certification and Artisanal and Small-scale Mining: An Emerging Opportunity for Sustainable Development*, a report by Communities and
Small-Mining (CASM), June 2008.

167 AND WEDDING RINGS ARE ONLY "IDEX Online Research: Jewelry sales hit record," *National Jeweler*, Feb. 4, 2013, retrieved Sept. 12, 2013. See also: http://www.jckonline.com/2013/12/24/report-us-jewelry-and-watch -sales-expected-to-reach-79-billion-in-2013, accessed May 25, 2014.

168 ADD ACCESS TO LEGAL MICRO-CREDIT For a deeper discussion of how alternatives to illegal mining in Ghana might develop see: Hilsen, Gavin, and Banchirigah, Sadia Mohammed (Feb. 2009). "Are Alternative Livelihood Projects Alleviating Poverty in Mining Communities? Experiences from Ghana," *Journal of Development Studies*, Vol. 45, Issue 2, pp. 172–96.

CHAPTER 8

176 IN OCTOBER 2006 HE STATED Lana Cristina (July 1, 2005). "Lula Blames Slavery for Brazil's 'Social Abyss,'" *Brazzil Magazine*.

176 PERHAPS FOR THE FIRST TIME IN THE HISTORY It is probably the topic for another book, but it is worth remembering that most countries abolished legal slavery without having a civil war as occurred in the United States and Haiti. At the same time, most countries also fudged their emancipation, creating parallel systems that allowed enslavement in spite of its illegality. Today, as national governments scramble to address slavery within their borders most do so in a way that is marked by knee-jerk reactions, half-measures, and a deep ignorance of the problem, all the while trumpeting the allocation of ludicrously small resources as a great victory for freedom. Brazil's record on contemporary slavery is far from perfect, but at least they treat it seriously.

178 SADLY, THE NUMBER OF http://old.antislavery.org/archive/submission /submission2005-brazil.htm.

180 HE HAD REPORTED THOSE I often wonder why we hear so little about these heroes. They are putting their lives on the line to get people out of slavery and protect the environment, meanwhile we get in-depth reports celebrating the grade-B TV actor or actress who's managed to get through drug rehabilitation.

180 THE PARALLEL AND CONTRAST WITH THE UNITED STATES In 1534 the King of Portugal divided up the country into fifteen hereditary "captaincies" each one given to a noble family. Their job was to convert or eradicate the original inhabitants, and while some failed others prospered cultivating sugar.

181 INEQUALITY AT THIS LEVEL IS DANGEROUS Tatyana Soubbotini and Katherine Sheram (2000). *Economic Growth: Meeting the Challenge of Global De-*

velopment, Chapter 5—Inequality, accessed at: http://www.worldbank.org /depweb/beyond/beyondco/beg_05.pdf, Sept. 6, 2011.

182 A CALM, PENSIVE, BOUNDLESS LANDSCAPE Walt Whitman (1982). "Specimen Days," *Walt Whitman: Poetry and Prose*, Justin Kaplan (ed.), New York: Library of America, p. 864.

183 IN KANSAS ALONE THE BONES S. C. Gwynne (2010). *Empire of the Summer Moon: Quanah Parker and the Rise and Fall of the Comanches, the Most Powerful Indian Tribe in American History*, New York: Scribner, p. 5.

185 "'YOU'VE GOT TO GO'" In Portuguese, this is the Centro de Defesa da Vida e dos Direitos Humanos de Açailândia (CDVDH). Located in the town of Açailândia in the western part of Maranhão state and with links to the Comboni lay Catholic community, the Center for Defense of Life and Human Rights of Açailândia promotes and defends the human rights of the people of western Maranhão state. The center's efforts to combat slave labor include providing social service referrals for those freed from slave labor, supporting income- and employment-generating projects to help reduce the lure of slave labor among "at-risk" populations, assisting those wishing to make a formal denunciation of alleged slave labor practices, and promoting local awareness and prevention campaigns against slave labor. I was especially impressed with their work with young people in this area where regular jobs are few and far between and higher education opportunities are lacking. I saw projects producing slave-free charcoal, furniture from responsibly managed trees, a radio station teaching production skills, and classes in English and Spanish.

189 IN SEPTEMBER 2011 ASTRONAUTS You can see this photo on the NASA Earth Observatory website, access at: http://earthobservatory.nasa.gov /IOTD/view.php?id=71256, May 25, 2014.

190 FOR THE DAYS TO COME I want to give a special shout-out to an Austrian relief and development organization called MIVA (www.miva.at). They fight poverty and promote social justice in a very tightly focused way: they provide vehicles—bicycles, motorcycles, cars, and trucks—to those doing important work. They're supporting mobility in more than sixty countries—and the pickup truck that carried me (and others and food, medicines, books, and at one point a squealing piglet) into Amazonia was a MIVA vehicle. Thank you, MIVA.

196 WITH GROWING AWARENESS SYMPHONY MUSICIANS See the League of American Orchestras' work on pernambuco at http://americanorchestras .org/advocacy-government/travel-with-instruments/endangered-species -material/pernambuco-exemption-and-conservation.html (accessed May

25, 2014); and the International Pernambuco Conservation Initiative at http://www.ipci-usa.org (accessed May 25, 2014).

196 GROWING AS TALL AS A FIFTEEN-STORY BUILDING Consider what this longevity means for carbon sequestration. While most Amazonian trees live and die in a few decades, releasing their stored carbon as they decompose, some Brazil nut trees are still storing carbon today that they fixed the year the Magna Carta was signed in 1215. The preservation and propagation of Brazil nut trees is a small but vital step in addressing global warming.

200 As ONE OF THEIR CLOSE FRIENDS I'm not going to name their close friend here. This person works against the slaveholders and those who destroy the environment. In Brazil this is dangerous, too often deadly, work. I'm hoping their friend can be a little safer by not being named.

202 WAS EARNING $157 BILLION accessed at: https://www.fidh.org/IMG/pdf /report_brazil_2012_english.pdf.

205 THEY WILL LIVE WELL From TEDx Amazonia—an "independently organized TED event"—available here: https://www.youtube.com/watch?v =OSS2ALiU1ss in Portuguese with English subtitles.

206 "IT WAS TERRIBLE" John Collins Rudolf (May 28, 2011). "Murder of Activists Raises Questions of Justice in Amazon," *New York Times,* accessed at: http://green.blogs.nytimes.com/2011/05/28/murder-of-amazon-activists -raises-justice-questions/#more-103425, Jan. 30, 2012.

CHAPTER 9

213 THIS IS ONE OF THE REASONS The USA is an interesting example of this. In spite of being a big country with lots of farmland, our balance of payments for food is only just about breaking even. In 2010 America exported food, animal feeds, and beverages to a total of $146.5 billion. At the same time we imported food, animal feed, and beverages to a total of $132.3 billion. So it would seem that the USA has a positive balance of payments of $14.1 billion, until you take into account the $15.2 billion that was paid out in farm subsidies from taxes. It's worth noting that the top 10 percent of subsidies, the agribusinesses, get an average subsidy of over $30,000; the 80 percent of other farmers (like small family farms) get an average subsidy of $587. See "US International Trade in Goods and Services, November 2011" US Census Bureau, US Bureau of Economic Analysis, Dept. of Commerce, Press Release Jan. 13, 2012, accessed at: http://www.census.gov /foreign-trade/Press-Release/current_press_release/ft900.pdf, Feb. 2012;

and Farm Subsidy Database, Environmental Working Group, accessed at: http://farm.ewg.org/region?fips=00000&regname=UnitedStatesFarmSub sidySummary, Feb. 7, 2012.

214 COCOA TREES ARE UNDERSTORY If you are used to forests in eastern North America, under tall oaks and other canopy trees, you'll find the understory includes species like redbud, dogwood, pawpaw, and hornbeam.

214 AS GROWERS WRUNG OUT A FEW YEARS A good explanation of the forces at work in cocoa in Brazil can be found in: Leiter, Jeffrey, and Harding, Sandra (2004). "Trinidad, Brazil, and Ghana: Three Melting Moments in the History of Cocoa," *Journal of Rural Studies*, 20, pp. 113–30.

215 "THERE HAVE BEEN DAYS" Joanne Silberner (June 14, 2008). "A Not-So-Sweet Lesson from Brazil's Cocoa Farms," National Public Radio, accessed at: http://www.npr.org/templates/story/story.php?storyId=91479835, Feb. 8, 2012.

222 IN 2008 BRAZIL OVERTOOK THE UNITED STATES Reporter Brasil, an award-winning investigative human rights organization, helped me to get my head around the complexities of Brazilian agriculture and government policy. Two publications were especially helpful: *Brazil of Biofuels: Impacts of Crops on Land, Environment and Society* (2008), and *Sugarcane 2009* (2010), both were products of the Biofuels Watch Center of Reporter Brasil (www .reporterbrasil.org.br).

224 THE IMF SPOKE OF SERIOUS IMPLICATIONS Edith M. Lederer (Oct. 27, 2007). "UN Expert Calls BioFuel 'Crime Against Humanity,'"*LiveScience*, accessed at: http://www.livescience.com/4692-expert-calls-biofuel-crime -humanity.html, May 9, 2012.

224 BY 2011, THE GOVERNMENT THERE ESTIMATED The information in this paragraph was drawn from a number of research papers, including: 1. Timothy A. Wise (May 2012). "The Cost to Mexico of U.S. Corn Ethanol Expansion," Global Development and Environment Institute Working Paper No. 12-01, Tufts University. 2. Action Aid (May 2012). *Biofueling Hunger: How US Corn Ethanol Policy Drives Up Food Prices in Mexico*, Washington DC: Action Aid. 3. Marco Lagi, Alexander S. Gard-Murray, and Yaneer Bar-Yam (May 2012). "Impact of Ethanol Conversion and Speculation on Mexico Corn Imports," New England Complex Systems Institute, http://necsi.edu/research/social/foodprices/mexico/. 4. Institute for Agriculture and Trade Policy and Global Development and Environment Institute (Jan. 2012). *Resolving the Food Crisis: Assessing Global Policy Reforms since 2007*, Tufts University.

225 COMMUNITIES AND ECOSYSTEMS Shelby J. Hayhoe, Christopher Neill, Stephen Porder, Richard McHorney, Paul Lefebvre, Michael T. Coe,

Helmut Elsenbeer, Alex V. Krusche (May 2011). "Conversion to Soy on the Amazonian Agricultural Frontier Increases Streamflow without Affecting Stormflow Dynamics," *Journal of Global Change Biology*, Vol. 17, No. 5, pp. 1821–33.

226 WHERE THE FORESTS ARE DESTROYED McCullough, David (1987). *The Johnstown Flood*, Simon & Schuster, New York.

227 HELL IT MUST HAVE BEEN Schwartz, S. (1985). *Sugar Plantations in the Formation of Brazilian Society: Bahia, 1550–1835*, Cambridge University Press, UK, pp. 133–34, 257.

231 IN A 2011 REPORT The Social Observatory was created in 1997 by the Central Workers Union (CUT), with the support of the Centre for Contemporary Cultural Studies (Cedec), the Inter-Union Department of Socioeconomic Studies (Dieese), and the Inter-University Studies and Research on Work (Unitrabalho). Its foundation arose from concerns about the monitoring of social and environmental clauses in international trade agreements. More at: http://www.observatoriosocial.org.br/portal/.

234 TODAY PEOPLE CONTINUE TO DRAIN See: Fitzgerald, Daniel C. (1994). *Faded Dreams: More Ghost Towns of Kansas*, Lawrence: University Press of Kansas.

237 WORSE, THE BRAZILIAN JUDICIARY CAN'T DECIDE There is one decision from High Court (Dec. 2006) about jurisdiction over slavery, but this ruling was not considered definitive and is likely to be reversed at any moment. In practice, since 2007, federal courts tend to judge this crime.

CHAPTER 10

244 JONATHAN SAFRAN FOER NOTED Jonathan Safran Foer (2009). *Eating Animals*, New York: Hamish Hamilton, pp. 258.

245 WENDELL BERRY SAID THAT EVERY TIME Wendell Berry (2003). *The Art of the Commonplace: The Agrarian Essays of Wendell Berry*, edited by Norman Wirzba, Berkeley: CA: Counterpoint.

INDEX

ABOUT THE AUTHOR

———

KEVIN BALES is Professor of Contemporary Slavery at the Wilberforce Institute for the Study of Slavery and Emancipation. He co-founded the global anti-slavery group Free the Slaves that has liberated more than 10,000 slaves in India, Nepal, Haiti, Ghana, Brazil, Ivory Coast, and Bangladesh, and works with them to build new lives of dignity. His book *Disposable People: New Slavery in the Global Economy*, published in ten languages, was named one of "100 World-Changing Discoveries" by the Association of British Universities. The film version won a Peabody and two Emmys. He has received numerous awards including the $100,000 Grawemeyer Prize.

kevinbales.net
facebook.com/kevinbalesauthor